COMMUNISTS, COWBOYS, AND QUEERS

COMMUNISTS, COWBOYS, AND QUEERS

THE POLITICS OF MASCULINITY IN THE WORK
OF ARTHUR MILLER AND TENNESSEE WILLIAMS

David Savran

University of Minnesota Press • Minneapolis, London

Published by the University of Minnesota Press
2037 University Avenue Southeast, Minneapolis, MN 55414
Printed in the United States of America on acid-free paper

Library of Congress Cataloging-in-Publication Data

Savran, David
    Communists, cowboys, and queers : the politics of masculinity in the work of Arthur Miller and Tennessee Williams / David Savran.
        p. cm.
    Includes bibliographical references and index.
    ISBN 0-8166-2122-5 (hard). — ISBN 0-8166-2123-3 (pbk.)
    1. American drama—20th century—History and criticism.   2. Politics and literature—United States—History—20th century.   3. Williams, Tennessee, 1911–1983—Political and social views.   4. Miller, Arthur, 1915- —Political and social views.   5. Political plays, American—History and criticism.   6. Masculinity (Psychology) in literature.   7. Sex role in literature.   8. Men in literature.   I. Title.
PS338.P6S28 1992
812′.5209358—dc20   92-4267
                                                                              CIP

The University of Minnesota is an
equal-opportunity educator and employer.

For Ronn, without whom not

Contents

Preface

This book happened by accident. I set out two years ago to write a
study of masculinity on the contemporary American stage and got only
as far as the introduction. In composing a brief critical overview of the
work of Arthur Miller and Tennessee Williams, I became so fascinated
by the different ways in which they each negotiated questions of gender
and sexuality in Cold War America—and so amazed by the shortsight-
edness of most critics in analyzing their drama—that I knew I had to
devote an entire volume to these two. What follows is the result of two
years of passionate involvement.

As I was working on this book, however, and immersed in research,
a marvelous surprise awaited me: the lesser-known works of Tennessee
Williams. For the most part, I retained the image of Williams as a great
poet of the theater and a discreetly closeted homosexual that I had
deduced from critical clichés and the popular plays between *The Glass
Menagerie* (1944) and *The Night of the Iguana* (1961). But I was quite
unfamiliar with his many short stories, two novels, *Memoirs* (1975),
letters, and later plays. Steeping myself in these works, I was overwhelmed to discover a figure completely different from the one I had
been teaching. Here was a writer who called himself a revolutionary
and meant it, a playwright who produced a new and radical theater that
challenged and undermined the Cold War order. Taking Williams at his
word and crediting this revolutionary promise, I realized that this book

had to move from Miller to Williams (despite the latter's seniority), in
order to demonstrate the possibility of *undoing* the hegemonic notions
of gender, sexuality, and political praxis that have prevailed in the United
States since World War II.

In expanding my original introduction, I have approached the works
of both men as an anthropologist studies cultural productions, seeing
them less as individual or idiosyncratic artifacts than as *instances* of two
distinct cultural moments, each with its own implicit social hierarchy,
dominant values, and symbolic code. (I designate Miller's cultural
moment as anxious Cold War liberal; Williams's, as skittish radical.)
This book deliberately focuses on the discontinuity between these unstable contemporaneous moments in order to underline the difference
between an oppressive, masculinist sexual politics and the (admittedly
remote) possibility of an egalitarian, antihomophobic, and emancipated
body politic and body sexual. In more personal terms, this book represents my own attempt to theorize a male subjectivity and sexuality
less destructive and stultifying than the one on which I grew up, and it
has been structured in the hope of leading the reader to a radical position,
along a pathway, I might add, that corresponds neatly to my own
political transformation: from a bouncing, anti-Communist exemplar of
the postwar baby boom, to a rebellious adolescent during the headiest
days of the 1960s, to a seditious academic eager to valorize and reclaim
the promises of the New Left, the women's movement, and gay and
lesbian liberation. It is my attempt to understand the network of sexual,
economic, and racial subjugation by and in which I have been articulated
as a subject—the apparatus that I once took for granted and against
which I subsequently rebelled—as a historical formation. The introduction and chapter 1 map that formation; chapters 2 and 3 suggest ways
of deconstructing and subverting it.

Unquestionably, this book owes an incalculable debt to the work of
feminist theorists, and with it I hope to repay a part of what I owe
Catherine Belsey, Sue-Ellen Case, Teresa De Lauretis, Elin Diamond, Jill
Dolan, Janelle Reinelt, and many others who have revolutionized the
study of gender and sexuality in theater. It also marks my attempt to
compose what I hope is a felicitous disequilibrium of the discourses of
Marxism, feminism, and gay and lesbian studies (a triad reflected in the
title), in the belief that a subtle dissonance among several positions is
more productive theoretically than some imaginary or imaginable unity.
For this project, I have been particularly grateful for the incisive criticism
of the manuscript I have received from Sue-Ellen Case, Elin Diamond,
and Gary Thomas, and for the assistance of Janaki Bakhle and Robert
Mosimann at the University of Minnesota Press. In addition, I want to

thank the English Department at Brown University for its Walter C. Bronson Fellowship as well as my many friends and students who have given me invaluable feedback, including Graham Bass, Stacie Chaiken, Peter Cohen, Matt Doull, Brian Herrera, Yvonne Shafir, and especially Gwendolyn Parker, who has helped me follow through with what has been at times a very difficult investigation. I am deeply grateful to my colleagues in the English Department for their much-needed support and close reading of this manuscript: Karin Coddon, Coppélia Kahn, Neil Lazarus, and especially Paula Vogel, who offered me the blueprint to this material. I owe a very special thanks to Sandra Rich and Tammis Day—for a cherished summer in Provincetown and this eagle's nest of an office high above the dunes in which I am writing these words. And finally, my great and loving appreciation to Ronn Smith for helping me straighten out all my willful, unruly ideas, for his brilliant editorial skills, his gentleness, and his infinite patience. This book was written for him.

David Savran
Provincetown, Massachusetts

Introduction

KHRUSHCHEV: I defend the real policy, which is to assure peace. How can peace be assured when we are surrounded by military bases?
NIXON: We will talk about that later. Let's drink to talking—as long as we are talking we are not fighting.
KHRUSHCHEV: [Indicating a waitress] Let's drink to the ladies.
NIXON: We can all drink to the ladies.

—Exchange between Nikita Khrushchev and Richard Nixon, as reported in the *New York Times*, July 25, 1959

When the American National Exhibition opened in Moscow with great fanfare during the summer of 1959, then Vice President Richard Nixon journeyed to the Soviet capital to open the show, bringing the good wishes of President Dwight D. Eisenhower and cutting a symbolic red ribbon. The civility of the occasion, however, was unfortunately sabotaged by a day-long heated debate between Nixon and Soviet Premier Nikita Khrushchev over nuclear weapons, foreign military bases, the free exchange of ideas, and the merits of American capitalism, home appliances, and jazz. James Reston described the encounter the next day in the *New York Times* as "the most startling personal international incident" since the end of World War II.[1] And in many respects, this dispute between Stalin's relatively liberal successor and a politician who had cut his teeth on the House Committee on Un-American Activities remains one of the most revealing exchanges of the Cold War. Trading scarcely veiled threats, each man claimed that although he wanted peace, the other's policies made peace impossible. Citing the potentially disastrous consequences of military engagement, Khrushchev called for a peace treaty in Europe and the elimination of both "bases from foreign lands" and "the point of friction in Berlin." Nixon, to borrow the *New York Times*'s word, "sidestepped" the issue of foreign bases and urged the foreign ministers of the formerly allied powers then meeting in Geneva to settle the question of Germany. The debate went on and on, accusation

1

meeting accusation, and, like so many other encounters during the Cold War, it ended in a stalemate.[2]

The foundation for this historic confrontation between two of the most prominent Cold War antagonists was laid during the closing days of World War II and the partitioning of Europe. Unlike Franklin Roosevelt, who had taken a relatively conciliatory position at Yalta in 1945, Harry Truman pursued a much more belligerent campaign against the Soviets. James F. Byrnes, secretary of state to the new president, swore in August 1945 (the same month two atomic bombs were dropped on an already prostrate Japan) that capitalism and communism are absolutely inimical, and insisted that "an expanding world economy" could be based only "on the liberal principles of private enterprise, nondiscrimination, and reduced barriers to trade." The same year, Under Secretary of State William L. Clayton declared to Congress: "We've got to export three times as much as we exported just before the war if we want to keep our industry running at somewhere near capacity."[3] Knowing that the prosperity of the U.S. economy was dependent on its securing the worldwide domination of markets during this historic realignment, the president formally announced the Truman Doctrine in 1947, opposing capitalist "freedom" to Communist "tyranny," and pledging to keep the world open to American goods.[4] Even more decisively than Winston Churchill's "iron curtain" speech of 1946, the Truman Doctrine divided the world into two utterly opposed camps and provided the justification for what was to be the largest arms buildup in world history (despite the fact that polls at the end of the war indicated that a majority of Americans believed that the Soviets could be trusted).[5]

The rationale for the Truman Doctrine was provided by George F. Kennan, an attaché to the U.S. embassy in Moscow, who, in a legendary 1946 telegram to the State Department, warned that Communism was on the march globally and had to be *contained* by the Western powers. Inspired by the doctrine of containment, the Truman administration pursued a vigorous anti-Soviet policy, overseeing the defeat of leftist rebels in the Greek Civil War in 1948–49 and founding the Central Intelligence Agency, in part, to influence elections and shore up conservative regimes in France, Italy, and Germany. As Lawrence Wittner has pointed out, Washington quickly learned (and, under the Reagan-Bush program, continues to believe) that "with sufficient U.S. assistance, even the most venal, oppressive, and unrepresentative" of foreign regimes could be appropriated by U.S. interests "to quell domestic revolts in the name of anti-Communism."[6] When the Korean War began in 1950, it put the Communist world on warning and provoked a revealing comment from one American general, who noted that "there had to be a Korea either here or someplace in the world" and called the war "a blessing."[7]

Yet the most successful of all American interventions (at least in the short term) was the Marshall Plan, developed in 1947 to rebuild and stabilize capitalism in Western Europe in the belief that the loss of European markets would be disastrous for the expanding U.S. economy. Despite the fact that the Marshall Plan gave "tacit approval to the continuation of European colonialism in most of Asia and Africa," the Truman administration simultaneously set forth its own imperial agenda, insisting that the British Empire be opened to U.S. trade, fortifying its economic and political domination of Latin America, and doubling its share of Middle Eastern oil holdings (they jumped from 31 to 60 percent between 1946 and 1953). At the same time, it set the stage for the next phase of Western imperialism by its founding of the Export-Import Bank in 1949 to guarantee private investments in an emerging Third World.[8] For the most part, these American initiatives worked as planned. The domestic economy and foreign investment boomed as never before, and myriad consumer goods beckoned an increasingly prosperous middle class. At the same time, however, the gulf between the rich and the poor, both in the United States and internationally, steadily widened. For many living on the fringes of the "free world"—in the poor villages and slums of Latin America, Africa, and Asia—and for most African-Americans, the postwar boom was a bust.

So when Nixon and Khrushchev faced off in 1959, they took up the positions prescribed for them by a narrative of conquest and imperial domination that long antedated their heated words. Despite their pre-occupation with the world stage, the most revealing part of their exchange had little to do with affairs of state. According to the *New York Times*, their debate reached its "high point" in front of an American middle-class kitchen installed in a model house at the exhibition.[9] Nixon extolled the luster of capitalism by citing the wondrous array of consumer goods that the U.S. economy had produced—from color televisions to washing machines—and stressed the importance of "diversity, the right to choose." He explained that "Americans were interested in making life easier for their women," a remark that prompted Khrushchev to criticize "the capitalist attitude toward women." Nixon argued, however, that "this attitude . . . is universal" and he continued his encomium to the commodity. Only at the end of their debate did the two reach agreement. Khrushchev proposed a toast to the elimination of bases, which Nixon disallowed. So Khrushchev took a different tack. Sighting a waitress, he declared, "Let's drink to the ladies," to which a disarmed Nixon replied, "We can all drink to the ladies."[10]

What is most remarkable about this exchange is its disclosure of a point of strategic agreement that transcends the Cold War: the politics of masculinity. For despite Khrushchev's earlier criticism of "the capitalist attitude toward women," his toast quietly and emphatically approved the veracity of Nixon's claim of a "universal" attitude that produces women as objects of male desire. Simultaneously, it splits the world in half along a different axis, subsuming the antithesis between West and East beneath another one far more deeply (and violently) inscribed in Cold War culture, on both sides of the "iron curtain." In this friendly toast, the antagonism between capitalism and communism is displaced and reconfigured as an opposition between man and woman, producer of discourse and silent accessory, ogling subject and object of the gaze. Rhetorically, Nixon's declaration, "We can all drink to the ladies," accomplishes far more than the Geneva Convention ever could, coupling the two Cold Warriors under the aegis of "all," of a "universal" desiring subject—belligerent, inflamed, masculine, and heterosexual—who, in his unspeakable arrogance, carves up the world and then threatens to annihilate it.

Communists and Queers

The global realignment that followed World War II had an almost incalculable impact on American politics. As many historians have observed, the Truman Doctrine bred an anticommunism fervor that gripped the national psyche, becoming the ideological currency for an America on an imperial spree. Senator Joseph McCarthy and other leading Republicans conducted an exhaustive search for alleged Communist dupes and traitors in the State Department, labor unions, universities, and the entertainment industry, sponsoring some of the harshest and most repressive social legislation in U.S. history. Because of the publicity given to Hollywood's most celebrated former Communists, the fact is sometimes obscured that homosexuals were targeted by McCarthy with a level of violence and hatred that often surpassed even the baiting of "Reds." As many historians have noted, and as this book will explore, when the architects and administrators of the Cold War turned their attention to policing the American body politic, they aimed precisely at Communists and homosexuals in the conviction that both groups were plotting to undermine and destroy the American way of life. As was so often the case during this tumultuous period, Senator McCarthy put it most memorably and viciously, railing against the "egg-sucking phony liberals," who, with their "pitiful squealing," held "sacrosanct those Communists and queers" in the American government who were betraying American interests.[11] During the late 1940s and 1950s, with one or another foreign Communist government or so-called front group at home as a pretense, the baiting and brutalization of "Communists and queers" dominated the national agenda.

Although this symmetry was constructed and exploited by one of the most ignominious figures in American politics, it has coincidentally determined the structure of this book, which opposes the two most prominent and respected figures of the postwar theater, Arthur Miller (b. 1915) and Tennessee Williams (1911–1983), the alleged Communist and the proven queer. Because of their ostensible misdeeds, both men unhappily found themselves marginalized politically and/or culturally at different times in their lives, despite the fact that both, earlier in their careers, had embraced that marginalization, consciously taking up a stance in opposition to the dominant culture and attacking its orthodoxies. In the late 1950s, Miller was branded a radical and hailed before the House Committee on Un-American Activities, while Williams was stigmatized more subtly for his homosexuality and chose to reflect it obliquely in his plays (but not his short stories) until late in his career. There are other points of agreement as well. Both Miller and Williams produced bodies of work that fall broadly under the heading of American realism, both collaborated with many of the same directors and actors, both are most celebrated for their serious—or, if one prefers, tragic—plays, both worked to establish a new degree of independence from European models for American drama, and both wrote their most successful and widely respected works between the mid-1940s and the early 1960s.

Yet despite these correspondences, despite their near contemporaneity and their shared preeminence in the American theater, Miller and Williams make strange bedfellows. Undeniably, they cultivated very different public images, were preoccupied with different concerns, and preferred different styles of writing. For most theatergoers, academic critics, and the popular press, Miller remains the exemplary intellectual, leftist playwright; Williams, the apolitical poet of passion and the flesh. The one is celebrated for politically driven male heroes and his forthright style; the other for his female protagonists and more indirect mode of writing. The one seems to personify masculine play writing; the other, a feminine, or even vaguely aberrant, theater. Although these unmistakably gendered character sketches continue to be widely disseminated, they are, to my mind, fraught with difficulties, and my goal in this book is to take them apart rigorously and replace them with more nuanced and incisive portraits. In order to do so, I will analyze the differences between the two playwrights' representations of genders and sexualities, and detail the ideological implications of these differences. Or, enunciated in more historical terms, I will examine how each playwright negotiates the same politics of masculinity that those Cold War archenemies, Nixon and Khrushchev, both embraced and symbolized.

In questioning the popular images of these two playwrights, this book is designed, in part, as an answer to the double-dealings, recriminations, obfuscations, and amnesia that seem to have afflicted so many writers and critics at the height of the Cold War and that, deplorably, remain widespread in highly visible portions of the theatrical and intellectual communities. This book represents my critique both of the formalism of the 1950s and of its continued domination of much of the scholarship on Miller and Williams. Although attempts have been made in recent years to historicize their work, most notably by C. W. E. Bigsby, theatrical and critical fashion continues to champion the ostensibly "universal" qualities of plays such as *Death of a Salesman* (1949) and *Cat on a Hot Tin Roof* (1955). I believe, however, that the most important cultural work being performed by these plays will become apparent only upon a close examination of their relationship with the national and international crises of the 1940s and 1950s, the historical struggles these works simultaneously conceal and illuminate. Because theatrical production is so deeply and intricately ideological, and because, during the postwar period, the Broadway theater was a genuinely popular art (at least for the middle classes), the works of Miller and Williams provide, I believe, an unusually graphic and emotionally charged field in which to explore the packaging and marketing of Cold War masculinity for an impassioned consumer culture.

The Nuclear Family

Although the Cold War was aimed explicitly at containing the Soviet threat, the American family was, in many respects, even more deeply affected than the Soviet military. Many historians have noted that the popular image of the United States in the 1950s—a land of prosperous and happy families in their comfortable suburban homes, of domesticated sexuality and stable gender roles (an image produced and fortified by "Father Knows Best" and "The Adventures of Ozzie and Harriet," and reconstructed more recently by the stylishness of 1950s nostalgia)—is woefully inaccurate. Beneath this image lies a much more complex and disturbing reality. In an important work of social history, *Homeward Bound: American Families in the Cold War Era*, Elaine Tyler May analyzes the politics of domesticity during the late 1940s and 1950s, examining the interrelationship between U.S. foreign and domestic policies and carefully unraveling the institutionalization of various modes of oppression (economic, sexual, and racial) in the United States. In particular, she explores the construction of the middle-class nuclear family as a seemingly autonomous unit of production in what she designates "the domestic version of containment." At the center of this family is a hardworking husband-father and wife-mother for whom the most important commission is the propagation and education of children who grow up to be like their parents—property-owning husbands and housewives living a life of affluence and abundance. In an increasingly anxiety-producing and dangerous world, the nuclear family provided a refuge, the one sphere in which "people could control their destinies and perhaps even shape the future."[12] The preferred setting for the nuclear family is, of course, the suburban ranch house (usually at a considerable distance from the rest of the extended family), within whose walls

> potentially dangerous social forces ... might be tamed, where they could contribute to the secure and fulfilling life to which postwar women and men aspired. ... More than merely a metaphor for the cold war on the homefront, containment aptly describes the way in which public policy, personal behavior, and even political values were focused on the home.[13]

At the heart of this "domestic version of containment" was the strict prescription of masculine and feminine roles defined by the interrelationship of men and women in both home and marketplace. Although there are countless examples of these mandated "sex roles," one postwar sociologist provides an especially vivid portrait of the normative family in the following 1950s domestic idyll:

> Father helps mother with the dishes. He sets the table. He makes formula for the baby. Mother can supplement the income of the family by working outside. Nevertheless, the American male, by definition, *must* "provide" for his family. He is *responsible* for the support of his wife and children. His primary area of performance is the occupational role, in which his status fundamentally inheres; and his *primary* function in the family is to supply an "income," to be the "breadwinner." There is simply something wrong with the American adult male who doesn't have a "job." American women, on the other hand, tend to hold jobs *before* they are married and to quit when "the day" comes; or to continue in jobs of a lower status than their husbands. And not only is the mother the focus of emotional support for the American middle-class child, but much more exclusively so than in most societies. ... The cult of the warm, giving "Mom" stands in contrast to the "capable," "competent," "go-getting" male. The more expressive type of male, as a matter of fact, is regarded as "effeminate," and has too much fat on the inner side of his thigh.[14]

The ideology of familialism and the theory of "sex roles" conceived the distinction between men and women as a binary opposition that set the aggressive, "go-getting" businessman and father against the "warm, giving," and "expressive" housewife and mother whose responsibility it was to embrace domesticity and contain her sexuality. Simultaneously, this ideology severely disparaged and marginalized those who did not fit the prescribed molds: women who preferred the company of other women or who opted for careers rather than children, and "effeminate" men with more fat on "the inner side" of their thighs than most of their Cold War buddies. Individuals who seemed to fit both of these stereotypes were, at best, made the butts of wisecracks; at worst, they were silenced, reviled, and driven to suicide.

As May points out, however, these normative models put severe and often impossible pressures on men, on women, and on the nuclear family as an institution, leading married women, in particular, to experience "a great deal of discontent" for which they had little expression and less recourse. As she notes, many felt stifled, trapped, and isolated, having been forced to sacrifice their educations, careers, and close relationships with extended family to be "the focus of emotional support" for husband and children. And many, trained not to recognize the systemic character of their subjugation, blamed themselves for feeling discontented and angry.[15]

Men's problems were of a different sort. Because they were rarely as efficacious, powerful, or fulfilled in the workplace as they expected to be, they fashioned their families as the sites in which they could exercise their authority and prerogatives as "breadwinners." Bureaucratized at work and autocratic at home, both working- and middle-class men were often restive and disillusioned. May, by way of example, cites one successful man who realized in retrospect that his ideal of marriage, of "a young couple, much in love, . . . looking forward to a happy life," was "a farce."

> Today, what do we have to look forward to? Civil defense tests,
> compulsory military training, cold wars, fear of the atomic bomb, the
> diseases that plague man, the mental case outlook?[16]

For many middle-class women and men, the happiness and fulfillment promised by the so-called domestic revival were elusive and imaginary, as much a fabrication as Senator McCarthy's infamous list of 205 State Department employees accused in 1950 of being "card-carrying" members of the Communist party.[17]

As the two most serious and speculative playwrights of the Cold War era, Miller and Williams not only provided a voice for the many discontented American men and women living under the postwar settlement, but also—both in their writing and in their lives—vividly illuminated the pressures and anxieties circulating around the normative constructions of masculinity and femininity. And because both playwrights have left several autobiographical and quasi-autobiographical texts and taken prominent public stands in notable cultural struggles, their discursive self-fashioning must be regarded as being as much a part of their work as their plays and fiction. Examining this work then in this broader sense, I have become convinced that Miller's work tends to reinforce, albeit nervously and guiltily, these hegemonic constructions of gender, and simultaneously reveal with unusual clarity the anxieties circulating around both male and female sexuality. Williams's work, on the other hand, challenges these same constructions by offering subtly subversive models of gender and sexuality that, I believe, suggest a way beyond those "sex roles" that continue to exercise a powerful hold over the American domestic *imaginaire*. Chapter 1 examines the fashioning of Miller's male subjects as heroic rebels in connection with the playwright's own ideological affinity with both the Old Left of the 1930s and the Cold War masculinity that was one of its most problematic stepchildren. Chapters 2 and 3, by way of contrast, explore Williams's enunciation of a decentered and fragmented subject and valorize Williams's own claim to being a revolutionary by investigating both his conflicted relationship with the dominant and the "deviant" notions of sexuality during the 1940s and 1950s and his professed affinity with the liberation movements that emerged out of the New Left during the late 1960s.

The Sex / Gender System

The "domestic version of containment" charted by Elaine Tyler May with such care was a crucial component in the implementation of American imperial designs during the Cold War. The intensive level of surveillance posted over the circulation of sexuality in and around the nuclear family facilitated an unprecedented level of social control and is closely linked to the impressive rise in the birthrate during the 1940s and 1950s (known as the baby boom), which coincidentally furnished the rapidly expanding U.S. economy with a large future labor force. The theoretical ballast for the "domestic theory of containment," meanwhile, was provided by the above-noted principle of "sex roles," a theory of gender and sexuality whose hegemony attested to the (often unwitting) collusion of the intellectual and scientific elite with Cold War policy. Elaborating on the concept of the "social role" popularized during the 1930s, sociologists under the leadership of Talcott Parsons developed elaborate hypotheses on the inculcation and definition of complementary and asymmetrical "sex roles." In Parsons's narrowly Freudian view of personality, "sex roles" were the necessary result of "the anatomical differences of the sexes," which "constitute fundamental points of reference for the development" both of "orientations" and of "the differentiations of roles."[18] As the Freudian family romance played itself out in Parsons's scheme, these "orientations" and "roles" were efficiently implanted and consolidated and made virtually synonymous with membership in the nuclear family.[19]

The rise of the New Left and the rebirth of feminism in the 1960s radically changed the shape of the social sciences in the United States. During the next decade, as so many disciplines began to be (often contentiously) reshaped, feminist critics and historians, in Sue-Ellen Case's words, began "to produce a new kind of cultural analysis" based on "the interplay of cultural and socio-economic evidence" that new feminist histories had brought into play.[20] Central to this analysis was a challenge posted to the notion of biology-as-destiny that clearly underlies the politics of domesticity and the doctrine of "sex roles." In its place, many feminists theorized a crucial (and sometimes irreducible) distinction between *sex* as biology and *gender* as social and ideological production. From the vantage point of the 1970s, the elision of sex and gender in the postwar consensus had worked to naturalize the subjugation of women by founding this subjugation in the "universal" exigencies of a biology that was itself deeply masculinist. In 1978, Suzanne J. Kessler and Wendy McKenna set forth one of the classic formulations of the "social construction of gender," which they understood to be a crucial "part of reality construction" with which even—or especially—the scientific community has been complicit.

> The natural attitude toward gender and the everyday process of gender attribution are constructions which scientists bring with them when they enter laboratories to "discover" gender characteristics. Gender, as we have described it, consists of members' methods for attributing and constructing gender.[21]

In their highly influential thesis, Kessler and McKenna argue that gender functions as a dichotomizing system of categorization and representation, a process of "attributing" and "constructing" relations between gendered subjects. They emphasize that, when used to provide the basis for the binary gender system, biology is in fact "no closer to the truth" than (to use their example) theology.

During the 1980s, the work of Kessler and McKenna, Gayle Rubin, and others provided an increasing body of support for feminists in many fields intent on producing an antiessentialist theory of gender and elaborating on the ideological implications of what Rubin calls the "sex /

gender system.''[22] In theater studies, American feminist critics called for a radical reconfiguration of the discipline based upon their recognition that acting, play selection and production, spectatorship, textual interpretation, the convictions of the press, and hiring practices in theaters and universities have been deeply inscribed by patriarchal discourses and practices. Most notably, Sue-Ellen Case and Jill Dolan, with their notion of a materialist-feminist critique; Elin Diamond, with her theorization of a "gestic feminist criticism"; and Teresa De Lauretis, with her analysis of the genderization of narrative and the various "technologies of gender," have transformed the field.[23] Despite different areas of specialization—De Lauretis, for example, writes primarily on film—and some substantial disagreements, all are intensely committed to exploring the relationship between feminist and Marxist theory, or, in Diamond's admirable phrase, to practicing "the passionate analysis of gender in material social relations."[24] All are intent on reading dramatic literature, theatrical bodies and performances, and the various discourses circulating around and through theater as gendered practices inextricably linked to complex economic, cultural, and political forces. All insist that gender is a construction—that, in Dolan's words, it "is not innate," but rather "dictated through enculturation." All emphasize the decisive role of history in gender studies, with Dolan pointing out that materialist (or Marxist) feminism "views women as historical subjects whose relation to prevailing social structures is also influenced by race, class and sexual identification."[25] And Case, underscoring "the role of class and history in creating the oppression of women," observes that a materialist feminist critique will both account women status as a social class (albeit one constituted very differently from an economic class) and emphasize the primacy of "the spheres of labour and production" in both analyzing and combating the subjugation of women.[26]

In her essay "The Technology of Gender," Teresa De Lauretis provides a powerful reconceptualization of gender through her rewriting of the Althusserian concept of ideology. In answer to the "limitation" of an essentialist "notion of gender as sexual difference" propounded by some cultural (or "radical") feminists, she offers instead a historically rigorous and richly multivalent elaboration of gender as "the product of various social technologies, such as cinema, and of institutionalized discourses, epistemologies, and critical practices, as well as practices of daily life."[27] Citing the later work of Michel Foucault, she carefully notes that gender is not an ontology, but "'the set of effects produced in bodies, behaviors, and social relations,' . . . by the deployment of 'a complex political technology.'" De Lauretis then proceeds to four basic propositions. First, "gender is [a] representation" of "a particular social relation which pre-exists the individual and is predicated on the *conceptual* and rigid [struc-tural] opposition of two biological sexes." She emphasizes that this "social relation" is necessarily historical, that it "is always intimately intercon-nected with political and economic factors." Second, she notes that the "representation of gender *is* its construction" and emphasizes that con-struction is an ongoing and self-renewing process. Third, she takes up (and amends) Althusser's notion of the "ideological state apparatus" to invoke the primacy of gender—as an ideology—in constituting individ-uals as subjects who can speak, produce meaning, and represent them-selves and each other. And finally (and most controversially), De Lauretis notes both the ubiquity and the radical potential of hege-monic notions of gender, pointing out that "the construction of gender is also effected by its deconstruction." For her, gender functions (like the Derridean supplement) as an "excess," simultaneously marginal and deci-sive, an effect both "outside" discourse and "a potential trauma which can rupture or destabilize, if not contained, any representation." This fourth proposition leads to her conclusion that "a different construction of gender" can begin to be envisioned only in what she calls "the else-where of discourse here and now, the blind spots, or the space-off," that is, in the "spaces in the margins of hegemonic discourses."[28]

Although De Lauretis critiques Althusser's fashioning of an ostensibly gender-blind theory of ideology as masculinist, she, like the other anti-essentialist feminists cited above, relies heavily on the Althusserian notion of ideology as a way of theorizing the engagement of subjectivity, the interpellation (or address) of the individual into representation as a subject. According to Althusser (drawing, in turn, on Lacan), ideology is a system of representations—texts, images, performances, mythologies—that constitutes the necessary preconditions for all cultural practices, all social interactions, including art, literature, theater, and politics. Reacting against the definition of ideology as false consciousness, Althusser emphasizes that ideology is neither a mystification nor the result of a con-spiracy fomented by the agents of capital. For him, ideology is a semiau-tonomous superstructural network that represents "not the system of real relations which govern the existence of individuals, but the imaginary relations of those individuals to the real relations in which they live."[29] So ideology (like gender), in designating the lived (or "natural") relationships among individuals, describes, in fact, only an "imaginary" relation, which is to say, a fictional construct—or even collective hallucination—that is necessary for the operation of culture and yet always exceeds the understanding of the individual subject (who is articulated by ideology, and not the other way around). Elaborating on this theory, Diamond points out that gender "provides a perfect illustration of ideology at work since 'masculine' or 'feminine' behavior usually appears to be a 'natural'— and thus fixed and unalterable—extension of biological sex."[30] When gender (like ideology) is working efficiently, it does not coerce the individual into taking an appropriately gendered subject position, but allows him or her "freely" to choose it (in the same way that the worker under American capitalism is allowed "freely" to exchange labor for wages, "freely" to select from an alluring array of commodities, or "freely" to choose between Democrats and Republicans).

Despite its efficiency, however, ideology, constantly intersecting with the sex-gender system, is unable to naturalize its productions completely. As a result, it always allows for the possibility that it will be recognized as an "imaginary" relation. Catherine Belsey, a British cultural materialist and feminist whose work (primarily on Renaissance drama) bears some striking similarities to that of the American theorists cited above, capitalizes on the "imaginary" and vulnerable situation of ideology by characterizing it as

> a set of omissions, gaps rather than lies, smoothing over contradictions, appearing to provide answers to questions which in reality it evades, and masquerading as coherence in the interests of the social relations generated by and necessary to the reproduction of the existing mode of production.[31]

Because it only masquerades as coherence, ideology, in effect, can form the basis of its own critique, of a disclosure of the omissions, gaps, and contradictions that constitute it. Like the ideology critiques practiced by the feminists cited above, this book is dedicated to exposing the fissures and contradictions inherent in hegemonic constructions of gender by mapping them critically on a field of material social relations—that is, by uncovering the presuppositions on which they are based and the historically determined anxieties they aspire to allay. I have undertaken this project in the belief that the "sex roles" and gendered relations normalized by the "domestic theory of containment" were deeply oppressive for both women and men, and continue, in striking ways, to cast a powerful ideological spell over American culture. Furthermore, I believe that the process of unmasking and mapping these unusually durable gendered subjects (so vibrantly represented in the work of Miller and Williams) can provide the possibility of framing alternatives or, in De Lauretis's words, of intuiting the terms in which "a different construction of gender can be posed." As De Lauretis urges, I often look to the edges of the texts in question, to characters and discourses that are systematically marginalized (such as the laughing Woman in *Death of a Salesman* or a strain of antihomophobic utterance in *Cat on a Hot Tin Roof*) in order to suggest a way of both deconstructing these texts and envisioning "a different" and less onerous and despotic "construction of gender."

At the same time, I believe that the exposure of contradictions within hegemonic notions of masculinity and femininity can, in effect, restore a degree of agency to the subject of ideology, the subjected being who "freely" submits to the ubiquitous network of power relations that (re)produces him or her. Because the individual is continually being articulated by an ideological apparatus that is contradictory and riddled with cracks, he or she is always constituted not as a seamless whole but as a radically divided or fragmented subject. As Lacan and many poststructuralists have pointed out in their critiques of the Cartesian *cogito*, this subject, rent by the inaccessibility of the unconscious and the inadmissibility of repressed desire, only appears to be self-possessed, the author and origin of meaning. The speaking "I" can never be fully present to itself, nor can it ever take up an identity as "an autonomous and self-grounding subject," but only *posture* as one, to borrow Judith Butler's word.[32] Despite the subject's desperate and feverish embrace of a masculine or feminine posture, it can never resolve the ideological incoherencies supervising its interpellation into representation and into culture. This does not mean, however, that the gendered subject is condemned simply to repeat automatically its own schizoid enculturation. In a deeply political and utopian intuition, Belsey deftly turns these ideological incoherencies around to reveal the revolutionary potential inherent in the divided subject, a subject who, though

> the site of contradiction, and . . . consequently perpetually in the process of construction, thrown into crisis by alterations in language and in the social formation, [is] capable of change. And in the fact that the subject is a *process* lies the possibility of transformation.[33]

Because gendered subjectivity is not a *telos* but a constantly (self-) renewing process, it is always vulnerable, always prone to being refashioned and restruck, to becoming a casualty of those very historical struggles over which it proudly claims victory. An exposure of these struggles—and of the historically bound contradictions by which the gendered subject is articulated—allows the reinstatement of choice through the subject's recognition that what was once taken to be timeless and universal is itself the product of discrete historical forces and, thus, subject to change.

Masquerade

During the 1980s a number of theorists, drawing on the work of psychoanalysts Joan Riviere and Jacques Lacan, developed the concept of femininity (or "womanliness") as masquerade. In Riviere's widely influential

1929 essay on conflict resolution and gender, she strategizes an antiessentialist "womanliness," one that "could be assumed and worn as a mask"
by a woman circulating and working among men (and "wish[ing] for
masculinity"), "both to hide the possession of masculinity and to avert
the reprisals [from men] expected if she was found to possess it."[34]
According to Riviere, masquerade allows a woman to expropriate the
masculine prerogative while playing the womanly part, while dissimulat-
ing femininity. This permits her, in Judith Butler's estimation, to take on
"a masquerade knowingly in order to conceal her masculinity from the
masculine audience she wants to castrate," or disarm, and thereby avert
the retribution of the men upon whose privilege she encroaches.[35] Yet the
most startling allegation in Riviere's essay is not about conflict resolution
at all, but the ontological status of femininity:

> The reader may now ask how I define womanliness or where I draw
> the line between genuine womanliness and the "masquerade." My
> suggestion is not, however, that there is any such difference; whether
> radical or superficial, they are the same thing.[36]

In this extraordinary insight, Riviere completely disallows the possibility
of a "womanliness" outside of or prior to masquerade. In her estimation,
it is always a copy without an original, an act of endless mimicry, a
performance designed specifically for an audience of men. In this masquerade, in disguise as "a castrated woman," according to Stephen Heath,
"the woman represents man's desire and finds her identity as, precisely,
woman."[37]

Elaborating on Riviere's essay in Lacanian terms, Butler pursues the
implications of masquerade for a theory of the gendered subject within
a heterosexual system of exchange. She points out that in Lacanian
psychoanalysis the distinction between genders (and sexual positions) is
founded upon the difference between "having" and "being" the Phallus—
the forever elusive paternal signifier, the Law of the Father, the "fullness
of being" that, because it is always just beyond reach, also denotes a
lack in being.[38] She notes that although both man and woman must
finally be understood as "nonpositions" (because of the nonpresence of
the Phallus), man is nonetheless theorized as "having" (or never quite
"having") the Phallus, while woman is understood as "being" (or never
quite "being") the Phallus. In "being" the Phallus, woman becomes the
object of man's heterosexualized desire:

> For women to "be" the Phallus means, then, to reflect the power of the
> Phallus, to signify that power, to "embody" the Phallus, to supply the
> site to which it penetrates, and to signify the Phallus through "being"

> its other, its absence, its lack, the dialectical confirmation of its
> identity.[39]

Butler observes that within the Lacanian phallic economy, women appear to "embody" or "be" the Phallus (and so reflect it back to the one who "has" it) through masquerade, through "the performative production of a sexual ontology, an appearing that makes itself convincing as a 'being.'"[40] Femininity as masquerade is precisely this performance, this womanly impersonation of the Phallus that will convince an audience of desiring (and vindictive) men that the woman in question could not possibly threaten their exclusive possession of the perpetually deferred signifier.

Although the Lacanian elaboration of masquerade is clearly intended to map the female, heterosexualized subject, it need not be restricted simply to the one who appears to "be" the Phallus. It is my goal here, by expropriating this notion of femininity, to develop a corresponding theory of *masculinity as masquerade*. As I have indicated, within the Lacanian system, man is understood as the one who "has" (and yet never quite "has") the Phallus and all "the privileges of the symbolic" to which it provides access, despite the fact that the penis he does have, the "anatomical appendage" that authorizes him to check the box marked "M" on a census form, can never be synonymous with the Phallus.[41] The latter always exceeds subjectivity, presence, the Law. And yet, as Stephen Heath points out, this impossibility does not forestall a man's claim to masculinity: "The man's masculinity, his male world, is the assertion of the phallus."[42] It is this act of assertion, of phallic identification, that I designate by the term *masculinity*. Like "womanliness" for Riviere, this performative masculinity dissolves the distinction between the genuine and the masquerade. It is always a display, a sham, a mask of power articulated by what Butler describes as the Lacanian "comedy of sexual positions."[43] If, as Lemoine-Luccioni notes, "the penis was the phallus, men would have no need of feathers or ties or medals" or any of the extravagant representative machinery they use to symbolize their elusive phallic potency. "Display [*parade*], just like the masquerade, thus betrays a flaw: no one has the phallus."[44]

Despite masculinity's status as an illusion without ontological foundation, a sequence of postures, it has a profoundly real—and, many would say, devastating—impact on the world. And although a construction central to the operation of all patriarchal cultures, it is, like "womanliness," constantly subject to the vicissitudes of history. The masculinity of Cold War America, for example, is characterized very differently from that of the 1920s—or the 1990s, for that matter. Despite its constant reconfiguration, however, masculinity in the United States during the twentieth century has remained relatively invariable in relation to certain issues (many of its most salient characteristics can, in fact, be traced back to the consolidation of bourgeois subjectivity in the early eighteenth century). Perhaps most crucially, it has been consistently inscribed within a strictly heterosexual framework, or what Judith Butler (with a nod to Monique Wittig and Adrienne Rich) designates as the "heterosexual matrix," a

> hegemonic discursive/epistemic model of gender intelligibility that assumes that for bodies to cohere and make sense there must be a stable sex expressed through a stable gender . . . that is oppositionally and hierarchically defined through the compulsory practice of heterosexuality.[45]

Understood within this matrix, masculinity relates the male subject both to women and to other men. In the former case, it functions as a form of display that facilitates the exchange of women between men, a performance designed both to attract "the opposite sex" and to establish masculine proprietary authority over it. In the latter, it is the sign of male aggression, of competition between those who pretend to the Phallus for those who "are" the Phallus. As a number of feminist theorists have pointed out (see chapter 1) both instances, in granting primacy and priority to (sexual) relations between men, are irreducibly contradictory and put an extraordinary degree of stress on the ostensible heterosexuality of the normative male subject who is expected to repress what Butler calls the "unresolved homosexual cathexes" in which, she argues, are rooted "the very notions of masculinity and femininity." [46] As my analysis of *Death of a Salesman* demonstrates, the compulsory heterosexuality of this rather pathetic—if tyrannical—subject is always ghosted and disrupted by its forbidden other.

The brutal masquerade of Cold War capitalists and Communists that flourished within this heterosexual matrix admirably exemplifies what R. W. Connell labels "hegemonic masculinity." A strictly hierarchical set of relations, it secures its dominance by lording itself over "various subordinated masculinities." [47] And the hierarchy in which it participates and the subjects constituted by it are particularly sensitive to differences in race, ethnicity, and social class. The masculine posture, for example, of the white middle-class "organization man" of the 1950s is clearly distinct from that of the working-class African-American man. Yet these different qualities of masculine display cohere worldwide around at least

one issue. As the single point of agreement between Nixon and Khrushchev demonstrates ("We can all drink to the ladies"), hegemonic masculinity is "centred on a single structural fact, the global dominance of
men over women." [48]

Despite the deadly earnestness of Nixon and Khrushchev locked in
debate before a model American suburban bungalow, their exchange can
also be read through a feminist (or psychoanalytical) lens, which reveals
their masculinity as a series of grotesque poses and threats that is all a
part of the potentially lethal game of nuclear deterrence. In so reconfiguring the two world leaders as despots posturing in Cold War drag,
this rereading of nuclear brinksmanship underlines the status not just of
masculinity, but also of the Cold War itself, as an ideological construction, a masquerade produced for particular economic and geopolitical
ends. In a recent article on the politics of feminine masquerade, Sue-
Ellen Case advocates what she calls a "butch-femme aesthetic" as both
an ideology critique and a way of undermining heterosexist constructions
of gender. As she points out, in this cultural performance, as in masquerade, an "atmosphere of camp" permeates "the *mise-en-scène* with
'pure' artifice" and "a strategy of appearances replaces a claim to truth."
Gendered roles, as a result, "are played in signs themselves and not in
ontologies." [49] In Case's theorization, the " 'pure' artifice" of gender is
thereby reclaimed for a revolutionary practice.[50] (Read through this lens,
it is difficult not to interpret the aggressive posturing of Nixon and
Khrushchev simultaneously as overcompensation for their notorious lack
of masculine allure.)

When reconsidered as "butch" masqueraders—hired guns for capitalism and communism, respectively—both Nixon and Khrushchev
appear as variations on the one figure referred to (but not yet analyzed)
in the title of this book: the cowboy. In many respects, the cowboy
most clearly exemplifies the hegemonic masculinity of the late 1940s and
the 1950s in all its violent contradictions. The historical American cowboy was, of course, a product of nineteenth-century expansionism, during which he exemplified the "self-made man." Working among exclusively male comrades-in-arms, he defined his masculinity through a form
of male bonding that retained, at the least, ambiguous sexual resonances
(see chapter 1). And as a key player in an imperialist adventure, the
cowboy, in Andrew Ross's estimation, found his vocation—a vocation
surprisingly similar to that of Nixon and Khrushchev—in "the exploitation of land and labor through the codes of 'lawlessness,' the justification of genocide through the codes of 'manifest destiny,' and the legit-
imation of wild misogyny through the codes of maverick male

autonomy." [51] What the Dakotas were for the cowboys, Taiwan and Hungary were for Nixon and Khrushchev.

Despite the popularity of the cowboy in films and on television during the late 1940s and the 1950s, neither Arthur Miller nor Tennessee Williams is exactly renowned for his use of the western genre. And yet cowboys haunt the work of both men in uncanny ways. Miller wrote the screenplay for one western, *The Misfits* (1961), a caustic examination of the ethos of the modern cowboy and the disappearance of the old West, a remarkable film that remains his most critically disparaged major work (and which I analyze in chapter 1). Although he never wrote a western, Williams allows the image of the cowboy to infiltrate his fiction strangely and obliquely. In his paired short stories, "The Mysteries of the Joy Rio" and "Hard Candy," both published in 1954 (and which I examine in chapters 2 and 3, respectively), an aging male homosexual protagonist journeys to a "third-rate cinema" to engage in furtive sexual encounters with young men who have come innocently to watch the "cowboy pictures" playing there.[52] And yet the difference between *The Misfits* and "The Mysteries of the Joy Rio," between the cowboy as the stuff of tragedy, as "straight" entertainment (in Miller), and the cowboy as the pretense for a cunning and grotesque farce, as "camp" (in Williams), emblematizes the different attitudes toward hegemonic masculinity on the part of the two playwrights. Moreover, I have introduced the cowboy, the quintessential American masculine icon, into the title of this book *between* Communists and queers—neither of which, please note, is definitively gendered—in the hope of disrupting the symmetry between them and of revealing Cold War masculinity to be both a gruesome exercise in nuclear "chicken" and a charade, both a deadly earnest con game and a dirty joke.

One

Arthur Miller
"Why can't I say 'I'?"

> I don't believe that in the history of letters there are many great books
> or great plays that don't advocate. That doesn't mean that a man is a
> propagandist. It is in the nature of life and it is in the nature of
> literature that the passions of an author congeal around issues.
>
> —Arthur Miller, Testimony before the House Committee on
> Un-American Activities, June 21, 1956

> Arthur Miller, playwright, disclosed today a past filled with
> Communist-front associations and a future filled with Marilyn Monroe.
>
> —*New York Times*, June 22, 1956

On the morning of June 21, 1956, in testimony before the House Committee on Un-American Activities, Arthur Miller refused to name those
with whom he had associated in so-called Communist front groups.
Invoking the right to free speech guaranteed by the First Amendment
and echoing the words of John Proctor from *The Crucible* (1953), Miller
declared that while he was willing to be "perfectly frank" about his own
activities, he "could not use the name of another person and bring trouble
upon him."[1] Before the mighty committee, Miller freely answered scores
of detailed questions about his previous commitment to leftist causes
and his involvement with several organizations the committee alleged
were Communist controlled.

In the midst of a long and, at times, aggressive interrogation, Miller
never wavered in his determination not to inform. His finest moment,
however, was his vigorous defense of the political character of all artistic
production. He insisted that writing is a form of political practice and
that the writer who is forbidden to take a political stand cannot function
as an artist: "My understanding of [the Smith Act] is that advocacy is
penalized or can be under this law. Now, my interest, as I tell you, is
possibly too selfish, but without it I can't operate and neither can literature in this country."[2] Miller's none-too-"selfish" assertion, spoken
against those who had been crusading since 1947 to silence the left-wing
writer and to forestall any progressive political views on the stage and

in film, describes a crucial moment in his lifelong commitment to the political instrumentality of art.

Miller's understanding of the ideological network in which artistic productions are necessarily entangled has earned him a singular position, not just in the imaginations of those who saw *The Crucible*, his heroic indictment of McCarthyism, in 1953, but also in the consciences of a subsequent generation of American theater artists.[3] For his critics, as well, Miller remains the foremost social dramatist of his generation, the American playwright who has most successfully, in C. W. E. Bigsby's words, "touched a nerve of the national consciousness."[4] Almost unanimously, those in both popular and academic theater have embraced him as the leading proponent of "social commitment," as the playwright who knows that "the theatre must dedicate itself to public matters," as "an energetic, socially conscious thinker and [as] an accomplished dramatic craftsman."[5] Beginning with the plays he wrote as a student at the University of Michigan during the 1930s, Miller has consistently dedicated his writing to the exploration of manifestly political issues, including the alienation and commodification of the individual subject in bourgeois society, the mechanics of ostracism, and the ethics of informing on one's colleagues. As a renowned advocate and intellectual, he has persevered in his political activism for more than fifty years, working as a delegate for Eugene McCarthy in 1968, serving as president of International PEN, and protesting in support of persecuted and imprisoned writers in Turkey, the Soviet Union, Czechoslovakia, and numerous other countries.

Despite Miller's vigorous commitment to social justice, his political position has been and remains—as most of his critics acknowledge—extremely complex and contradictory. Even the significance of Miller's testimony before "the committee" is far more equivocal than his simple refusal to name names would indicate. Unlike the so-called friendly witnesses (such as Elia Kazan, who had directed *Death of a Salesman* [1949] and would direct *After the Fall* [1964], Miller's analysis of Kazan's betrayal), Miller refused to play the informer. However, by the time he testified, the most intense wave of anti-Communist furor had subsided and "the committee" no longer wielded the power it had when it began its investigation of writers in the 1940s (McCarthy himself had been censured by the Senate in 1954). Even in the face of its diminished prestige, Miller did not challenge the committee's right—as the Hollywood Ten had done in 1947—to question his own political beliefs and activities. Despite his citation for contempt of Congress (his conviction was later reversed on a technicality), Miller was not considered a hostile witness, but (in the words of historians) "cooperative," "credible," and "reasonable."[6] Although he denied having been a "dupe" of "Communist organizations," he freely volunteered at the end of the hearing to declare it "a disaster and a calamity if the Communist Party ever took over this country," and noted grimly, "I have had to go to hell to meet the devil."[7] Chairman Francis E. Walter, in his closing remarks, expressed satisfaction with what he took to be Miller's recantation and noted that the playwright had evidently "learned a great deal" from his "errors" and could serve as "a very loud warning to a lot of other people."[8] As he had done and was to do countless times on a different stage and before a different kind of audience, Miller had walked a rhetorical tightrope, his discourse suspended between heroic and principled assertion and artful and guilty equivocation. His politics, as always, was "ambiguous."[9]

The Old Left

During the late 1930s and the 1940s, Miller proudly identified himself as "a confirmed and deliberate radical" and revolutionary.[10] And in his 1987 autobiography, *Timebends*, he remembers those years as a time when he "believed with passionate moral certainty that in Marxism was the hope of mankind."[11] In the course of his testimony before the House Committee, Miller defended his support for a number of causes and organizations that the committee deemed subversive. Despite his repeated assertions, however, Miller's plays remain squarely and demonstrably within the tradition of American liberalism, flattening out class conflicts and prizing individual initiative far more than collective action. In his memoir, for example, Miller criticizes the principle he alleges lies "deep within Marxism," that "power is forbidden to the individual and rightly belongs only to the collective." Rather than consider collective agency or the opening up of a possibility beyond the (liberal) fixation with individual versus society, he appears to see "Marxism" only as the destroyer of personal freedom and the symptom of "a despairing passivity before History."[12] Bigsby, in what is unquestionably the most vigilantly historicized critique of Miller's work, has cogently examined the differences between the playwright's professed radicalism and the liberal values his plays espouse.[13] Although I generally agree with Bigsby's assessment, I want to examine the context of Miller's beliefs in greater detail in order to demonstrate how enmeshed in a particular historical moment his politics has always been.

As a member of a generation of intellectuals (often referred to as the Old Left) that had a decisive impact on mid-century American culture, Miller came of age during the Great Depression of the 1930s, which coincidentally was the period in which the American Communist party exercised its greatest political power and recruited its largest membership.

It is important to note, however, that the Communist party of the mid- and late 1930s was dramatically different from its more unequivocally Leninist and revolutionary predecessor. In his excellent history, *Marxism in the United States*, Paul Buhle points out that "the insurrectionary fever had largely passed by 1933–34" and that "over the next half-dozen years, . . . American Communists were transformed from a persecuted pariah into a semi-legitimate left-of-center force within national poli- tics."[14] This was the era of the Popular Front, an enormously important development in the history of American Marxism. As formulated in 1935 by the Seventh Congress of the Communist International, Popular Front communism gained ascendancy in the United States from 1936 until the Hitler-Stalin pact of 1939. Although the party never abandoned its tra- ditional Marxian analysis of American capitalism, its commitment to a politics of class struggle, or its long-term goals during those years, it did move toward a politics of reform, virtually endorsing Roosevelt's reelection and his Second New Deal of 1936 and recruiting an impressive level of support from the leaders of labor unions, the ethnic working class, African-Americans, and even the progressive wing of the Demo- cratic party. As Buhle underlines, the newly respectable party of the Popular Front "reflected the . . . triumph of the new middle class," and championed democratic ideals in the face of fascism. Earl Browder, one of the leaders of the Communist party from 1919 and a staunch opponent of the New Deal in 1932, declared four years later that "the direct issue of the 1936 elections is not socialism or capitalism, but rather democracy or fascism."[15] Reconceived as a citadel of antifascism, Popular Front communism—on which Miller and so many others were nourished— prospered enormously. By the end of the 1930s, the party's membership had risen from 10,000 to 65,000, and in 1942 reached an all-time high of 85,000.

As is well known, the American Communist party virtually collapsed after World War II for a multitude of reasons, and its history from 1945 to 1960 is branded not only by the sting of McCarthyism, but, just as rancorously, by the animosities of its former supporters trading accu- sations and counteraccusations over the errors and crimes of Stalinism.[16] During this period, the Right successfully managed the disintegration of the American Left and the effective disappearance of both oppositional politics and an intelligentsia predisposed to an incisive critique of the new Cold War order. The only major intellectual figures in the United States who did register criticism (albeit subdued and measured) of the forces of reaction were the Cold War liberals, many of whom had been members of the Communist party (or at least sympathizers) during the fervid days of the Popular Front. While these Cold War liberals ranged from relative moderates such as Arthur Schlesinger, Jr., to rabid apostates such as Sidney Hook, they were united (not unlike the neoconservatives who came to prominence during the 1980s) by an unflinching opposition to communism that often demanded the renunciation of their own past beliefs.

Despite the unique terms of its inception, Cold War liberalism did not mark a fundamental shift in the liberal ideology that has remained hegemonic in the United States since the end of the colonial period. Like its many variations, it is clearly linked to the rise of mercantile capitalism during the sixteenth and seventeenth centuries, to the consolidation of European imperialism, and to the philosophies of Descartes, Hobbes, and Locke that provided the ideological support for the new economic system and world order. In its classic formulation, liberalism takes the sovereign individual as the fundamental social unit, and private property and the unrestricted market as the bases of a "free" economy. It champions a representative and limited government and the rule of law, prizes freedom above equality (although usually giving lip service to the latter), and places a premium on rationality, progress, and individual initiative. As Anthony Arblaster points out, "Liberal individualism is both onto- logical and ethical," granting primacy to an ostensibly independent and integral subject who is seen as the repository of free will, moral respon- sibility, sovereign desires, and the power "to follow the dictates of his or her own conscience."[17] In the years following World War II, traditional American liberalism was recruited to combat "totalitarianism" and embrace what was called "the end of ideology," a position supposedly beyond politics and beyond social classes (which, according to orthodox liberalism, are only temporary expedients anyway, easily transcended by the hardworking, self-reliant individual). In Arblaster's estimation, Cold War liberalism represents "an almost terminal stage in the decline of Western liberalism" in which it "ceased to retain any vestige of rad- icalism," becoming "wholly defensive and fundamentally conservative."[18] (As the inheritors of the Cold War mantle, most so-called liberals dur- ing the Reagan-Bush years are more accurately described as "liberal- conservatives.")

Despite the obvious differences between the programs of the Old Left and the Cold War liberals, both were agreed that politics—and literature—are preeminently masculine affairs.[19] The Communist party leaders of the 1920s and 1930s were almost entirely men, as were the officers of the American Writers' Congress, who, meeting in 1935, con- stituted a virtual "who's who" of male leftist artists (both in the popular imagination and in fact, the Old Left Communist was almost always gendered masculine).[20] The virtual exclusion of women went hand in hand with the production of a vehemently masculinist and homophobic theory of literary production. Writing in 1930, Michael Gold, a member of the staff of *New Masses*, labeled as "chambermaid literature" the art of the "genteel bourgeoisie" and viciously attacked Thornton Wilder, describing the narrator of one of his novels as "a typical American art 'pansy'" and berating Wilder for his "homosexual bouquet."[21] In its place, Gold demanded a virile and heroic proletarian literature, trumpeting:

> Send us a giant who can shame our writers back to their task of
> civilizing America. Send a soldier who has studied history. Send a
> strong poet who loves the masses and their future.... Send an artist.
> Send a scientist. Send a Bolshevik. Send a Man.[22]

Twenty years later, across the great divide separating the Old Left from Cold War liberalism, the arbiters of politics and culture were applying a similarly gendered rhetoric. Schlesinger's *The Vital Center* (1949), for example, lays out a program to bring "a new virility into public life." In Elaine Tyler May's summary, this virility is explicitly contrasted with

> the "political sterility" of leftists and the "emasculated" ruling class....
> Ideologues were "soft, not hard" and displayed "the weakness of
> impotence," compared to tough-minded American capitalists.
> Communism was "something secret, sweaty and furtive like nothing so
> much, in the phrase of one wise observer of modern Russia, as
> homosexuals in a boys school."[23]

Clearly, women and "pansies" had no place in either of these brave new worlds.

Judging from *Timebends* and the evidence of his testimony before the House Committee, Miller, like so many of his contemporaries, gradually changed between the early 1940s and 1956 (in his own words: "It was a slow process") from a Popular Front Communist to a Cold War liberal.[24] And while he never seems to have held the violently reactionary views of a Sidney Hook or an Irving Kristol, the liberalism that Bigsby correctly describes in his work in many respects exemplifies the one variety endemic to Cold War America. Even his long, celebrated note in act 1 of *The Crucible* on the international political order implicates the writer on the far side of "ideology." In positing a symmetry between the American and Soviet empires as "two diametrically opposed absolutes" (and refusing the demonization posed by the McCarthyite "absolute"), his analysis unequivocally sets Miller himself (like the exemplary Cold War liberal) outside the dualism, which is to say, beyond both Communist "ideology" and its mirror image.[25] Furthermore, Miller's recantation before the House Committee also neatly conforms to the attack on utopianism launched by the Cold War liberals who persistently associated it with "totalitarianism." Miller's final, mournful confession, "I was looking for the world that would be perfect," in its use of the past tense, effectively banishes utopia from his imagination (although utopia still manages to inform his dramatic discourse in perhaps surprising ways).[26]

Colonizing the contradictory space between the Popular Front and Cold War liberalism, Miller's work—like that of Gold and Schlesinger—posits a virtual equation between political commitment (whether progressive or liberal) and masculinity. Relentlessly, it associates the persecuted hero, fighting for victory against a battalion of suffocating and destructive forces, with an embattled virility. And while Miller's position is hardly unique, his plays do provide an unusually clear view of the set of presuppositions underlying the construction of the liberal, masculinized hero, as well as the ideological and sexual configuration of the forces against which this hero struggles. In analyzing the trials of this hero, I will answer the following questions: What dramatic forms and conventions does Miller mobilize in order to dramatize this conflict? How is the heroic male subject configured, materially and ideologically? What is his story? Who is his opponent? How are the profiles of these antagonists redrawn in the course of Miller's career? And, most important, why do the forces of the repressed invariably return to haunt, undermine, and finally destroy the best-laid plans of his heroic male protagonists?

The Personal and the Political

During a short recess in Miller's testimony before the House Committee, America's foremost social dramatist announced that within the month he was going to marry America's foremost "love goddess," Marilyn Monroe.[27] Miller did not refer to her by name during the hearing, but mentioned her in passing as "the woman who will then be my wife" and would accompany him to London for the British premiere of *A View from the Bridge* (1955).[28] The announcement of Miller's betrothal, however, was far less inconsequential than this mention makes it out to be. In most newspaper reports, it completely upstaged the hearing, producing "enormous" headlines and burying the nuances of Miller's equivocal performance before the committee in the sizzling details of his now sensational personal life.[29] What is most striking, however, is the curiously snide and prurient tone with which the press reported the incident. Even the stolid *New York Times* did not flinch from a sarcastic lead: "Arthur Miller, playwright, disclosed today a past filled with Communist-front associations and a future filled with Marilyn Monroe."[30] Richard Rovere's use of innuendo is even more revealing of the contemporary attitude toward the impending marriage: "There can be little doubt that if the average American were asked today what he thought of Arthur Miller he would respond not with a denunciation but with a wink."[31] Rovere (for whom the "average" American is, tellingly, a lecherous, heterosexual male) feigns amusement at Miller's publicity coup to criticize him for his manipulative maneuver to disarm the public. Victor Navasky, meanwhile, criticizes Miller for not taking a more aggressive stance before the committee, given the fact that he had "the nation's reigning sex queen" at least figuratively "at his side."[32]

Each of the aforementioned accounts supposes that Miller deliberately staged his announcement to coincide with the day of the hearing—and there is no evidence to contradict this supposition—in order to deflect attention from his testimony and clear his name in the public eye. Each assumes a calculated link between his performance in the political arena and his betrothal to Monroe. What is perhaps most remarkable about this incident, however, is that the relationship between public and private that Rovere and Navasky presume exactly replicates the one implicit in Miller's plays. On June 21, Miller had, in effect, become the protagonist in a drama uncannily like one of his own. If one is to believe the press, Miller, like the fictional John Proctor, had tried to capitalize on the rhetorical force granted the release of withheld information about a sexual liaison, using his relationship with a powerful and bewitching woman to vindicate a controversial political stand. At the same time, the drama of June 21 presages the complications that would plague Miller in regard to his next play, *After the Fall*: the capricious yet inexorable slippage between sexuality and politics, and the difficulty in separating oneself from one's texts (or the construction of autobiography from the writing of fiction).

In "The Family in Modern Drama," an essay published just two months before the hearing, Miller attempts to regulate the relationship between the domestic and the political by setting up an elaborate scheme of interrelated binarisms: family and society, private and public, realism and expressionism, among others.[33] Taking up the mantle of Cold War liberalism, Miller privileges the first term in the pair, insisting that "the family relation," which is "received by us unawares before the time we were conscious of ourselves as selves," constitutes "the very apotheosis of the real." In comparison, "the social relation," located "outside" the self, is consciously learned; it is known rather than felt, derived rather than essential; it "is always relatively mutable, accidental, and consequently of a profoundly arbitrary nature to us."[34] According to Miller,

these modalities are distinguished not just ontologically and epistemo-
logically, but linguistically as well: the natural speech of the family is
"the language of the private life—prose," while "the language of society,
the language of the public life, is verse."[35]

At the end of the essay, Miller seems cognizant of the difficulty in
maintaining the radical breach between "family" and "society," and he
announces his intention of closing it. He speaks out forcefully against
plotless "mood plays" (by which he means the dramas of Tennessee
Williams) that pursue what he believes to be the wrong kind of reconciliation, seeking "poetry precisely where it is not: in the private
life, . . . the area of sensation, or the bizarre and the erotic." In its place
he seeks to install a "tragic" drama that will "unite" both private and
public, investigate "the whole gamut of causation," and "embrace the
many-sidedness of man."[36] The rhetoric of Miller's essay, however, unites
the private and public only in an abstraction, in "the high order of art,"
situated on some elevated, "tragic" plateau. Significantly, Miller produces
this amalgamation by dissolving the concreteness and specificity of the
binarism into a set of imprecise and quasi-mystical universals: truth,
man, the drama, total art. As he does unremittingly in his theater essays,
Miller produces these false universals by disregarding the specificity of
a particular cultural moment and eliding two profoundly dissimilar historical constructions. Thus, in searching out a precedent for his own
project, he equates "the later Greek plays," with their separation between
"society" and the "privacy of life," with twentieth-century theatrical
realism and its dramatization of the "widening gap between the private
life and the social life." By projecting his own bourgeois liberalism,
with its indispensable schism between individual and society, back
twenty-four hundred years, Miller tries diligently (and, to my mind,
unsuccessfully) to convince the reader that his own "tragic," dialectical
synthesis will restore the "everlastingly sought balance" between "private
lives" and "the life of the generality of men."[37]

Like so many patriarchal discourses, "The Family in Modern Drama"
is based upon the ostensible dichotomy of genders, exemplifying the
proposition, in Sue-Ellen Case's words, that "public life is the property
of men, and women are relegated to the invisible private sphere."[38] And
despite Miller's attempt at a Hegelian synthesis, the public and the private
are finally rendered as irreconcilable as all those binarisms related to
gender and sexuality that are so vigorously deployed throughout Miller's
plays: male versus female; honest woman versus whore; and the heroic,
masculine man versus the weakling, the "anemic," or the "weird."[39]

The rigor with which these interlocking binarisms are applied bears
witness to Miller's determination to regulate the production of genders

and sexualities and to police the distinctions between political and personal, and between masculine and feminine. Obsessively and determinedly, he tries in his plays to forestall potential transgressions by containing unruly women and homosexual men (in both literal and proverbial closets) and by punishing those, like Abigail Williams and Eddie Carbone, whose desires obscure the boundaries of orthodox sexuality, whether by threat of adultery, incest, or homosexuality. What passes unrecognized, however, in those who see Miller simply as a stern and tragic moralist, is that these sets of oppositions are so deeply contradictory and unstable as to stand, from the beginning, already discredited. As the reportage of Miller's testimony before the House Committee makes clear, the political body and the sexual body are coupled in complex and elusive ways. Far more concretely than Miller seems to understand, the personal *is* the political, the familial *is* the social, the honest woman *is* the whore, and the heroic male subject harbors his other inexorably within him.

The Subject of Liberal Tragedy

> BIFF: Somebody got in your bathroom!
> WILLY: No, it's the next room, there's a party—
> THE WOMAN, *enters, laughing. She lisps this*: Can I come in? There's something in the bathtub, Willy, and it's moving!
> *Willy looks at Biff, who is staring open-mouthed and horrified at The Woman.*
>
> —*Death of a Salesman*, act 2

> The hero defines an opposing world, full of lies and compromises and dead positions, only to find, as he struggles against it, that as a man he belongs to this world, and has its destructive inheritance in himself.
>
> —Raymond Williams, *Modern Tragedy* (1966)

Arthur Miller's body of work serves as a vast stage on which the liberal humanist subject—that allegedly seamless individual, conceived as author and origin of meaning and action—attempts to construct a linear, unified history. As Miller acknowledges, each of his plays pivots round a male protagonist, the "lead character," who determines the play's "central reality." Its plot, meanwhile, "is carried forward by [that] one individual wrestling" with a moral quandary, and the sequence of scenes is tightly controlled to focus the action squarely on the protagonist's anguished confrontation with his ever-intensifying "dilemma."[40] Miller's draft of *Death of a Salesman* began with an image of "an enormous face the height of the proscenium arch" and with the title *The Inside of*

His Head.[41] *After the Fall*, meanwhile, takes place unabashedly "in the mind, thought, and memory of Quentin," the play's protagonist.[42] Both plays are literally psychodramas that stage the dynamics of liberal humanist subjectivity: the interplay of will, desire, fantasy, and memory. Both expand the conventions of domestic realism by using expressionistic devices to concretize and render more vividly the plights of their tormented protagonists. Insistently, the nonlinear, theatricalized elements in both plays (associations and recollections) serve to reinforce, rather than undercut, the spectator's belief in the substantiality of the male psyches under examination. Both plays serve as a testament not merely to the compatibility of expressionism with realism, but to the almost incessant cross-fertilization between the two since the Renaissance.

In her analysis of early modern tragedy, Catherine Belsey argues that a psychological drama slowly emerged during the sixteenth century (coincidentally with the liberal humanist subject) as the autonomous characters of late medieval drama became internalized as psychological forces. In a play such as *Doctor Faustus*, the soliloquy, as a kind of dialogue for one speaker, relocates the conflicting voices of the morality play within Faustus's mind and thereby generates the illusion of interiority and psychological depth.[43] At the other end of the modern era, during the late nineteenth and early twentieth centuries, as the bourgeois subject was becoming increasingly isolated and bureaucratized, the process of internalization was, to some extent, reversed. In the work of Strindberg and his successors, expressionism developed as the external (or naturalistic) mimesis was supplanted by a kind of psychic mimesis that allowed for the projection of psychological forces upon both the environment and the entire *dramatis personae*.[44] Between 1912 and the mid-1920s, expressionist drama became codified as a form of confessional narrative that dramatized the various stages in the development of a protagonist.[45] Walter Hasenclever's *Humanity* (1918), for example, appropriating the form of the quest (like Goethe's *Faust*), dramatizes the search of its protagonist, Alexander, for his own lost and fragmented self through a brutally dehumanized world. Although the play attacks social and political organizations on both the right and the left, it is hardly a paean to bourgeois individualism. None of its characters experiences the kind of personal enlightenment from which Faust or the traditional tragic hero profits. The shattering of syntax, the dislocation of linear dramatic form, and the use of flat, emblematic characters disallow an empathic response on the part of the reader or spectator, and so refuses a cathartic release. In its very form, then, the play enacts—without explicitly offering a cure for—the atomization of German "humanity" in the wake of the Great War and the ensuing economic collapse. In doing so, it works to redefine political theater less as a catalyst for personal growth than as an incitement for reconceptualizing the body politic.

In *Death of a Salesman* and *After the Fall*, Arthur Miller combines the formal pliancy and confessional orientation of German expressionism with the structure of the well-made play to produce a unique hybrid. The well-made play, a long-lived and sturdy dramatic paradigm, was codified by Scribe in the 1830s and developed by Ibsen into psychological drama in the 1870s. In its latter formulation, it furnishes Miller with the backbone for virtually all of his plays.[46] Following his Norwegian master, he provides a causal link between scenes, building an argument dialectically and leading the action to a single climactic peripety. Almost invariably in Miller, this moment of reversal functions as a psychoanalytical fulcrum, either releasing information about a traumatic moment in the protagonist's past (as in *Death of a Salesman*) or suddenly betraying an unconscious and previously inadmissible desire (as in *After the Fall*). In either case, the peripety functions as the solution to the mystery, the key to character psychology that allows the spectator to share a moment of recognition with the protagonist.

In underscoring the already unmistakably Freudian orientation of the well-made play, Miller's dramaturgy remains strictly teleological, moving toward a future that has already happened, a peripety that is always a disclosure of the past. In so doing, it discovers a continuity between past and present, the traumas of youth and the crises of manhood. This continuity, however, does not guarantee that the present merely repeats the past. In most of his plays, Miller admits the possibility, however hazily defined, that the "individual wrestling with his dilemma" can, like Biff or Quentin, begin to correct past mistakes and forge intimate bonds that do not simply replicate the dysfunctional relationships that shaped his personality. Miller mitigates Ibsen's formal and psychological rigor both by positing a less severely deterministic model of behavior and by mollifying the undecidable contradiction toward which the Ibsen last act invariably moves. (Consider, for example, how Ibsen presents Nora Helmer simultaneously as a robust, protofeminist champion and as a deluded romantic heroine fleeing wildly into the night.) In his adaptation of *An Enemy of the People* (1950), Miller turns Dr. Stockmann into an unambiguous hero by cutting the arrogant and fanatical speeches that Ibsen pointedly assigns Stockmann to problematize his moral position. Consistently, Miller interprets Ibsen—and the social and psychological issues with which Ibsen was preoccupied—less as a producer of plural and interrogative texts than as a polemicist who "used to present answers."[47]

Miller's misrecognition of Ibsen's project did not inhibit him, however, from becoming, like his forebear, the preeminent playwright of his generation to develop and use consistently the dramatic form that Raymond Williams designates as liberal tragedy. As cultivated by Ibsen, this form pits an aspiring individual (who is almost always male) against a repressive or destructive society that can neither understand nor accommodate him. Inevitably, however, the liberating individual discovers that he, too, has unwittingly been tainted by corruption, "that as a man he belongs to this world, and has its destructive inheritance in himself."[48] Ibsen's liberal tragedy, despite its often brutal critique of the social inequities and crimes underwritten by monopoly capitalism, distrusts the collectivity (and the failed proletariat revolutions of 1848 and 1870) and conceives opposition in the person of the solitary crusader. By so crippling the liberator and, simultaneously, erasing the possibility of collective action, Ibsen guarantees his hero's—and his society's—tragedy. Miller, following his mentor's lead, critiques commodity capitalism from the perspective of the oppressed individual, the Willy Loman who is unable to prosper in the fiercely competitive marketplace. But even more unequivocally than Ibsen, Miller (especially in his later plays) obviates collective opposition by taking up an almost Hobbesian ethical stance. Unlike Ibsen's plays, in which corruption remains societally based, *After the Fall* posits an original sin, a defective human condition that transcends a particular historical situation. Against this corruption, Miller, like Ibsen, sets the struggling individual. However, in Miller's work this subject is problematized far less radically than in Ibsen's. Miller's hero remains, like the "free" agent of commodity capitalism, capable of triumphing over the past and his inherited neuroses by a sheer act of will.[49]

The sovereign subject that towers above Miller's work is particularly well suited for representation by an actor trained in "the Method," a solemnly psychological approach to acting rooted in the same late nineteenth-century European culture that produced psychoanalysis. During the 1930s American acting was revolutionized by the teachings of Konstantin Stanislavsky, as disseminated directly by the master's own texts or as adapted by his many American disciples, including Lee Strasberg, Stella Adler, Harold Clurman, and Elia Kazan. These acting teachers and directors together consolidated and codified the Method, energizing both theater and film and producing three generations of America's most celebrated actors, from Morris Carnovsky, Marlon Brando, and Marilyn Monroe to Robert De Niro and Meryl Streep. The psychological approach that the Method promotes reinforces a sense of both actor and character as fully developed (which is to say, *split*) subjects made up of a supple exteriority, an "outer life" (in Stanislavsky's words), that harbors a rich "subconscious" within—a transhistorical "inner life of the human spirit." The Method insists that the actor discover an "inner justification" for everything he or she performs and that all theatrical action be "logical, coherent, and real," thereby reinforcing the much-desired stability of the individual and producing the illusion of a seamless subjectivity.[50] Above all, the Method attempts to foreclose the endless chain of deferral that constitutes theatrical performance based on a written text by denying the actor's contingency. It undertakes to turn the actor into an author, restoring his or her full presence by demanding that all the "material" received from playwright or director "become part" of the actor's self, that he or she "bring to life what is hidden under the words" and put his or her "own thoughts into the author's lines."[51] Having thus wholly appropriated the "material," the actor *becomes* the character and stands revealed as a fully present, fully centered subject, whose "each and every moment" is "saturated with a belief in the truthfulness of the emotion felt."[52]

All of Miller's plays from *All My Sons* (1947) to *After the Fall* work congruently with the Method (many of whose most celebrated practitioners have collaborated with Miller) to reinforce confidence in the liberal humanist subject's (imaginary) authority, solidity, and depth. Together, liberal tragedy and the Method try to contain a subjectivity grown increasingly restless and divided by carefully regulating the production of binary oppositions (Miller's family/society, private/public corresponds felicitously to Stanislavsky's subconscious/conscious, inside/outside). In *Death of a Salesman*, for example, widely regarded as "one of the greatest American plays ever written"[53] and the preeminent postwar liberal tragedy, Miller, like Hasenclever and the other early expressionists, demonstrates a remarkable ability to map the divisions within subjectivity. Unlike Hasenclever, however, Miller mobilizes the mechanisms of empathy and catharsis in an attempt to close over, with elegance and efficiency, all the fissures he has exposed. Its concluding "Requiem," rather than being an extension of the play's constituent contradictions, is an active and sentimental forgetting of the second act's daunting revelations. The confusion between self and other, present and past, is clarified, private becomes primly separated from public, and the subject—whether dead or alive—is rendered powerful and whole.

Hom(m)o-sexuality and the American Classic

In *Death of a Salesman* the sovereign subject is under siege, assailed from without and within. Willy and Biff are its embodiment, liberal tragic heroes (and "organization men") struggling against a society grown increasingly mechanized and indifferent. Both are crushed by the highly competitive postwar economy, with which they are ill equipped to cope, and crippled by their well-intentioned lies and desperate self-deceptions. Both long for the frontier—an unspoiled world that lies far beyond the suburbs of an oppressive city whose "angry" sheen glowers over the salesman's fragile house.[54] Willy vacillates between a wish for "a little place out in the country" where he can discover "peace of mind" and a secret, far deeper desire for the untamed wilderness of Alaska or Africa, a dream landscape that holds inestimable adventures and riches, a place for "me and my boys in those grand outdoors!" (pp. 72, 85). For Willy, this realm of freedom is embodied in his brother Ben, who, following in his father's footsteps, set out into the wilderness to become "a genius, . . . success incarnate," the "authoritative" individual who "knew the answers," the man who appears in Willy's visions with "an aura of far places about him," always accompanied by "idyllic music" (pp. 41, 44, 45, 133). For Biff, the untrammeled and mythic American West remains the locus of his dreams and desires, the place "to be outdoors, with your shirt off," the land where it's "cool" and where "it's spring . . . now" (p. 22).

For both father and son, the frontier represents a haven from the reaches of multinational capital, which, in 1949, was consolidating its grip by generating increasingly voracious consumers of a seemingly endless stream of commodities. Willy's utopian fantasy—which owes far more to Emersonian individualism than to Marxian socialism—hearkens back to a less competitive phase of capitalism in which it was more plausible that individual initiative and acts of daring would bring wealth and success.[55] This fantasy romanticizes the so-called self-made man so prized by American liberalism, both in Ben's achievements and in the melody of the solitary flute that pervades Willy's consciousness and evokes his flute-playing father, who deserted his family to hunt for treasure in Alaska. By way of contrast, Biff's utopian longing is even more removed than Willy's from the exigencies of the marketplace. Spurning society altogether and prizing independence and adventure far more than the acquisition of wealth, Biff longs to buy a ranch and become a cowboy. A man for whom "nothing [is] more inspiring or—more beautiful than the sight of a mare and a new colt," he seems to prefer commerce with the natural world to human society (p. 22).

Despite the apparent rejection by both Willy and Biff of the body politic, their fantasies are deeply enmeshed in the production of gender, fashioning two closely related masculine ideals. For Willy, Ben embodies a rugged and heroic virility ("What a man!" Willy exclaims after his first vision of Ben; p. 53) that the failing salesman keenly desires. For Biff, meanwhile, the dream of being a cowboy represents an attempt to recover the power that deserted him when he discovered his father's adulterous liaison in Boston. Before his fateful visit to Willy's hotel room, Biff had been the incarnation of a charismatic and reckless masculinity: star athlete, captain of the football team, and a man "too rough with the girls" (p. 40). After his disenchantment, however, Biff flounders and, like his father, turns to fantasy as a way of recouping masculine power.

Although drawing on stubborn American myths, both of these masculinist ideals are significantly different from the prevailing stereotype of Cold War masculinity, which decreed, in the words of Talcott Parsons, that "virtually the only way to be a real man in our society is to have an adequate job and earn a living," that is, to support a family.[56] Both Willy and Biff, however, scorn these domesticated breadwinners in favor of a more heroic and maverick ideal that, during the 1940s and 1950s, always ghosted the "organization man" and determined the shape of his dreams. For both Loman men, the most striking characteristic of this ever-present fantasy is its rigorous exclusion of women. In Willy's imagination, Ben comes unencumbered with wife or children. He looms instead as the conqueror and plunderer of a natural realm that is unmistakably feminine and unresistant, a tenebrous continent whose glittering jewels he holds out to beckon the suicide-to-be: "The jungle is dark but full of diamonds" (p. 134). Instead of a family, Ben offers Willy the glory of "comradeship" (p. 127). Biff, as well, longs for a male community in which men are free to "raise cattle, use our muscles." He dreams of a partnership like the one his father desires: "Men built like we are," Biff exclaims, "should be working out in the open" (p. 23). The Loman Brothers ride again.

In examining the character of desire in Miller's work, Robert W. Corrigan identifies a "streak of puritanism" that, he alleges, marks the playwright's "view of women." Comparing Miller to Tennessee Williams, Corrigan notes that "desire is not a central part of Miller's universe," and that "his plays are manifestly lacking in the sensual."[57] While Corrigan is certainly correct to point out the relative scarcity of heterosexualized eroticism, his observation neglects what is, I believe, the primary mode of desire in Miller's work, which is, to borrow Luce Irigaray's neologism, determinedly hom(m)o-sexual. According to Irigaray, hom(m)o-sexuality describes the system of exchange under patriarchy that always refers "the production of women, signs and commodities . . . back to men." It is a social monopoly in which "wives, daughters, and sisters have value only in that they serve as the possibility of, and potential benefit in, relations among men." In this system, "man begets man as his own likeness" and women function as conduits, esteemed only insofar as they articulate male homosocial relations, relations between men.[58] Despite a certain ahistoricism in Irigaray's thought, a tendency to collapse distinctions between different economic systems and different stages of capitalism, her notion of hom(m)o-sexual exchange provides an indispensable guide to the dynamics of male desire in Miller's work.[59] It helps one to understand how, throughout his plays, women function as objects of men's desire, like the mare and newborn colt in Biff's fantasmatic corral, denied access to the most utopian and unsatisfiable desires that circulate solely among men, in their collective dreams of freedom and self-sufficiency.

Although *Death of a Salesman* foregrounds hom(m)o-sexual desire, it does not by any means unequivocally endorse the utopian idylls of Willy and Biff. In fact, their elaborate fantasies are more a sign of their self-deception than of their perspicacity. The play's critique of Willy's and Biff's delusional expectations does not, however, lead me to believe that it questions the assumptions that underlie the protagonists' dreams. Unfailingly, the play eulogizes the contents of the Loman *imaginaire* by its romanticization of a self-reliant and staunchly homosocial masculinity and by its corroborative and profound disparagement of women. Throughout the play, women are associated with a chaotic and disruptive natural realm that must be subjugated and rigorously controlled so that it cannot undermine the three cardinal masculine characteristics: achievement, responsibility, and authority.[60] Like Ben's dark jungle or the mare and colt that Biff finds so thrilling, women ("that worshipped, tortured species")[61] are rendered sources of inspiration and beauty only when subdued by the conquering male. In almost all of Miller's plays, they are presented as being closer to nature than men, more deeply involved in biological process, their bodies the source of a dangerous sexuality that threatens to destroy the projects of culture to which the men are dedicated. Cast as the natural and unstable Other, women exhibit a tendency toward extremes, or what Sherry B. Ortner calls a "greater symbolic ambiguity" than men.[62] In Parson's sociology, the prevailing "ambivalence" is configured in the opposition between the "asexual and 'good'" woman and the "glamour girl."[63] In *Death of a Salesman*, this ambiguity is encoded in the dichotomy the play desperately attempts to establish in order to separate the honest woman from the whore, wives from "strudel" (p. 100), and the dutiful Linda Loman from the unnamed laughing Woman in Boston.

Try as it may to install this binarism, the text of *Death of a Salesman* inadvertently ends up taking it apart. The more closely one examines the opposition between Linda and the sinister laughing Woman, the less securely it holds. From the beginning, the two figures are indissolubly intertwined in Willy's imagination. His outburst of "great feeling" for his wife in act 1 is juxtaposed against his memory of The Woman who appears "dimly" in the background, "as behind a scrim." Immediately afterward, he replays a brief scene with her in his hotel room that ends as The Woman bursts out laughing and "Linda's laughter blends in" (pp. 37–39). Furthermore, the two are linked metonymically by the new pair of stockings that Willy gives The Woman rather than Linda, thereby forcing his wife to mend her old ones. Most strikingly, however, the two are connected by a curious slip in the text. In their first scene, Biff and Happy discuss their relationships with women. Biff claims he wants to find a "steady" girlfriend, "somebody with substance." To this assertion he adds: "Somebody with character, with resistance! Like Mom" (p. 25). What is so startling about his pronouncement is his attribution of resistance to the most acquiescent female character in all of modern American drama. From the beginning of the play, Linda Loman is defined entirely by her relationship to her husband, whose "longings . . . she shares," although she "lacks the temperament to utter and follow [them] to their end" (p. 12). Throughout, she doggedly supports him and actively reinforces his delusions. The one woman in the play who resists Willy— and whom Biff has accidentally encountered—is, of course, the laughing Woman who emerges out of the bathroom, lisping, at the climactic moment of revelation in act 2.

Biff's slip of the tongue should not be read psychologically, as being indicative of any unconscious confusion on his part between his mother and The Woman, but as a sign of the text's inability to keep the two characters distinct and separate. The blending of the one into the other discloses the play's profound anxiety over the status and power of women and, in particular, over women's speech. Despite her several elaborate disquisitions, Linda is more frequently interrupted than any other character in the play. Insistently, the men (in particular Willy) cut off her sentences before she can finish them. Miller even calls attention to this practice by having Willy ironically and viciously reproach her for interrupting him (pp. 62, 64). But even more revealing of this anxiety (because more gratuitous) is the scene in act 2 in which Howard demonstrates his wire-recording machine to Willy. Howard and his five-year-old son blabber cheerfully into the machine while his wife is intimidated and reduced to an embarrassed silence: "His Wife, *shyly, beaten*: 'Hello.' *Silence.* 'Oh, Howard, I can't talk into this'" (p. 78).

Unlike these submissive women, The Woman in Boston is conspicuously unruly and garrulous. In act 1, she vainly "primps" at an imaginary mirror and utters just enough—"I picked you," ends her first speech— to accept responsibility for the liaison and thereby, at least in part, to absolve Willy (p. 38). In act 2, she pointedly criticizes Willy in an ungrammatical and infantile idiom: "You are the saddest, self-centeredest soul I ever did see-saw" (p. 116). Most important, unlike the restrained Linda (with whom she shares a fantasmatic seesaw), she laughs continually and irrepressibly in Willy's memory. Indeed, it is her uncontrollable laughter in act 2 that betrays her presence in the hotel bathroom to the astonished Biff, and brings ruin on both father and son.

Throughout *Death of a Salesman*, the obedient women are distinguished from the unruly ones by their ability to govern their speech. And yet, the devastating power of uncontrolled female discourse betrays the fact that something far greater than phonemes is at stake here. Verbal transgression is associated insistently with sexual transgression, with the failure of women to contain a desire that threatens to undermine and destroy the order of culture that men have carefully carved out of an unstable, feminized nature whose volatility they must continually control. As a result, the oral slips inexorably into the genital, and verbal transgression becomes a mark of sexual transgression. In *Salesman*, The Woman's wild laughter is the sign of the sexual threat she poses to the institution that for Miller (and "the domestic version of containment") best guarantees an ordered and civilized world: the nuclear family. In *The Crucible*, Abigail Williams's public accusation of Elizabeth Proctor and, indeed, the whole Salem witch-hunt, is motivated by her uncontrollable lust for a married man, John Proctor.[64] Of all of Miller's works, however, it is the relatively meditative play, *The Price* (1968), that discloses the most horrifying feminine oral transgression. The climactic revelation there is the description of a crucial moment of betrayal, which, like the scene in the Boston hotel room in *Salesman*, has permanently traumatized an impressionable young son. At the climax of act 2 of *The Price*, Victor remembers the day his father confessed to his family that he was bankrupt:

> It was right on this couch. She was all dressed up—for some affair, I think. Her hair was piled up, and long earrings? And he had his tuxedo on . . . and made us all sit down; and he told us it was all gone. And she vomited. *Slight pause. His horror and pity twist in his voice.* All over his arms. His hands. Just kept on vomiting, like thirty-five years coming up. And he sat there. Stinking like a sewer.[65]

Throughout Miller's work, the female body is constantly in danger of overflowing its limits. It is unstable and unfixed, its boundaries always in dispute, its interior—constituted indifferently of speech, sexual desire, or partially digested food—always threatening to erupt and engulf men in a sea of laughter, chaos, and stink. Confronted with this danger, the male subject must constantly be on guard, must constantly rein in the female body and demand that it maintain a Linda Loman-like "iron repression," remaining incapable, like Linda, even of crying over her husband's grave (pp. 12, 139). Aligned with a sovereign rationality, this subject seeks to install itself as the guarantor of order and of limits, and to exert incontrovertible control over both its own needs and the desires of others, since, as Victor J. Seidler has argued, "within a rationalist tradition, . . . emotions and desires" are seen as being most menacing to the social order.[66] Since the sixteenth century, however, the male subject's will to regulate others has been secretly subordinated to a silent injunction to self-discipline, to the policing of his own body and his own desires, an injunction accomplished at a crippling cost: the expense of permanent estrangement from the object that has been henceforth known as his own body. As Francis Barker has demonstrated, control of this Other within the self is deemed the basis of bourgeois culture, politics, and art.[67] When this self-control is extended to the control of others, meanwhile, it is deemed masculinity. It is the power—always striven for but only fitfully attained—that enables the men in Miller's work to master and regulate women's promiscuous desires and to stem the vomit, to keep the female body from spilling over and, like a sewer, contaminating the self-controlled, self-contained, and self-reliant male subject.

In Miller's work masculinity is, to borrow R. W. Connell's formulation again, jealously hegemonic and hierarchical in its construction, being set "in relation to various subordinated masculinities as well as in relation to women."[68] As a result, the men in *Salesman* are as subject to the exigencies of masculinist surveillance as the women, for, in addition to controlling unruly women, the fully masculine male must disdain effeminate men. In Willy's act 1 judgment, Charley is reckoned "disgusting" and "not a man" because he can't handle tools (p. 44). Charley's son, Bernard, meanwhile, is judged "an anemic" and "a worm" because he lacks athletic prowess (pp. 33, 40). (In act 2, however, Willy's evaluation changes as Charley and Bernard become far more successful in business than Willy and his sons. But what fully redeems Bernard's masculinity is his appearance before the Supreme Court and, even more important, his neat trick of fathering two sons, like Willy and Willy's father, and thereby assuming the role of the patriarch.) Despite Charley's and Bernard's belated successes, however, they are unable to appreciate the need for male camaraderie that fires Willy's and Biff's fantasies, the "desire," in Biff's words, "to be outdoors, with your shirt off," among cattle herders and farmhands (p. 22). Even Happy is swayed by Biff's homosocial reverie to profess his own frustration with the effete world of business: "Sometimes I want to just rip my clothes off in the middle of the store and outbox that goddam merchandise manager" (p. 24).

Both Biff and Happy dream of a male body whose boundaries—unlike those of the unruly female body—are clearly defined, one that opposes hard muscle to a pregnable natural world. At the same time, they envision a male community whose borders are clearly demarcated, one that uses ritualized combat as a form of social control (to express and contain aggressive impulses) and pointedly excludes both women and effeminate men.

The fantasy of a community defined by strictly homosocial bonds and yet aggressively heterosexual in its professed orientation puts enormous stress on the already fractured male subject, the one who must exert a control as rigorous over his own desires as over the desires of others. For in addition to demanding the exclusion of effeminate men, this fantasy also requires him to police the feminine within him, those wild and disorderly desires that threaten both the material integrity of the body and the coherence of the social group. In *Salesman*, neither Willy nor Biff is able to coax his masculinist fantasy into reality insofar as both are, in very different ways, tainted by the feminine. Willy's guilty secret, his adulterous liaison with an ungovernable woman whose effusions infect not only his own integrity but Biff's as well, is his ruin and threatens both his own masculine self-sufficiency and the very stability and durability of the patrilineal economy. Since that fatal day in Boston, Biff has lost his way, become a compulsive liar and thief, declining in initiative, feeling "mixed up very bad" (p. 23), the prey of despair and "self-loathing" (p. 124). Unlike his more alluring brother, to whom "sexuality" clings "like a visible color," Biff has a "worn air" (p. 19). Questioned by Happy, he denies that he "still run[s] around a lot" with women and protests mournfully, "I don't know—what I'm supposed to want" (pp. 25, 22).

For Biff, the moment of catastrophe (and the play's climactic disclosure) is his witness of the primal scene between his father and the woman "with resistance" who does not happen to be his mother. As replayed in the salesman's memory, Willy hears the knocking at his hotel room door and convinces The Woman to take refuge in the bathroom. When Biff enters, he explains to Willy that he flunked math and will not be able to graduate and go on to be a football star at the University of Virginia, as both had expected. Willy tells Biff that he will talk to his math teacher, Mr. Birnbaum, and, in an effort to get rid of Biff, asks him to go downstairs and inform the clerk that he is checking out. Rather than leaving, however, Biff suddenly decides to tell his father why Mr. Birnbaum "hates" him (although Biff's delay is requisite to the plot, his proffered information is purely gratuitous):

One day he was late for class so I got up at the blackboard and imitated him. I crossed my eyes and talked with a lithp.

Willy is greatly amused by the story and so Biff continues, in imitation of his lisping teacher:

The thquare root of thixthy twee is . . . *Willy bursts out laughing; Biff joins him.* And in the middle of it he walked in!

At that juncture Willy laughs again, and "The Woman joins in offstage." When Biff asks if someone's there, she laughs a second time and he naively voices his alarm: "Somebody got in your bathroom!" At this point she enters, lisping like Mr. Birnbaum, "Can I come in?" while Biff just stares "open-mouthed and horrified at The Woman" (pp. 117-19).

This scene explicitly thematizes a symmetry between the two lisping individuals who barge in unexpectedly and sabotage the hopes of Loman father and son: The Woman and Mr. Birnbaum. I believe, however, that this scene has such undeniable power because of another, less explicit, but far more disruptive identification. Just as The Woman and Linda Loman are indissolubly linked (as the uncontained is to the contained) to become the sign of an acute anxiety regarding female discourse and the geography of women's bodies, so are Mr. Birnbaum and Biff linked (as an original is to its imitation) to become the sign of the fear that the feminine always inheres inside the male subject. I make this point not to imply that Biff—or the hapless Mr. Birnbaum, for that matter— is homosexual, but rather to demonstrate the constitutive role that the dread of a feminine male plays in the construction of the authoritative Cold War masculinity for which Miller's protagonists yearn.

Among Miller's plays, *A View from the Bridge* provides the most elaborate example of the jealous and guilty Miller protagonist using the fear of effeminacy to justify his malice. Alarmed over the loss of his niece, Catherine, for whom he feels "a powerful emotion," Eddie Carbone turns in rage upon her suitor, Rodolpho, who, he somewhat arbitrarily decides, is homosexual, "a weird," and "a punk."[69] In the climactic scene of the play, desperately trying to humiliate and impede the two lovers, Eddie, in response to Catherine's declaration of her independence ("I'm not gonna be a baby any more!"), suddenly "kisses her on the mouth." As Rodolpho attempts to stop him, he whirls on the young, blond Italian, "pins his arms, laughing, and suddenly kisses him."[70] Most of Miller's critics read Eddie's last kiss as evidence of his largely unconscious "homo-sexual attraction" toward the seducer of his niece.[71] For Benjamin Nelson, for example, Eddie's "savage" kiss "obviously reveals more about Eddie than about Rodolpho."[72] I believe, however, that Eddie's kiss reveals more about the structure of Cold War masculinity than about the peculiarities of Eddie's psyche. More clearly than any other of Miller's plays, *A View from the Bridge* demonstrates how the fear of effeminacy slides into homophobic panic, which, almost inevitably, slides into homosexual desire. It documents the difficulty in Miller's work of separating erotic fascination from erotic dread and of the extraordinary anxiety produced by a man's confrontation with the Other, the feminine within. It proves the precariousness of a masculinity that is far more dependent on hom(m)o-sexual bonds than on heterosexual intrigue, a masculinity for which the relatively stable and impermeable male body is a far more important source of definition than a female body always in danger of transgressing its boundaries.

Returning to the pivotal scene in *Death of a Salesman*, I want to emphasize that the power of that supremely phobic moment is not dependent on hypothesizing conscious or unconscious homosexual desire on Biff's part (although there is certainly enough material in the text for an actor to do so, and thereby to intensify the "tragic" irony of a son who ends up embracing all his father despises). Rather, the scene derives its force from its success in conjuring all that Willy—and doubtlessly many of his spectators and readers—most fears, trapped between a reckless, laughing woman on one side and a prodigal, lisping son on the other. For Biff, an oral transgression, the imitation of his math teacher, marks his attempt to rescue his athletic achievements and embattled manhood by impersonating and casting off the feminized man. The possibility that this scapegoating ritual will not work, that his effeminacy will suddenly burst forth, like the passion of Eddie's last kiss, or that, like the perfect Method actor, he will become the lisping mister he imitates, is the unacknowledged nightmare of those masculine myths to which the play—and Cold War masculinity—so desperately clings.

Dead Men

> Killers! Murderers! You liars, all of you, liars! You're only happy when
> you can see something die! Why don't you kill yourselves and be
> happy? You and your God's country. Freedom! I pity
> you. You're three dear, sweet dead men.
>
> —Roslyn, in *The Misfits*

The Misfits (1961), directed by John Huston, with a screenplay by Arthur Miller, occupies a unique position among the playwright's works. It is his first original screenplay, written as a "gift of words" for his wife, Marilyn Monroe, who plays the part of Roslyn.[73] It is the first of Miller's works in which no character dies. It is the first to be situated in a minutely detailed social and cultural context. And it is the first to break with the conventions of liberal tragedy and the well-made play by focusing not on the individual rebel but on a community of the marginalized and disenfranchized, a band of misfits struggling for individual and collective self-realization. More important, however, *The Misfits* is the first—and only—work of Miller's to offer a radical critique of the conventions of male heroism and to clear a site of female resistance. In so doing, the film provides an unusually distinct image of the ideological and economic contours of contested masculinity in American culture during the late 1940s and the 1950s.

The characters, ambience, and outline of the film were suggested to Miller during his six-week stay in 1956 in a rented cabin at Pyramid Lake, fifty miles north of Reno, while awaiting a divorce from his first wife, Mary Slattery. His short story "The Misfits" (1957) recounts the exploits of three cowboys he had met who rounded up the mustangs of the Nevada mountains and sold them to a slaughterhouse, at six cents a pound, for dog food.[74] Miller used this story—together with an even shorter one, "Please Don't Kill Anything" (1960)—as the basis for a film that was to become legendary even as it was being shot, one that brought Clark Gable and Marilyn Monroe, Hollywood's most fabled icons of masculinity and femininity, together with several other illustrious actors, a preeminent film director, and America's leading intellectual playwright. The project was plagued by problems and mishaps, however, which ranged from the stifling heat of the Nevada desert to Monroe's "complete breakdown" halfway through shooting that necessitated her hospitalization in Los Angeles for two weeks.[75] It was also the last film that either Gable or Monroe would complete. The enterprise, which Miller hoped would restore his failing marriage, proved its ruin. A week after the end of shooting, Monroe announced her separation from the writer. Six days later, Clark Gable died of a heart attack. By the time it was released, *The Misfits* had become the most expensive black-and-white film that had been made up until that time, and probably the most ill-fated.[76]

When it opened, *The Misfits* received mixed to negative reviews and failed at the box office. It has since been criticized more caustically by Miller's critics than any work falling between *All My Sons* and *After the Fall*. Nelson considers the film's movement "circular, erratic, and bewildered," its dialogue "vague, self-conscious, often pretentious," and its characters "for the most part poorly conceived."[77] Leonard Moss deems the film "undoubtedly the poorest product of the dramatist's mature years."[78] (Almost alone, Robert W. Corrigan finds *The Misfits* "unaccountably neglected" and judges it, with some justification, "the pivotal work in Miller's career as a playwright.")[79] Huston's critics, as well, have consistently disparaged the film. Scott Hammen considers it "often clumsy in its staging, frequently pretentious in its dialogue," and "unsatisfying" in its "dramatic structure," although conceding that it is "an interesting failure."[80] John McCarty, while calling it one of Huston's "best-directed efforts," does not rank it as "one of his most distinguished."[81] Huston, however, never apologized for or denigrated the film. When he first read the screenplay, he judged it "magnificent," and even in his memoirs he calls it "excellent."[82] Miller, in contrast, although deeply committed to the film during its making, is in retrospect strikingly disdainful of the project and of Hollywood generally, insisting that he "always looked down on screenwriting." Although, he writes, he was "prepared to dedicate a year or more of [his] life to [Monroe's] enhancement as a performer," he otherwise "never would have dreamed of writing a movie."[83]

Miller's short story "The Misfits," which originally appeared in an abridged version in *Esquire* in October 1957, is a brilliant and disturbing piece of work—and an excoriating indictment of male brutality. It is the story of three men—Gay Langland, an aging cowboy; Perce Howland, a young rodeo rider; and Guido, an audacious pilot—who flush five mustangs out of the Nevada hills and bind them to heavy truck tires in preparation for selling them to a slaughterhouse. In the *Esquire* version (shorn of the extensive portraiture that opens the unabridged story) the narrative moves swiftly to the capture of the wild horses on the desolate alkali flats.[84] The three men (like the misfit horses) appear as the last of a dying breed: three independent, self-reliant men who disdain the domestic sphere—"Driving [Roslyn's] car, repairing her house, running errands wasn't what you'd call work"—in favor of itinerant labor.[85] Throughout both the story and the film, the line "It's better than wages" is constantly tossed back and forth among them. Like the cowboys of Biff's dreams, these three are bound in a cooperative brotherhood, on the edges of a market economy, "free," like Guido, "to pitch and roll with time in the bars," like Gay, to sleep "in Roslyn's house," or like Perce, to make "a try in some rodeo."[86] When the mustangs descend onto the flats, the men rope them dexterously. Only Perce, the youngest and most feminine of them, has second thoughts, wishing the colt could escape.[87] But in the end, he accedes to what the others have decreed is an irrevocable fate for a vanishing breed.

This summary of the action, however, omits the most compelling part of the story: Miller's extraordinarily visceral description of the capture of the mustangs, exhausted and frantic, soaked with sweat, blood dripping from their nostrils, their knees stained a deep red. In appalling detail, Miller relates the lassoing of each horse, focusing on the defeat of the stallion and the mare, along with her defenseless colt, tethered to its mother by invisible filial bonds. At the end of the story, as the three conquering men depart into "a future," into "something to head for," Miller suddenly and unexpectedly cuts back to the parched mustangs. In a wrenching scene, he describes how they pawed the ground for water and caught the scent of the distant pastures in which they had grazed. As night descended, the colt huddled "close to the mare for warmth," and the horses slept. When dawn broke, the colt "stood up and, as it had done at every dawn, it walked waywardly for water." Just at that moment, however, "the mare shifted warningly" and the colt returned to her side to wait, "its nostrils sniffing the warming air."[88]

Miller's last paragraph forces a peripety by turning the reader's sympathy decisively away from the conquering men (if any at all should remain with them at that point) and toward their helpless victims. In so doing, it deftly exposes the murderous brutality that underlies the freedom these men so esteem. It points up how repugnant the culture is that values these wild horses only as commodities to be sold for dog food. At the same time, the pathos that Miller generates depends upon the struggle between these "free" men and what is unmistakably an equine nuclear family. As is so frequently the case in Miller's work— and especially, I will argue, in the next play Miller would write, *After the Fall*—the decisive familial bond is that between a mother and her offspring. Among the horses, the relationship between mare and colt (like the one that Biff envisions) is protective and life affirming. Among human beings, however, it is far more complex and problematic.

In turning "The Misfits" into a full-length screenplay, Miller greatly expanded the characterizations of the three men, providing all of them with traumatic pasts, dysfunctional families, and histories of deception and abandonment by wives or mothers. In the film, all three come betrayed: Gay (Clark Gable) by his wife's adultery with an old friend, Guido (Eli Wallach) by the sudden death of his wife in childbirth, and Perce (Montgomery Clift) by the remarriage of his widowed and "changed" mother to a man who effectively steals his inheritance, his father's ranch.[89] As elsewhere in Miller's work, the men have been cozened by transgressive and unruly women. However, these women, haunting the men's backgrounds, are resolutely overshadowed by the most powerful (and arguably the most sympathetic) female figure in Miller's work, Roslyn, whose development into the pivotal character is the film's most significant elaboration on the short story. In the latter, she is mentioned only in passing as the woman Gay lives with, yet another disruptive influence who will "probably razz [the men] about all the work they had done for a few dollars."[90] As played in the film by Marilyn Monroe in her most serious dramatic role, Roslyn emerges as a complex and vital woman struggling to break free of an unsavory past, as Gay's cautiously skeptical lover, and, most important, as the savior of the mustangs in the film's final sequence.[91]

In examining her function in the narrative, it is tempting to see her, as Stanley Kauffmann does, as a representative of "the Eternal Feminine," a woman aligned with nature, in sympathy with the animal world and "in tune with the universe."[92] But Roslyn is far more than an abstraction or a symbol. Although vain ("she can be obsessed with how she looks") and infantilized ("like a little child in a new school"), she possesses extraordinary strength and perspicacity, criticizing the men more forthrightly than any other character and handily unmasking Guido's selfishness and jealous cruelty (p. 7). From the beginning, Roslyn seems to understand the pathology that renders the self-reliant man emotionally withdrawn (or, in the vocabulary of "sex roles," committed to "instrumental" rather than "expressive" interests).[93] Speaking to Isabelle about her soon-to-be ex-husband, she asks, "Why can't I just say he wasn't *there*? I mean, you could touch him but he wasn't there" (p. 7). After the hearing, she attempts to maintain her independence, insisting on renting a car rather than driving out with the men to Guido's unfinished house, preferring "to feel I'm on my own" (p. 19). Later, as Guido waxes sentimental over his dead wife, telling her that she "stood behind me hundred percent, uncomplaining as a tree," Roslyn notes wryly, "But maybe that's what killed her" (p. 25). Perhaps her most complex moment of resistance in the film, however, is her gentle rebuke to Guido that his late wife may have been more responsive than he believes. (This sequence is brilliantly played by Monroe, who, while dancing with Guido, snaps her fingers distractedly in time with the jazz blaring from the radio.)

> ROSLYN: Whyn't you *teach* her to be graceful?
> GUIDO: You can't learn that.
> ROSLYN: How do you know? I mean, how do you *know*? You see, she died and she didn't know how you can dance! To a certain extent, maybe we're strangers.
> GUIDO: I don't feel like discussing my wife.
> ROSLYN: Oh, don't be mad. I only meant that if you loved her you could have taught her anything. Because we're all dying, aren't we? All the husbands and all the wives, every minute, and we're not teaching each other what we really know, are we?[94]

Throughout the film, Roslyn cautiously carves out a site of resistance by confronting the men with their fears (here, the immanence of death) and thereby challenging their sense of mastery and self-sufficiency. Significantly, her admonition does not earn her the revulsion heaped upon the laughing Woman in *Salesman*.

For the mapping of gender in *The Misfits*, Roslyn's most crucial function is to effect a tentative reversal of the binary opposition between "nature" and "culture" that *Death of a Salesman* and Miller's other plays work so zealously to sustain. Throughout the film, Miller characterizes the cowboys, in Isabelle's affectionately mocking words, as "the last real men" (p. 21), as self-employed, independent subjects who scorn the domestic realm—Guido never finishes his house after his wife's death—in favor of a home on the range, in "the open country."[95] Miller makes it very clear that the mythologized West they inhabit is vanishing, becoming "suburban," and that the cowboys now imitate their commercialized simulacra, wearing "the tight shirts and jeans they saw in movies" (p. 58).[96] Unlike the cowboys of Biff's fantasies, however, Gay, Perce, and Guido, whether at work on the range, at the rodeo, or in the sky, are never completely in control of their tools or of the forces of nature with which they are wrestling: the mustangs are dying out, Gay's truck is falling apart, Guido's plane is faltering. The new cowboy, rather than being master of an unstable natural world, is its embodiment, "a natural man," in Miller's words, whose imminent passing is identified with the impending extermination of his prey.[97]

In the final sequence of the film, Roslyn functions as a civilizing agent, one of the "nervous people," without whom "we'd still be eating each other" (p. 90). She effects the release of the captured mustangs and tames Perce ("I wish I'd met you a long time ago," he tells her, "save me a lot of broken bones"; p. 121). Although identified with the horses because of her compassion for their plight—their seizure is as violent in the film as in the short story—she vehemently opposes herself to the "natural man" and finally denounces him, in the most impassioned attack on machismo in all of Miller's work:

> Killers! Murderers! You liars, all of you, liars! You're only happy when
> you can see something die! Why don't you kill yourselves and be
> happy? You and your God's country. Freedom! I pity you. You're three
> dear, sweet dead men.[98]

Although the men's action clearly motivates Roslyn's outburst (which occurs immediately after the division of the paltry spoils), it is framed in the film in a strangely equivocal way. The scene of the men bargaining is filmed in a medium shot. The camera then cuts to a close-up of Roslyn, who suddenly turns away and runs from them, toward the middle of the dry lake bed, where, a mere speck in the vast landscape (this is probably the longest shot of the film), she launches into her assault. The camera turns back to the men for their reaction, in a medium shot, and then closes in on Gay and Guido, the latter responding to her attack with a tirade of his own, his eyes "fanatical, as though he had been seized within by a pair of jaws which were devouring him" (p. 118):

> She's crazy. They're all crazy. You try not to believe it. Because you need them. She's crazy. You struggle, you build, you try, you turn yourself inside out for them, but it's never enough! So they put the spurs to you. I know—I got the marks![99]

The camera then cuts back to Roslyn screaming, "I pity you. You're three dead men," back to Gay and Guido, and, finally, to a medium shot of the colt, who, with its hoof, is stroking the neck of its prostrate mother.

Given the nearly excessive ferocity of Roslyn's attack and the idiosyncratic camera work, this sequence—clearly the film's peripety—is extremely difficult to interpret. Although Roslyn displays startling insight into the murderous and potentially suicidal nature of the trials on which the men rely to prove their masculinity (lassoing wild horses, rodeo riding, daredevil flying), her judgment is, if not called into question, at least qualified by the way the scene is filmed.[100] Unlike Guido, who speaks with a self-possessed, angry intensity, Roslyn screams wildly at the men, almost reduced to the "pair of jaws" that Guido believes are "devouring" him. Kauffmann describes her fit as "hysteria" and remains unpersuaded by her argument.[101] The impression of hysteria is reinforced, to some extent, by the fact that the camera, for the whole sequence, is kept close to the men and far from Roslyn, who appears as a small, infantilized, out-of-control figure. In other words, the shot/reverse shot formation interpellates the (male) viewer into the action as the silent partner of the men, as an intimate in their conspiracy. Roslyn, in contrast, is articulated as a thing in the distance whose screams and anger are muted by her remoteness. The filming of this scene thus submits her to the objectifying gaze both of the cowboys and of the viewer, a gaze whose significance, like this entire pivotal sequence, is overdetermined. Throughout the film, the camera presents Roslyn in a deeply ambiguous way, as though not quite knowing what to do with her, at times offering her face in close-up or her point of view sympathetically, at other points treating her as an object of scopophiliac desire, indeed, as Hollywood's reigning sex queen. This voyeuristic stratagem is not lost on Kauffmann: "Too bad that [Huston's] camera occasionally peers lubriciously down the girl's bodice or elsewhere to remind us that Roslyn is really Marilyn Monroe."[102]

The manipulation and objectification of Roslyn—and Monroe—for the visual pleasure of the interpellated (male) viewer is of course a crucial aspect of the film's technique. Like classic Hollywood cinema generally, *The Misfits* (despite its unusually sympathetic portrait of Roslyn) is clearly constructed for the pleasure of the heterosexualized male viewing subject whose gaze is captured and held by the images of Monroe/Roslyn. Capitalizing on the power of male desire, it carefully (re)constructs Roslyn as both object and commodity in what is, in fact, a fine example of a historic alignment of masculinity with consumer capitalism. And yet, as Laura Mulvey has argued, in the economy of the cinematic gaze woman is always articulated as contradictory: the site of both pleasure and anxiety, the object of voyeuristic delight (because she "is" the Phallus), and the sign of the threat of castration (because she simultaneously designates the lack of the Phallus).[103]

In dramatizing this contradiction, *The Misfits* is patently incapable of maintaining a uniform and stable perspective on Roslyn, who, as an object, reflects back to the heterosexualized male viewer both his desire and his fear. Hence, the deeply conflicted representation of Roslyn's indictment of male brutality, which seems calculated both to objectify her and to remove her from the camera's "lubricious" observation, as if both to reinforce and to cancel the power of the masculinized gaze. At the same time, however, the film ends up dividing the male subject as well, when Guido's fury inadvertently turns back upon him. Through the violence of his misogynist rhetoric, Guido unwittingly splits himself into a voyeuristic self that still passionately desires Roslyn and a hateful and guilty self that is appalled by his own desire. Moreover, by asserting that "crazy" women "put the spurs to you," he ironically transforms himself into the very animal he pursues and puts Roslyn into the proverbial saddle. As a result, both men and women in *The Misfits* are articulated as divided subjects. Guido is split by the interdependency of anger and desire, misogyny and lust. Roslyn, meanwhile, is divided by her status as fetish, by both "being" and not "being" the Phallus, representing both object of desire and source of anxiety. This division, furthermore, is redoubled by her association with a "culture" whose contradictory meanings are inscribed upon her: on the one hand, she embodies the mastery over "nature" for which the men yearn; on the other, she exemplifies the force of a civilization that is destroying the cowboy's world and the self-reliant masculinity he embodies. And even Gay is split, a "free" and loving killer, one of "the last real men" whose very name contains his sexual Other.

The ending of the film does not resolve the contradictions that have been raised. Gay reluctantly accedes to Roslyn and, through her, to a new civilized and domesticated world, but not before his "last totally free act": a battle with the stallion, which he single-handedly defeats, so that he, rather than Roslyn, can be credited with the release of the horses.[104] After this final proof of masculinity, she agrees to leave with him in his truck and the two become reconciled as Guido's accusatory cries ring out: "Where will you be? Some gas station, polishing windshields? . . . Or making change in the supermarket" (p. 130). Their final conversation, however, includes a speech for Roslyn—which is not included in the film—that startlingly reverses their roles:

> For a minute, when those horses galloped away, it was almost like I gave them back their life. And all of a sudden I got a feeling—it's crazy!—I suddenly thought, "He must love me, or how would I dare do this?" Because I always just ran away when I couldn't stand it. Gay— for a minute you made me not afraid. And it was like my life flew into my body. For the first time. (p. 131)

The viewer has just watched Roslyn become the agent of Gay's conversion, but suddenly and unexpectedly the text demands that she renounce that authority by ascribing the transformative power to *him*. I suggest that this recantation be interpreted not as the signal of a change in Roslyn, but rather as a last-ditch attempt by patriarchal discourse to reclaim the power it has lost, and by the forgetful male subject to restore to himself the very life-giving properties he has just been accused of squandering. Without this speech, the film ends more ambiguously, with Roslyn retaining a modicum of authority. But Gay, driving the truck, literally leads the way. He also has the last word, in answer to Roslyn's question: "How do you find your way back in the dark?" "Just head for that big star straight on," Gay tells her. "The highway's under it; take us right home" (p. 132). But even Gay's reassurance is called into question when one remembers that their home remains an unfinished structure, with permeable boundaries, unable to separate the outside decisively from the inside, or "nature" from a frighteningly ambiguous "culture."

Like its protagonists, *The Misfits* is a deeply conflicted film, harboring contradictory perspectives on the society of the spectacle that is cannibalizing the old West, on both the resistant female and the "free" male subject, and on voyeuristic pleasure. Is *The Misfits* critiquing or ratifying the objectification of Roslyn? Is it attacking a destructive, guilty, and schizoid masculinity? Or is it ridiculing all that Roslyn represents? Monroe, apparently, believed that the fury of Roslyn's denunciation was deliberately calculated to undercut her strength.[105] Whether or not it does, it certainly betrays a sense of deep uneasiness in regard to the relationship between masculine authority and female resistance, an anxiety crystallized in the two strangely out-of-place adjectives embedded in Roslyn's accusation: "You're three dear, sweet dead men." Why "dear"? Why "sweet"? Are these qualifiers intended to reveal Roslyn's equivocal feelings, her need for these men despite their brutality? Or, on the contrary, do they not betray the profound misgivings of a masculinity forced to condemn its own murderous practices?

Working Women

The manifold contradictions performed by *The Misfits* in regard to the exercise of male and female power are by no means the product of one— or, indeed, several—idiosyncratic imagination. Rather, they are deeply enmeshed with complex historical forces and remain incomprehensible unless contextualized with the social and demographic upheavals that marked the late 1940s and the 1950s in the United States. As is characteristic of Miller's work, these upheavals leave their mark most plainly on the dysfunctional family, of which the emblem is Reno itself, divorce capital of the United States and a "confusin'" place (p. 2). Family structure, however, is not the only victim of cultural change in *The Misfits*. Just as important (if less obvious) is a crisis in work and employment. I have already examined the conflicting attitudes toward the cowboy's vocation and the passing of the old West. The livelihood of the women in the film, however, is even more problematic. At one extreme is Isabelle's stable identity, as owner of a rooming house and friend to those, like Roslyn, in need of counsel. In contrast, Roslyn's occupation—and, indeed, her entire past—is mysterious and shady. Before her marriage, she was a pin-up girl and "interpretive danc[er]" in second-class nightclubs (p. 56). And although she has given up this work, she is clearly embarrassed when Guido notices "girlie photos" of her on the inside of the closet door (p. 46). There is another telling vignette in regard to female employment at the beginning of the film. Gay, at the train station, in his very first scene, says good-bye to an "expensively dressed" woman with whom he obviously has had an affair. She is reluctant to leave, however, and, while boarding the train, begs, "Will you think about it, Gay? It's the second largest laundry in St. Louis" (p. 12).

In each of these sequences, a woman is engaged in a distinctly feminine profession: one markets what voyeuristic men believe to be female sexuality, the other helps to maintain a domesticity long identified with the feminine sphere—one takes off her clothes, the other washes them. Despite the differences in social class between the two women, both, as women who work outside the home, produce a measure of discomfiture. The former is deemed slightly unsavory; the latter, slightly ridiculous. Yet both betray an uneasiness on the part of Miller—and the postwar culture he emblematizes—in regard to the relationship between home and marketplace, an uneasiness rooted in profound demographic changes taking place during and after World War II. With the coming of the war, at least eight million women (many of them married) joined the labor force, a quarter assuming jobs formerly filled by men in heavy industry. "Popular commentators," Mary P. Ryan points out, "were proclaiming the ability of women to perform all sorts of 'male' tasks."[106] A 1943 advertisement extolled the virtue of a new "Joan of Arc" working as an arc welder in a ship manufacturing plant.[107] A *Life* magazine article from the year before recounted the story of a former milliner who readily took over her husband's position as "president, secretary-treasurer, sales manager and personnel director" of a small machine shop when he was drafted. After three months on the job, *Life* proudly claimed, she "decided there is as much thrill in working with steel and grease as there was with felt and ribbon."[108]

When World War II ended, however, employment patterns quickly changed. Two months after the Allied victory, 800,000 women were fired by the aircraft manufacturers alone and two years later women had virtually vanished from heavy industry, despite the fact that surveys showed that 75 percent to 90 percent wished to retain their jobs.[109] Simultaneously, the years following the war bore witness to a domestic revival of unparalleled vigor and scope. The prewar division of labor was reinstated with a vengeance and the patterns of women's employment were radically readjusted, along with their prescribed roles and images. Women, in effect, were being compelled to forget the "new degree of psychological independence from men" that had been fostered during the war and to collaborate in the (re)production of a deeply conflicted society.[110] The rapidly expanding U.S. economy demanded the employment of large numbers of women, both married and unmarried (by 1952, there were two million more women in the work force than during the height of World War II). At the same time, however, the ideological accomplices of this economy were tirelessly attempting, with considerable success, to remake middle-class women into subservient wives and productive mothers. Of all women in 1951, one-third were married by age nineteen. Relentlessly, motherhood was glorified in women's magazines and on television while the working mother was disparaged.[111] In Benjamin Spock's classic 1946 text on child care, he strongly advised the new mother against returning to work, hoping that she would realize that "the extra money she might earn, or the satisfaction she might receive from an outside job, is not so important after all."[112] As a result of this intense ideological lobbying, the birthrate soared, reaching its height in 1957, as the feminism of the early twentieth century was mocked and derided as a "dead issue."[113] Although the number of working wives doubled between 1940 and 1960, most were shunted into low-paying positions as secretaries, salesgirls, and teachers. At the same time, the number of women working in the professions fell from 45 percent to 38 percent.[114]

During the 1950s the nuclear family became widely recognized as the primary social unit responsible for the maintenance of this economic organization. Sociologists such as Talcott Parsons wrote about the dwindling importance of the extended family and the increasing "isolation of the nuclear family," conceived as a haven from the exigencies of the economic and political realms. For Parsons (as for the Miller of "The Family in Modern Drama"), the autonomous, property-owning, middle-class family functions as the "social group in which . . . the child can 'invest' *all* of his [sic] emotional resources," as the fundamental force in the socialization of the child and as the mechanism that regulates the "balances in the personalities of the adult members of both sexes." If, as Parsons notes, "the modern child has 'farther to go' in his socialization than his predecessors," this circumstance places unprecedented pressure on the family as a mechanism of surveillance and discipline, one that would successfully inculcate those inescapable "sex roles."[115] Following a relative blurring of the boundaries between men's and women's work during World War II, the Cold War hegemony, working principally through the family, sought to exercise strict control over production by reimposing a rigorously gendered division of labor and a corresponding polarization of masculine and feminine "sex roles."

Considered in light of this division of labor, *The Misfits* is at once a subversive and a conservative text. On the one hand, it pointedly attacks a hegemonic masculinity (unlike *Death of a Salesman* or *View from the Bridge*) and attempts neither to squelch resistant femininity altogether nor to restrict women to the domestic realm. On the other hand, it simultaneously betrays the widespread anxiety generated by the employment of women outside the home, outside the sphere in which they could be most efficiently policed. The sexualized nature of Roslyn's work is especially telling, for, as Elaine Tyler May points out, "the entrance of women into the paid labor force" and the "increasing expression of female sexuality" were seen "as two sides of the same dangerous coin."[116] Both threatened the ideology of familism that the ending of the film clearly attempts to recuperate. The final reconciliation between a domesticated Gay and a reformed Roslyn, replete with the prospect of a child, promises to reclaim these misfits for a refurbished nuclear family that will complete Guido's house and take up residence behind its locked door. Yet even there, the contradictions will not be extinguished. Both the resistant vitality of Roslyn and her ability to teach what "we really know" militates against her capitulation to the very cultural order she embodies. (It is little wonder that the critics of Miller's work who are most sympathetic to *Death of a Salesman* have such problems with *The Misfits*.)

If *The Misfits* comes closer than any other Miller text to challenging the postwar hegemony and exposing the internal contradictions of its fractured subjects, then some of the credit must go to Miller's wife at the time, Marilyn Monroe, whom he credits with possessing an angry, "revolutionary idealism" more than passingly reminiscent of Roslyn's vigor.[117] In his autobiography, Miller writes that he knew while working on the film that "Roslyn's dilemma was hers," and he voices his hope "that by living through this role she too might arrive at some threshold of faith and confidence."[118] Given the inexorable slippage between the two "golden girls," Roslyn and Monroe, in Miller's autobiography and in virtually all the contemporary accounts of the film, it is tempting to read the role both as a cathartic psychodrama designed for his wife's therapy and as Monroe's spiritual biography (in which Roslyn's former career as an interpretive dancer, i.e., a stripper, is a thinly veiled allusion to Monroe's early work as a nude model).[119] I believe, however, that the contradictions in Roslyn's character have less to do with the psychological particulars of Miller's relationship with Monroe than with his status, during the domestic revival of the 1950s, as a writer whose wife's career not only eclipsed but threatened his own. (May notes that a wife's vocation "especially" became a problem for her husband "if she earned more than he did.")[120] In *Timebends*, Miller recalls with a sense of frustration his inability to write during their marriage, remembering that "during the shooting of *Let's Make Love* and *Some Like It Hot* I had all but given up any hope of writing."[121] In an era in which the American male's status "fundamentally inheres" in "the occupational role," how could a successful playwright not harbor equivocal feelings toward the woman whose income and renown far surpassed his own and who, in fact, redefined his identity as "Monroe's husband"?[122] What more efficient way is there to express his anxiety over his own career, and simultaneously to attempt to control and denigrate hers, than to write a screenplay for her that requires that she be a (former) stripper?

In reflecting upon *The Misfits*, John Huston is certainly correct to note that it is about "a world in change" and to nominate World War II as the pivotal moment of transformation. His assertion, however, that it documents a metaphysical crisis ("we have lost meaning now") ignores the economic and cultural changes that were reconfiguring both U.S. society and bourgeois subjectivity.[123] Although *The Misfits* is in many ways Miller's most uncharacteristic and alien work—an upper-middle-class New York intellectual's portrait of working-class men and women confounded by the passing of the old West—it provides a remarkably clear image of the contradictions bred by the Cold War domestic revival. As the film makes clear, demographic changes were placing enormous stress on the paradigms of masculinity and femininity and on the families that were being reorganized to police them. Were Roslyn and Gay successful in bringing the child they so desire into the world and making it "brave from the beginning" (p. 132), it is doubtful whether this new subject would resolve their own contradictory feelings or quell their anxieties any more than it would those of the myriad other new parents of the era. Benjamin Spock was well aware of the tensions generated by the conflicting demands of parenthood, and he prescribed a number of therapies for anxious parents that would help them forget, or provide an imaginary reconciliation of, these conflicting demands. To a new mother overwhelmed by the stress of raising a child, he urged so-called feminine diversions, suggesting she go "to the beauty parlor, or to get . . . a new hat or dress." Or alternatively, "to get relief," she could always "go to a movie."[124] I doubt he would have recommended *The Misfits*.

The Writer in the Text

QUENTIN, *to Listener*: But is it enough to tell a man he is not-guilty? *Glances at [Maggie]*. My name is on this man! Why can't I say "I"? *Turning toward her*: I did this. I want what I did! And I saw it once! I saw *Quentin* here!

—*After the Fall*, act 2

The play is a continuous stream of meaning. It's not built on what happens next in terms of the usual continuity of a tale—but upon what naked meaning grows out of the one before. And the movement expands from meaning to meaning, openly, without any bulling around. The way a mind would go in quest of a meaning, the way a new river cuts its bed, seeking the path to contain its force.

—"Arthur Miller Ad-Libs on Elia Kazan" (1964)

If *The Misfits* is the most widely disparaged of Miller's major works, then *After the Fall* remains his most controversial. When presented in January 1964 as the inaugural production of the Repertory Theater of Lincoln Center, directed by Elia Kazan, its reviews ranged from hushed panegyrics to incensed denunciations. At one extreme, Howard Taubman in the *New York Times* called on his readers to "rejoice" that Miller had returned to the stage after an eight-year absence with a "pain-wracked drama," which he judged Miller's "maturest" work.[125] At the other, Robert Brustein excoriated the play as "a wretched piece of dramatic writing: shapeless, tedious, overwritten and confused," peopled by characters "too shallow to be plumbed." Only a small part of Brustein's denunciation, however, was devoted to an analysis of what he claimed were the play's artistic failings. Most of the review attacked Miller for what Brustein called his "spiritual striptease" in a play deemed "a confessional auto-biography of embarrassing explicitness."[126]

Since its premiere, *After the Fall* has been dogged by questions about its status as autobiography and, in particular, about the ethics of what most critics saw (and some still see) as an exploitative exposé of Miller's relationship with Marilyn Monroe, who had committed suicide seventeen months before the play opened. *Newsweek* put a photograph of Jason Robards, Jr., and Barbara Loden (as Quentin and Maggie, the two char-acters allegedly based on Miller and Monroe) on its cover, and called the play "the most nakedly autobiographical drama ever put on public view." Even the chivalrous Taubman admitted that the play is "obviously" autobiographical.[127] For the reader intent on finding referents outside the text, the similarities between Quentin, the play's central character and consciousness, and Arthur Miller are almost too numerous to detail. As young men during the Depression, both Quentin and Miller witness their fathers' economic ruin and their mothers' contemptuous response to it, both become extremely successful in their chosen occupations, both appear before the House Committee on Un-American Activities and defend their histories of left-wing sympathy, both have as a second wife a performer popularly esteemed more for her sexual attractiveness than for her talent, both have a German-speaking third wife, and so on. Yet the similarities between Maggie and contemporary portraits of Marilyn Monroe are even more striking and inescapable. Both women are the illegitimate daughters of disturbed mothers; both are vain, exhibition-istic, neurotic, and infantile, yet idolized and desired by millions; both quit high school, have an affair with a senior professional associate, and are forbidden by his family to visit him on his deathbed; both suffer from addiction to alcohol and tranquilizers, are in psychoanalysis, and work·on their chosen craft with a fabled teacher; both end as suicides.[128] These similarities were no more lost on the theater-going public than they were on the critics. For two Sundays the "Drama Mailbag" in the *New York Times* was commandeered by a dozen impassioned letter writers. Most of them were incensed by what they took to be a hateful portrait of Monroe, attacking the play—and Miller personally—with an unusual level of indignation and furor. One woman wrote, "I came away, not uplifted, not purged, but feeling disgusted, shocked, threatened, stunned, betrayed by Mr. Miller," while another declared that Miller's "enormous ego and his self-righteousness, are beyond human endurance."[129]

Two weeks after the play opened, *Life* joined the fray, running a feature article on *After the Fall* that maintained that the play "insists" on the comparison between Maggie and Monroe, and another piece pointing out that Loden's portrayal, in a blond wig, was "frequently a Monroe impersonation."[130] In an essay accompanying the feature article, Miller avoids discussion of any similarities between the two, emphasizing punctiliously that Maggie "is not in fact Marilyn Monroe" but a fictional character, whom he then proceeds to analyze in dry, academic tones. In other contemporary accounts, he insists that autobiographical specula-tion is "irrelevant" and that "it honestly never occurred to me that anyone was trying for a literal resemblance, or that the audience would see one, because I didn't see one."[131] In *Timebends* he is more circumspect, arguing that although the play is "an attempt to embrace a world of political and ethical dilemmas," he realizes he was "blinding [himself] to the obvious" in trying to disconnect "the fictional character from any real person"[132]

Unlike the popular press, which has evinced an undying fascination for the play's alleged portrait of Monroe, Miller's more scholarly critics are uneasy with *After the Fall*. Most consider it a flawed work and have expressed serious reservations about its structure and language. Bigsby judges it "a remarkably sincere, if not wholly successful, attempt to pull together private and public acts of treachery"; Raymond Williams con-siders it "Miller's most confused play."[133] Although all of Miller's critics acknowledge the parallel between his life story and Quentin's—only the most oblivious formalist could ignore it—most consider it irrelevant to an analysis of the work. Characteristically, they allude to it in passing, relegate it to a discrete section of a longer analysis (or a mere footnote), or else rehearse it in detail only to proceed on to a thematic and structural investigation of the play that completely ignores questions of referen-tiality.[134] Unlike Bigsby and Williams, I find the play neither especially sincere nor confused, but read it as a self-serving construction designed by Miller to quell the gossip surrounding one of the most public marriages of the 1950s and to clear his name of responsibility for Monroe's suicide. As an amalgam of public and private discourses, *After the Fall* seems to me to be the completion (and dialectical negation) of the sequence of events that began in the House Office Building in Washington, D.C., on June 21, 1956. The first time he linked his name to Monroe's, Miller found himself almost magically lionized and absolved by the press and the public; eight years later, he would find himself almost universally condemned. I believe that one should take Miller at his word and judge the play as the "trial" he claims it to be.[135] Furthermore, I believe that *After the Fall* cannot be understood as testimony unless one closely examines how the play itself negotiates the distinction between autobiography and fiction.

Both historically and formally, autobiography describes a diverse and, at times, contradictory set of practices that become especially precarious when viewed from a poststructuralist perspective. In a provocative essay on the rhetoric of autobiography, Paul De Man notes the extreme difficulty in identifying and classifying autobiographical discourse as a genre and argues that the questions that must be asked to do so are "both pointless and unanswerable."[136] He challenges the sovereign position granted referentiality in most theories of autobiography by positing that the author—whether considered inside or outside the text—is always a textual production determined by the "resources of his medium." He also points out that self-portraiture is not a privileged activity but merely "one mode of figuration among others." De Man insists that reference is an "illusion," a fiction arising from the "structure of the figure," which is configured and positioned so as to acquire "a degree of referential productivity."[137] This assertion is perhaps the crucial critical maneuver in the essay, in that it allows De Man to shift the study of autobiography away from referentiality (which can only be an "illusion") and toward rhetoric. For De Man, autobiography is first and foremost a mode of address that produces—and is produced by—a particular transaction between text and reader, or speaker and listener. De Man defines the characteristic rhetorical trope of autobiography as prosopopoeia: "the fiction of an apostrophe to an absent, deceased or voiceless entity, which posits the possibility of the latter's reply and confers upon it the power of speech."[138] Of course, De Man's wholesale dismissal of reference in relation to allegedly autobiographical texts is extremely problematic (particularly since the discovery of his pro-Nazi publications of the 1940s). Furthermore, the formalist and ahistorical assumptions that underlie his notion of subjectivity (being determined by "the resources of his medium") make it of only limited value for a materialist analysis. However, I find the shift in emphasis toward rhetoric that De Man engineers extremely productive. First, it allows for a consideration of autobiography that is not dependent on the intention of the author but is, rather, "a figure of reading or of understanding."[139] Second, by conceiving confessional discourse as a mode of performance (requiring speaker, audience, and context), it establishes a useful gauge with which to assess a drama centered around a speaking "I."

When considered as rhetoric, *After the Fall* dissolves the distinctions between autobiography and fiction by its patently confessional pose. From the very beginning of the play, Quentin, the protagonist, enunciates "an apostrophe to an absent, deceased or voiceless entity," in this case, the silent and unseen Listener, who could be a spectator, intimate friend, clergyman, God, or (most likely) psychoanalyst. As in a classic autobiographical—and psychoanalytical—narrative, Quentin's confession superimposes retrospection and introspection in the hope of talking through a problem, of transfiguring the speaker.[140] The play built around Quentin's therapeutic narrative is, in Miller's words, "a continuous stream of meaning" that depends less upon an external mimesis than upon "what naked meaning grows out of the one before."[141] As a result, it eschews a straighforwardly linear (that is, causal) structure in favor of an associative one. It expands and heightens the quasi-expressionist form of *Death of a Salesman*, and simultaneously exploits the well-made play's method of gradually releasing withheld information. By melding memories, free associations, and fantasies and allowing characters to divide and coalesce, *After the Fall* gradually unveils a single "naked" psyche and discloses a moment of trauma to perform a classic "talking cure."

Moreover, *After the Fall* begs consideration as an example of autobiographical rhetoric because its central predicament is the same as the one facing the writer who prepares to compose a life story (or the patient who begins psychoanalysis): to confess or not to confess. All of the characters are racked by this dilemma. All harbor potentially calamitous secrets from relatives, friends, lovers, or "the committee." Father conceals his bankruptcy from Mother; Mother conceals the trip to Atlantic City from Quentin; Quentin conceals his real or imagined infidelities from Louise; Lou conceals his Communist past; Quentin and Dan debate concealing their mother's death from their ill father; and so on. Constantly, the characters contemplate the moral implications of speaking out. Lines such as, "I don't know what's permissible to say any more" echo throughout the play.[142]

At the center of *After the Fall* is Quentin, the confessor, the composer of a therapeutic narrative. Yet, even more conspicuously than Miller's other protagonists, Quentin is a deeply split subject: both the object of scrutiny and the inquiring self, the exhibitionist and the voyeur, the self embedded in its own narrative and the active speaker who always exceeds his self-representation. Furthermore, Quentin differs from Miller's other heroes in the way he administers his split subjectivity. On the one hand, he presents himself as the author of a sovereign, liberal humanist self behind which his self-division is concealed. He is a lawyer by profession, the creator of a legal brief so "majestic" it is "hardly like a brief at all" but "a classic opinion" (p. 24). On the other hand, this author of a classic text and a classic self is so compulsively conscious of his own activities that he cannot restrain himself from being displaced endlessly across text and stage. In act 2 of the original version of the play there is a fascinating sequence. Maggie enters the park in disguise, wearing a red wig, and greets an empty bench that, in her imagination, holds Quentin, while the "real" Quentin (the one impersonated by the actor) remembers:

> QUENTIN: . . . No, it's not that I think I killed her. It's—
> *An anonymous man passes Maggie, glances, and goes out.*
> MAGGIE, *to the empty bench*: See? I told you nobody recognizes me! Like my wig?
> QUENTIN: . . . that I can't find myself in it, it's like another man. Only the guilt comes. Yes, or the innocence!
> MAGGIE, *sitting beside "him" on the bench*: When you go to Washington tonight . . . you know what I could do? I could get on a different car on the same train!
> QUENTIN, *to Listener*: But is it enough to tell a man he is not-guilty? *Glances at her.* My name is on this man! Why can't I say "I"? *Turning toward her:* I did this. I want what I did! And I saw it once! I saw Quentin here![143]

Relentlessly, this sequence foregrounds its own fictionality, not just by means of Quentin's direct address to the audience but also by Maggie's disguise and her question to the empty park bench, "Like my wig?" Two figures are suddenly glimpsed incognito: Maggie passes unrecognized and Quentin does not sit where he sits. Neither is, in any sense, fully present. Instead, pairs of selves—Maggie in disguise and the "real" Maggie, the invisible Quentin and the "real" Quentin—graciously coexist next to each other, like two passengers, each "on a different car on the same train."

Unlike the two Maggies, who at least sit in the same position on the same bench, the two Quentins do not occupy the same scenic space. Indeed, the fact that one serves as audience for the other implies that these selves are not even contained by the proscenium arch. Rather, Quentin is disseminated across the theatrical space in such a way as to redefine male subjectivity *tout court* as a sequence of fractions, a protracted series of metonymic displacements in which a theatrical simulacrum is simply one point of articulation. Quentin is quite literally beside himself: "I can't find myself in it, it's like another man." By redefining himself as an indefinitely deferred presence, he provokes a kind of semiotic vertigo that calls into question the identity of the first-person pronoun: "Why can't I say 'I'?" This deconstruction of the sovereign subject radically problematizes the self-contained fictionality of the representation and constructs a figure with a remarkable degree of what De Man refers to as "referential productivity." Who can't say "I"? What is identity for this constantly shifting sign in a field of metonymic displacements? Who is speaking? The Quentin standing on stage, the invisible Quentin sitting on the park bench, Quentin's conscience? Or the man on which Quentin's name is superimposed: the actor playing Quentin? Or the man whose name is printed on the play's title page, that elusive signifier that has, at different times and in different circumstances, stood in for many different subjects, including a celebrated playwright, a former Communist "fellow traveler," the last husband of Marilyn Monroe, and the writer of a play that (deliberately) undermines the distinction between fiction and autobiography?

The passage cited above was suppressed in the final stage version of *After the Fall*. Drastically cut and rewritten, it was transformed into a moment of conventional skepticism about the accuracy of memory. The radical questioning is foreclosed. The slippage across a field of metonymically displaced subjects—from self to self, from character to actor, from sign to its many possible referents—is abruptly halted. In its revised form, this passage attempts to cover up what is the most radical deconstruction of the fully present subject in all of Miller's work, a destabilization that coincidentally undermines the high-minded tragic synthesis that Miller calls for in "The Family in Modern Drama." While prescribing a theater that would "unite" the political and the sexual, and "embrace the many-sidedness of man," Miller, no doubt, never expected that his next play would be interpreted, by most of the theater-going public and many critics, as a monument to his almost complete loss of control over the relationship between public and private.[144]

Beginning with the announcement of their betrothal during a recess of the House Committee, Miller and Monroe initiated a marriage that would blur the distinction between the political and the domestic, between society and sexuality. During the next four and a half years, they were followed closely by the press and Miller himself, especially at the beginning of their marriage, often seemed to delight in the role assigned him as consort—and possessor—of the most desired woman in the world (this is the flip side of his later discomfort with being cast as "Monroe's husband").[145] In one sense, *After the Fall* bears witness to the difficulty in separating the private from the public, the sign from the referent, in a culture that, despite its quasi-official position on the nuclear family as a sacred preserve from the political and economic realm, could never quite sustain the illusion of the family's autonomy. The "truth" contained in the original version of the play is its acknowledgment that in commodity culture, the slippage between private and public, sign and referent, cannot be forestalled. After the fact, Miller attempted desperately, in articles, interviews, and his revision of the play, to turn the metonymically displaced subject into a classical liberal humanist subject, thereby inhibiting the drift between Quentin and Arthur Miller and Maggie and Marilyn Monroe.[146] In its original version, however, *After the Fall* remains a testament to the impossibility of escaping that circle of voyeurism and exhibitionism in a society always in search of the most intimate, sexual details, in the belief that these alone constitute the truth of the subject. The inevitable slippage between public and private provides a key to interpreting those angry letters to the *New York Times* that criticized the activities of a character in a play by attacking the playwright, not as an artist but as a private man, and for the most ostensibly private of all his activities: "As for you, Mr. Miller, I find you nauseating as a lover. Throughout the play lovely women come throwing themselves at your feet. One wonders why."[147] This (mis)reading of Quentin as Arthur Miller is not necessarily the simple mistake of a naive theatergoer who cannot tell the difference between protagonist and playwright. More likely, it is the sign of this spectator's recognition— and denunciation—of the author's nervous deconstruction of the difference between the two roles.

Masculinity as Narrative

After *The Misfits*, which effectively undermines the masculinist idylls of Willy and Biff Loman, Miller reconceives masculine power in *After the Fall*. In the person of Quentin, the full male subject is repositioned and redefined as he who has reached the summit: the author of an appeal to the Supreme Court, husband to the reigning sex queen, and leader in his profession. He is the embodiment of the Law—whether understood as a body of juridical practices, as the legal authority granted the name on the play's title page, or as the rule of the Phallus. He is no longer a variation on the cowboy, but a development of Bernard, who also proves his manhood by arguing a case before the Supreme Court. The swagger of Biff, or of Gay and Perce, and their vision of a male community are consigned to the past, like Mickey's memories of "the Party": "a dream now, a dream of solidarity" (p. 35). Masculinity is no longer something to be aspired to, a mythology from the precapitalist past situated in a perennially deferred future, but an achievement upon which the heroic subject may reflect. Unlike Quentin's predecessors, Miller's new paradigm of masculinity is sober and disillusioned, no longer the romantic, striving individual, but the owner of recollections, a kind of landlord of the past.

Among the memories over which Quentin exercises proprietary rights, the most crucial are of women. Indeed, for the entire play he situates himself in relation to a string of women who are disallowed the complexity that Quentin alone harbors, denied the ability to be deconstructed that designates male subjectivity in *After the Fall*. Each woman acts as a foil for Quentin, the suffering confessor, "a light in the world," a "god," betrayed by those incapable of understanding his mission, a sacrificial victim who (like the expressionist hero of Kaiser's *From Morn to Midnight*) "spreads his arms in crucifixion" (pp. 67, 72, 75). Repeatedly in Quentin's memory, Felice and Elsie offer themselves to him, Mother gives him a toy sailboat in compensation for her absence, Maggie seduces him. Drawn from the pages of misogynist mythology, all are cast as either destroyers or protectors (like the women in *The Magic Flute*, the opera to which Holga takes Quentin in Salzburg). Among the destroyers are Louise, the banal and materialistic wife unable to understand her husband's struggle; Maggie's mother, who tries to kill her daughter; and Quentin's Mother, the angry, vindictive woman who browbeats her husband and sabotages the stratagems of her sons (and who seems even to have calculated the time of her death so that its announcement will most devastate her husband). Among the protectors are Felice, repeatedly raising her arms in blessing over Quentin, and Holga, the woman with the curative "Hello!" (p. 114), the heroic resister of the Nazis who dares, despite Quentin's past, to try to reclaim him.

Alone among Quentin's women, Maggie refuses to be categorized as either redeemer or destroyer, but instead is transformed gradually from guileless lover to malevolent temptress. After Quentin first meets her (in the original version of the play), he notes that she has "a strange, surprising honor."[148] He also believes that she has the ability to offer him moral clarity: "with Maggie, I think—for one split second I saw my life; what I had done, what had been done to me, and even what I ought to do" (p. 64). Yet in the course of the second act, Maggie turns into a monster, becoming totally narcissistic, vindictive, arrogant, abusive and suicidal, driving Quentin to reject her. Only in the original version is she invested with even a shadow of Roslyn's perspicacity or resistant power: "You taught me to speak out, Quentin, and when I do you get mad."[149] But she is too patently a destroyer to compromise Quentin's strength. The climax of the play—like that of *Salesman*, the revelation of a primal trauma—comes in the second act, when Quentin tries to wrestle Maggie's sleeping pills from her and he "suddenly . . . lunges for her throat and lifts her with his grip." As he does, in a flashback, he remembers locking himself spitefully in the bathroom while his mother pleads with him, "Darling, open this door! I didn't trick you!" Rather than being deceived by her ploy, however, he "stands transfixed as Mother backs into his hand, which of its own volition, begins to squeeze her throat" (p. 111).

With the ease of free association, one traumatic memory slides into another, and Maggie is reconfigured as Mother. Moreover, given the play's psychoanalytical logic, Mother is clearly made into the prototype for all the other dangerous women in the play. She is the woman whose very "soul" crawls with "blackness," who, with "contempt," attacks Father after he announces his bankruptcy, abuses him verbally ("I should have run the day I met you"), and makes him feel "as though stabbed" (pp. 17–20). Not only does she preside over this "emasculation" (Brustein's word) of her husband, she castrates her son as well, scaring him with the threat that he will "pee in bed" if he plays with matches (p. 16).[150] She is the epitome of the destructive, smothering "Momism" that, during the 1940s and 1950s, was often blamed for turning sons into weaklings, criminals, Communists, and "perverts."[151] Like the other unruly women in Miller's works, she is unable to restrain her angry and vindictive speech. Her cry of contempt, "You are an idiot!" ends all dialogue with Father and echoes savagely five times through the play in the mouths of Mother and the other women, conflating all of them except for the reserved Holga, the disciplined woman who has learned to suppress female discord, to embrace the "idiot" child within (p. 22). All the others are orally incontinent. Even Maggie's mother terrorizes her daughter by an oral transgression, smoking in the closet.

By rewriting *All My Sons* as "all my women" (to quote Quentin), *After the Fall* collapses all the women in the play except Holga into Mother (p. 14). In order to explain why Holga is granted a privileged position in the text, however, I want to examine the trajectory of male desire that runs through *After the Fall* and Miller's work in general (Miller himself has admitted that the play offers the "clearest revelation" of his vision).[152] The ambitiously psychoanalytical and expressionistic structure Miller uses permits an expansion of the definition of masculinity. It is not just a masquerade, an array of (metonymically displaced) male subject positions, or a rehearsal of patriarchal power; it is also a narrative. More clearly than any other Miller play, *After the Fall* redefines the heroic protagonist as what Teresa De Lauretis (following Propp and Lotman) designates as "a mythical subject," like Oedipus, or the hero of a folktale, whose drama has "the movement of a passage, a crossing, an actively experienced transformation of the human being into—man."[153] The traditional quest of a male hero for a woman—or unmistakably feminine prize, such as the grail—is represented in *After the Fall* as a quest for a magical third bride who will bestow upon the hero an honor very different from the rather dubious rewards brought him by his first two wives. According to the logic of this mythical narrative, the two women (together with the others who haunt his memory) function like the Sphinx, or Medusa ("You're so beautiful, it's hard to look at you," Quentin tells Maggie; p. 81), tempting him, questioning him, trying to destroy him. Only by turning his gaze from them, by outwitting their feminine wiles or strangling them, can Quentin fulfill his desires. (This is a very old story.) But what is most striking about this hero's quest is less the conventionally gendered set of obstacles he must overcome than the composition of the object and goal of his desire: Holga.

Unlike the other women in the play, Holga is characterized as a woman-who-is-almost-a-man, a figure able to rebuke Quentin so gently (at least in the original version) that it does not even count as a rebuke: "I've been told that [criticized for being emotionally sterile] before," he says to her, "but never so calmly."[154] She is, like the male subject in Miller, ostensibly independent and self-reliant: "I am not a woman who must be reassured every minute, those women are stupid to me" (p. 13). Most important, however, Holga is an almost magically effective bestower of patriarchal authority: an archaeologist and scientist, one devoted to the recuperation of lost cultures and lost lineages. She is also (in the final version) a woman without a mother, a woman whose only progenitor is her godfather, the commander of Nazi Intelligence and leader of a conspiracy to assassinate Hitler.[155] Although Holga is not given an active role in her godfather's plot—she is only a courier—she becomes his survivor and heir, and the itinerant sign of his heroism (pp. 14–15). Because Maggie functions as a trophy for Quentin, the indelible proof of his masculinity, Quentin can safely pledge himself to the heroic agent of patriarchy and renounce erotic desire in favor of a hom(m)o-sexual ideal—courage, glory, reputation. Unlike the dangerous Maggie, who arouses an uncontainable desire in Quentin, Holga is a stable commodity, a possession whose femaleness is guaranteed less by the erotic passion she elicits than by her status as the prize at the end of the narrative (and by the extraordinary force of the heterosexual matrix in Miller's work). Quentin's "grin" at the very first mention of Holga in the play seems far more the smirk of conquest than the ominous glow of eros (p. 3).

In dramatizing Quentin's quest, the plot of *After the Fall* reconstructs what De Lauretis calls the "two-character drama" of classic narrative, which is composed of a hero and his object of desire. It sets Quentin against the world, as "the human person" who must overcome a series of obstacles, who "creates and re-creates *himself* out of an abstract or purely symbolic other—the womb, the earth, the grave, the woman."[156]

As though (secretly) understanding the dynamics of this creation myth, Miller uses an apt metaphor in the description of *After the Fall* cited above, calling the play "a continuous stream," which, like a "mind," goes "in quest of a meaning," or like a "new river[,] cuts its bed, seeking the path to contain its force."[157] In *After the Fall* the active masculinized subject carves a path through resistant feminized terrain until it arrives at an end that enjoys a privileged relation to patriarchal authority and yet still retains its feminine identity because of its place in the landscape. In Miller's mythical geography (as a passage near the beginning of the play makes clear), the earth is a complex locale, the site of the confluence of several key terms. When Mother appears for the first time in the play, Quentin speaks:

> I still hear her voice in the street sometimes, loud and real, calling me.
> And yet she's under the ground. The whole cemetery—I saw it like a
> field of buried mirrors in which the living merely saw themselves. (p. 6)

Quentin's Mother is not only the embodiment of oral transgression, she is the very ground of difference itself, the mirror in which the subject (mis)recognizes himself and by means of which (to borrow a page from Lacan) he enters the symbolic order. She is the unself-conscious origin of a deathly self-consciousness, the one who, like Miller's own mother, "divided us against ourselves, unknowingly, innocently," and, at the same time, the voyeur who first turns the child into an exhibitionist, the one "secretly watching over me unseen, ... the mother, the first audience," the creator of theater.[158]

According to the mythical narrative that is enacted time and again in Miller's fantasmatic theater, the male subject is articulated as a field of metonymic displacements. The female subject, on the other hand, is configured as metaphor, as the ground of representation itself, as the mirror in which the male subject sees his infinitely displaced images and that he denounces because he believes it to be the very source of displacement, separation, and death.[159] As embodied by the laughing Woman, Abigail Williams, Maggie, or Eve (in *The Creation of the World and Other Business*, 1972), she is the origin and embodiment of chaos. Holga is excepted from this denunciation not because she is a different kind of woman but because she occupies a different position in this mythical (and psychoanalytical) narrative. Rather, like the death toward which Willy Loman, John Proctor, and Eddie Carbone rush, she is not the obstacle or the temptress or the Medusa, but the promised and glorious end itself: closure, the death of the narrative, which is to say, transfiguration, the cure.

That *After the Fall*, as a mythic narrative (or drama), condemns all the female demons along the hero's heroic pathway is hardly unusual in Miller (or in postwar literature generally). What is unique about the play, however, is the way in which the playwright guiltily calls attention both to his use of misogynist stereotypes and to his practice of collapsing all the unruly women who litter the hero's path into the figure of Mother. In the middle of act 1, Louise informs Quentin, "You have no conception of what a woman is," to which he is allowed no rebuttal (p. 28). Shortly afterward he muses, "Why is the world so treacherous?" adding, somewhat wryly, "Shall we lay it all to mothers?" (pp. 30–31). In the scene that follows, Louise tells him what he doesn't seem to understand: "I am not your mother! I am a separate person!" (p. 41). And near the end of the play, Maggie warns Quentin, "Don't mix me up with Louise!" (p. 109).

The composition of Quentin's mythical journey, his nonstop confession of his guilt over problems with Mother and wives is, I believe, a carefully calculated act. Assiduously, the confessor in *After the Fall* proclaims his culpability in order to diffuse (and defuse) it. By magnanimously accepting blame, he ensures that the play will function like a cathartic medicine, less to problematize his misogynist attitudes than to prove his good intentions and cure him of blame ("His guilt appears something of an indulgence," Bigsby remarks politely).[160] Miller's strategy of stigmatizing Quentin, however, is not an isolated pattern in *After the Fall*, but is embedded in the playwright's insistence upon a larger network of criminality. The play's entire moral order rests upon a stubborn claim of the universality of guilt, now understood, like the fall of Adam and Eve, as being more ontological than ethical in its complexion. Miller introduces the concentration camp tower into the play precisely to remind Quentin—and the spectator—of what is allegedly a universal network of crime and guilt from which no individual can ever be absolved. Looking at the tower, Quentin exclaims, "No one they didn't kill can be innocent again" (p. 21), a fatalistic—and profoundly unhistorical—conclusion that Miller carefully underscores (in his essay denying the identification of Maggie with Monroe) by asserting that the perception of "our own complicity with evil is a horror not to be borne."[161]

In *After the Fall* Quentin generously takes responsibility for his desire to throttle Maggie and his Mother by pointing out that these murderous fantasies are simply part of a universal pattern. In so doing, Quentin ingeniously engineers his innocence. He is, after all, no more guilty than anyone else. This strategy, however, is a peculiar one for a play that pretends to be a "trial of a man by his own conscience."[162] Rather than pursuing the investigation, it effectively destroys the possibility of moral evaluation, as Bigsby points out: "If we are all guilty we are all in some sense innocent and the basis for accusation, for the erection even of a contingent set of values by which to indict the criminal, is destroyed."[163] By judging himself irrevocably guilty, Quentin is, by a trick of logic, washed clean. This strategy was not lost on those first critics of the play who, like Brustein, noted that Miller seems oblivious to "how much self-justification is hidden in [Quentin's] apparent remorse."[164] By my own reckoning, Quentin's remorse is, in fact, an act of covert hostility that exemplifies the guilty yet violent masculinity that began to emerge during the early 1960s (coincidentally with the rebirth of feminism) as a result, in part, of the increasing disparity between men's institutional and personal power. On the one hand, the domestic revival facilitated a reconsolidation of patriarchal hegemony in the workplace (vide Quentin's professional triumphs). On the other hand, however, by strengthening women's control over the domestic sphere, it reinforced many men's belief in their relative powerlessness within the private and interpersonal space delineated by wife and children (vide Quentin's marital failures).[165] In After the Fall, this contradiction plays itself out not only in the opposition between public glory and private shame, but also (and more important) in the passive-aggressive fury with which Quentin assails "his" women.

Quentin, however, is not the only passive-aggressive character in After the Fall who wrestles with moral accountability only to be absolved of guilt. Alongside his allegedly private passion play runs an overtly political drama that strangely contradicts the moral position taken on the informer in The Crucible and A View from the Bridge. This is the drama of Mickey, an ex-Communist-turned-informer, and Lou, his former associate and a "saintly professor of law" (p. 23), whose relationship dominates act 1, both paralleling and foreshadowing the intrigue between Quentin and Maggie in act 2. Having been called a second time before "the Committee" (p. 32), Mickey has decided that he's "going to name names" (p. 33), including Lou's. Quentin suggests that Mickey "just tell about [him]self" (as Miller had done), but Mickey presses on sadistically, breaking Lou down, first making him feel "dazed," then to begin "physically shaking" and finally to "burst . . . into tears" (pp. 33, 36–37). Next to the hysterical and ineffectual Lou (who "never learned how to swim, always paddled like a dog"; p. 32), Mickey is fashioned as a tough man, one who respects a woman's "mystery" and believes, like Quentin, in taking responsibility: "I think a man's got to take the rap, Lou, for what he's done, for what he is" (pp. 31–32, 34). Like Quentin, Mickey is calculating, stubborn, a champion of personal accountability, and a misogynist: "I saw you burn a true book and write another that told

lies!"—Mickey tells Lou—"Because [Elsie] demanded it, because she terrified you, because she has taken your soul!" (p. 37). Like Maggie, Lou
is dishonest, weak, and a suicide. Although the supposed ubiquity of
guilt renders both partners in both couples equally culpable, the underlying pattern of scapegoating unanimously absolves *him* who has most
zealously and most manfully accepted responsibility, namely, Mickey
and Quentin (and, reaching further back, Eddie Carbone, John Proctor,
Willy Loman).

By providing absolution for the informer, *After the Fall* unexpectedly
transposes the relationship Miller had established in his preceding plays
between masculinity and politics. In *After the Fall*, the betrayal of one's
friends, not lone resistance to tyranny, becomes the proof of manhood.
Naming names is redefined as a courageous activity or, at the least, one
no worse than being a Communist and falsifier of documents. Albert
Maltz, one of the Hollywood Ten (and a great admirer of *The Crucible*),
maintains that *After the Fall* gives "as complete a justification" to the
informer as "to the man upon whom he informs." If Maltz is correct, it
is no wonder that Elia Kazan, opprobrious informer to the House Committee in 1952 and director of *After the Fall*, relished what he saw as
his vindication in the character of Mickey. According to Maltz, Kazan
reportedly paused one day during rehearsals and, pointing to Mickey,
"said proudly, 'That man is me.'"[166] Even more troubling than the absolution granted the informer, however, is Miller's own practice of *informing*
on others, on the destructive women whose identities slide compulsively
between the fictional and the historical: Quentin's Mother, Louise, and
Maggie. In *After the Fall*, Miller ironically repeated the process with
Barbara Loden that Norma Jean Baker had undergone to become Marilyn
Monroe—he gave her a different name and a different hair color.[167] And
as with Norma Jean Baker, so with Barbara Loden: the pseudonym
secured her identity and her fame. Miller's endorsement of Loden's blond
wig and her virtual imitation of Monroe (coupled with his deconstruction
in the text of the difference between fiction and autobiography) guaranteed that his second wife would be named. An actor in the original
production astutely described the situation: "The problem with Arthur
is that he *was* an 'informer.' . . . Gadg [Kazan] kind of had one over him
because he was really 'naming' Marilyn and the rest of them. The inva-
sion of privacy is what made it so sick."[168]

Miller turns what had never quite been private into a flagrantly public
performance in order to recuperate a desperate masculinity in *After the
Fall*. In the act of confession, he recklessly names names, attempting to
cloak the treachery of the informer and the hatred of the misogynist
beneath what is supposedly an inescapable network of universal guilt.

At the same time, the moral problems raised by the naming of names and the scapegoating are compounded by what amounts to the wholesale erasure of ethical distinctions (between Maggie and Quentin, Lou and Mickey, a mother's neglect and a Nazi concentration camp). By demanding that oppressor and victim be telescoped into a single figure (or, in Miller's words, that there be "a recognition of the individual's part in the evil he sees and abhors"),[169] *After the Fall* denies historical difference. By systematically equating all forms of brutality and collapsing morality into a bleary and melancholy ontology, it denies the possibility of any effective resistance. The vigor of a Roslyn is crushed by the combined force of Mother's contempt and Maggie's suicidal rage, and consequently written out of Miller's dramatic recipe. Bigsby is certainly correct in maintaining that *After the Fall* thereby testifies to the playwright's rejection of the belief "that evil is the product of a particular economic or political system" and hence of the last shred of Marxism in his work.[170] By equating the perpetrators of genocide with destructive parents, the gas chamber with the bathroom in which the young Quentin takes refuge, *After the Fall* collapses the distinction between the political and the domestic in a way that is startlingly different from what Miller calls for in "The Family in Modern Drama." In this play, the concentration camp is simply a grotesque extension of the nuclear family, the Nazi commandant a more efficient replacement for Mother.

The Last Real Men

Since *After the Fall* Arthur Miller has written only a handful of original plays, as opposed to adaptations, most of which have been poorly received by the American press and handled cautiously and somewhat indulgently by Miller's academic critics. Among them, *The Price* is deservedly the most widely performed (if not the most structurally or thematically provocative). Its popularity seems to rest primarily on the incidental role of Gregory Solomon, the octogenarian Jewish furniture dealer, who is one of Miller's more colorful characters. The remainder of the drama is a relatively conventional well-made play that dramatizes the struggle between two brothers, Victor and Walter, over their father's inheritance and repeats the patterns of male rivalry established in Miller's earlier plays. The play's only female character, Esther, Victor's wife, is another badgering, avaricious, unruly woman who can no more restrain her words of accusation and disgust than her late mother-in-law could her vomit.

Miller's plays of the 1970s and 1980s are, for the most part, even more labored than those of the 1960s and, I believe, would not have received attention from critics, audiences, and performers were it not for the proper name printed on their title pages. These plays fail, not because they deal with trivial matters, but because they address a number of important and provocative social, psychological, and aesthetic issues in ways that are often stilted and banal. Miller's dramatic situations are, for the most part, little more than clichés, and the prosaic, quasi-existentialist philosophizing that is superimposed on them is couched in the same kind of pretentious rhetoric that sabotages Quentin's universally criticized speeches in *After the Fall*. Although the action of most of the later plays is not monopolized by the single overreaching protagonist found in Miller's earlier works, it tends to repeat the mythological formula codified in *After the Fall*: the self-conscious and guilty masculine quest, through dangerous feminine terrain, for truth-beauty-power-glory-love-death.

Given the predominance of this mythological design, it is not surprising that Miller's later plays repeat the patterns of genderization codified in *After the Fall*. *The Creation of the World and Other Business*, for example, expands an originary misogynist narrative in a predictable way for a culture intent on reading female sexuality as dangerous and corrupting. In a Garden of Eden that was "perfect" before the first woman "showed up," a sensual Eve is tempted by Lucifer, who, "alone" among creatures, "understand[s]" her, and she sins, manipulating the first man into being her partner in crime.[171] In act 2, the abashed and pregnant Eve recounts to Adam her interpretation of the Fall, which could stand as a resumé of the mythical narrative underlying all of Miller's plays:

> With you the Lord was only somewhat disappointed, but with me He was furious. *Lucifer gravely nods.* And his curse is entirely on me. It is the reason why you've hardly changed out here in the world; but I bleed, and now I am ugly and swollen up like a frog. And I never dream of Paradise, but you do almost every night, and you seem to expect to find it over every hill. And that is right—I think now that you belong in Eden. But not me. And as long as I am with you, you will never find it again.[172]

As in *After the Fall*, the man is the heroic struggler, dreaming of Paradise, while the transgressive, swollen, and leaking woman is the obstacle blocking his reentrance to Eden.

Miller's subsequent plays, meanwhile, further reinforce this oppressive, masculinist mythology. *The Archbishop's Ceiling* (1976), set in an unnamed Eastern European country, is yet another parable of male desire that includes yet another promiscuous woman, this time the Scandinavian Irina, on the fringe of the drama, who reembodies the "strudel" of

Salesman as "a nice piece of Danish."[173] The primary female role, meanwhile, is given to Maya, the woman who learns English by reading *Vogue* and doesn't "like many women," a figure possessing "a sublime sluttishness," whose primary function is to cement the hom(m)o-sexuality of the play's three male protagonists, each of whom is her lover.[174] The three men, meanwhile, interlocked over Maya's flesh, continue Miller's series of self-portraits. Here they are writers—variously famous, rich, politically resistant, heroic, egotistical, and incomparably brilliant—gathered in the hope of rescuing the precious manuscript of one of them, Sigmund, from the hands of the tyrannical Communist authorities who have stolen it. Although the masterwork is supposed to be returned to Sigmund at the end of the play, it is never actually produced, remaining, like the "big play ... my big play" Arthur Miller promised in a 1986 interview, deferred, waiting tantalizingly and indefinitely offstage.[175]

Instead of a "big play," Miller's most recently produced work for the theater, *Danger: Memory!* (1987), consists of two one-acts: the rather slight *I Can't Remember Anything* and the more substantial and provocative *Clara*. Much like *After the Fall*, *Clara* is centered around the recollections of a protagonist (Albert Kroll) mourning the loss of a beloved woman, in this case, his daughter (Clara), who appears alive on the stage in his memory. Unlike *After the Fall*, however, which conjures a silent Listener, *Clara* incarnates the listener as Detective Lieutenant Fine, a police investigator and, from the evidence of his cunning and merciless examination of Kroll, something of an amateur psychiatrist as well. Clara, a social worker active in prisoner rehabilitation, is found murdered, and Fine undertakes to track down her killer. He believes that one of her former clients is responsible and enlists Kroll's aid in apprehending a released murderer with whom Clara had been sexually involved. The action of the play consists of Kroll's remembrance of Clara and, in particular, of his meeting with her Hispanic lover the preceding Christmas. Much like Quentin, Kroll is racked by guilt over Clara's death because he did not attempt to discourage her final romance, believing a convicted murderer preferable to the last "friend" of Clara's he had met, a woman, whom he had clandestinely observed kissing his daughter.[176]

Like the women in Miller's other plays, Clara is articulated as the ground of difference, as a metaphorical being (almost indistinguishable from the caged bird she cherishes), as environment (the outfitter and owner of the apartment-office in which the play takes place), as the "medal" her convicted murderer-boyfriend wears "on his chest," and as a kind of divine sorceress with the power to stop a "snarling, snapping" dog "in his tracks" (pp. 55, 38). Clara is the mirror in which Kroll sees himself, the embodiment of all he cherishes, the one whose "look of intense love" and "sublime smile" narcissistically reflect back upon Kroll the moral purity to which he aspires, despite—or, perhaps, because of—his questionable business dealings (pp. 40, 63). Simultaneously, Clara is the subject of intense textual violence, who appears as a fleeting image on a projection screen, "the bloodied body of a partially stripped woman," whom the reader or spectator later learns has been decapitated (pp. 35, 53). Unlike Kroll's wife, a former Rockette, consigned to the "kitchen cooking dinner," Clara has appropriated the goals and characteristics customarily reserved in Miller's dramatic arena for men: freedom, liberalism, dedication, self-sacrifice, heroism, even an (apparent) sexual passion for women—although without the masculine arrogance or the anatomy that usually accompanies these aims. Unlike Quentin, however, who recovers a fictitious wholeness, Clara not only dies for her desires, but is brutally mutilated and dismembered. This is what will happen—the play seems to warn—when women disrupt the inflexible rule of gender and the restrictive division of labor it supervises.

Ironically, however, this simple, cautionary fable is strangely destabilized by an exorbitance in the text. Clara's is not the only mutilated body. Kroll's, as well, has been literally wounded in battle—"I look down and my whole insides are falling out," Kroll recalls—and figuratively mangled by a traitorous friend (who "slit [him] right up the belly"; pp. 56, 43). In order to explain these incisions, I want to examine Kroll's project more generally, which, not surprisingly, is represented as Miller's most typical (and archetypal) quest: the search for a name—in this case, that of Clara's apparent murderer. This search for a fixed and exact patronym is the obsession of many Miller protagonists (and, arguably, of Miller himself, who seems determined to secure a preeminent status in the American theater). Beginning with the tomcat protagonist of Miller's 1941 radio play, "The Pussycat and the Expert Plumber Who Was a Man," and proceeding through John Proctor and Eddie Carbone, all the way to Albert Kroll forty-seven years later, the Miller hero is racked by anxiety over the possible ruination of his name. As the tomcat puts it: "The one thing a man fears most next to death is the loss of his good name."[177] Kroll, meanwhile, tortured by his inability to remember the name of his daughter's lover, needs to be broken down by the detective, who, using a Freudian stratagem (based on the assumption that "we block things we're ashamed to remember"), makes Kroll first confess his own guilt in the belief that this will remove the obstacle (p. 49). Only after admitting to his own petty crimes is Kroll able to name Clara's lover: Luis Hernandez.

Unlike John Proctor or Eddie Carbone, Kroll commemorates not his own name, but the name of another: a Hispanic murderer and ex-convict who works as a baggage handler at Kennedy Airport. Yet the psycho-analytical structure links Kroll's guilt so inseparably with that of the murderer that he cannot name the Other until he names himself. In an almost expressionistic manner, the intersection of remembrance and confession configures the murderer not as a distinct entity but as an Other within the self, as a man who, despite his superficial differences from Kroll, becomes his fantasmatic double. The subject is slit up the belly so that it will divulge the name of the Other, will reveal the murderer within, will confess carnally to all that its fictitiously whole simulacrum—one Albert Kroll by name—attempts to suppress.

In *Clara*, as elsewhere in Miller's work, the subject is cleaved, turned against itself, as it is forced to confess to the Other within. Yet the inevitable end of this confession is not an acknowledgment of the inescapability of division, but an emotional catharsis, a return to an illusory—and phallic—wholeness, like the one Kroll embodies at the end of the play, "standing erect and calm" (p. 68). The necessity of catharsis, however, puts enormous stress on the subject who, in the rush to closure, must attempt to conceal its self-division. Fortunately, for the mutinous reader, the anxious subject cannot suture all the incisions in the texts it generates, or (to denominate another crucial site of resistance) completely stifle the gloriously emancipatory laughter of The Woman in Boston. While *Death of a Salesman* tries desperately to condemn her (and other orally transgressive women), it also allows Willy, in Biff's words, to "spew . . . out that vomit from his mind" (p. 56). By recognizing these slips and inconsistencies, the reader is in a position to comprehend the multitude of contradictions that articulate the playwright known as Arthur Miller. Thus the disparity between the man who declares he was "never interested in being a 'realistic' writer," but whose work has been central to the institutionalization of the well-made play as the national form and realism as the national style.[178] Thus the distance between the former Communist and the playwright who prides himself on the knowledge that *Death of a Salesman* erases class distinctions.[179] Thus the vicious circle of criminality and guilt in *After the Fall* and *Clara* that bespeaks a "despairing passivity before History" far more stultifying than the one Miller attributes to Marxism.[180] Thus Quentin, the champion of an aggressive masculinity, who is always in danger of being revealed as the "fag" that Maggie half accuses him of being (not *in spite* of his denial but *because* of it): "I've known fags and some of them didn't even know themselves that they were" (p. 99).

For these divided male subjects—otherwise known as "the last real men"—frantically asserting a fictitious wholeness by suffocating the Other within, the very thought of uncensored speech induces a kind of panic. It is the ability to raise this fear that renders Quentin's Mother so pernicious ("She says anything comes into her head . . ."; p. 97) and the alleged murderer in *Clara* so dangerous ("They're liable to do anything comes into their heads"; p. 61). (Apparently, decapitation is the final solution for this unruly subject.) Unless discourse is rigorously policed, Miller's plays seem to be saying, it will unwittingly divulge all that the hegemonic masculinity of the domestic revival strives so desperately to conceal: its jealous and violent ownership of women and the past, the hom(m)o-sexuality of its desire, and the Other always lurking within, always threatening to slit open its name or trash its dream of Paradise. In the original version of *After the Fall*, the embodiment of this masculinity (and the one who harbors an astonishing "referential productivity") is Quentin, the one who tells Louise about his "latest conquest" and is "perplexed" when Louise, believing he expects her to "enjoy" the story, asks him, "You take me for Lesbian?" In reply, Quentin mutters a question left tantalizingly incomplete: "What's a Lesbian got to do with. . . . "[181] To do with what? With desire in narrative? With voyeuristic pleasure? With the politics of Cold War masculinity?

Two

Tennessee Williams I
"By coming suddenly into a room that I thought was empty"

> I think it is only in the case of Brecht that a man's politics, if the man is an artist, are of particular importance in his work; his degrees of talent and of humanity are what count. I also feel that an artist's sexual predilections or deviations are not usually pertinent to the value of his work.
>
> —Tennessee Williams, *Memoirs* (1975)

> You can't hardly separate homosexuals from subversives. . . . Mind you, I don't say every homosexual is a subversive, and I don't say every subversive is a homosexual. But a man of low morality is a menace in the government, whatever he is, and they are all tied up together.
>
> —Senator Kenneth Wherry (R-Nebr.), quoted by Max Lerner in the *New York Post*, July 17, 1950

In "The Mysteries of the Joy Rio," an early short story (written c. 1941, published 1954), Tennessee Williams creates what is probably his first homosexual protagonist, Pablo Gonzales, a searcher after furtive pleasures in the balcony of the Joy Rio, a derelict movie theater. Mr. Gonzales (as Williams chivalrously calls him) is the owner of a watch repair business bequeathed to him by his late patron and protector, Emiel Kroger, who has additionally passed along to his protégé both his "fleeting and furtive practices in dark places" and his fatal "disease of the bowels."[1] For this clandestine homosexual—unlike the less securely closeted Williams, who neither published this story until 1954 nor came out publicly until 1970—the dark balcony of the Joy Rio is an "earthly heaven," the site of his encounters with "male adolescents" and others who've come to see the "cowboy pictures and other films of the sort" that play in the decrepit "old opera house" (pp. 112, 105). Williams's narrative focuses on Mr. Gonzales one afternoon as he struggles up the theater's staircase and past George, the new usher, fornicating in the "ladies' room" with his girlfriend Gladys. When George hears Mr. Gonzales, he thrusts his paramour back "violently" against the basin and rushes out of the lavatory to accost the ailing "morphodite," to borrow George's quaintly abusive term (p. 112). Mr. Gonzales quickly retreats to the balcony for the last time, where he meets his late protector (or the ghost of him), who has appeared to guide the ailing Mr. Gonzales to a serene and comforting death.

Despite the vivid presentation of the "fury" that "burst[s]" forth from the virile young usher when, with "livid face and threatening fists," he brutally confronts the dying man (pp. 112–13), it is difficult to defend this story against charges of homophobia. Mr. Gonzales is a pathetic, although sympathetic, figure whose final, forbidden excursion to the balcony, under the "velvet rope with the sign 'Keep Out,'" seems to epitomize negative or prohibitive definitions of homosexuality. In "The Mysteries of the Joy Rio" homosexual desire appears, like its Mexican-American incarnation, to be diseased, "malignant," and deathly (p. 110). Furthermore, Williams's characterization of the violence of a normative heterosexual masculinity toward its cultural Other is not sufficiently condemnatory to bolster a reading of the story as an example of an antihomophobic text. Mr. Gonzales is not an especially resistant subject, and George's "fury" is soundly, if uncomfortably, triumphant. An analysis focused solely on characterization and conflict will find little in the story beyond a rehearsal of homophobic discourse and, I believe, will ominously foreclose the possibility of resistance to a patently oppressive and violent social order. For the primary site of resistance in the story is not an individual subject at all, but the social and architectural space in which the story's final scene takes place, "the mysterious upper galleries of the Joy Rio,"

> where practically every device and fashion of carnality had run riot in a gloom so thick that a chance partner could only be discovered by touch. There were not rows of benches, . . . but strings of tiny boxes, extending in semicircles from one side of the great proscenium to the other. In some of these boxes brokenlegged chairs might be found lying on their sides and shreds of old hangings still clung to the sliding brass loops at the entrances. . . . one lived up there, in the upper reaches of the Joy Rio, an almost sightless existence where the other senses, the senses of smell and touch and hearing, had to develop a preternatural keenness in order to spare one from making awkward mistakes, such as taking hold of the knee of a boy when it was a girl's knee one looked for, and where sometimes little scenes of panic occurred when a mistake of gender or of compatibility had been carried to a point where radical correction was called for. There had been many fights, there had even been rape and murder in those ancient boxes. (p. 107)

Although written at the very beginning of his career as a playwright, this description of the Joy Rio and the activities that take place therein provides an astonishingly apt and prescient metaphor for Tennessee Williams's project as a playwright: recolonizing an old-fashioned theater and turning it into an enigmatic, if slightly queer, site of resistance. Like the balcony of the Joy Rio, composed of a string of tiny boxes, each of Williams's plays does not present a grandly unified and seamlessly linear structure, but offers instead a composite of short and fragmentary episodes, each dramatizing a complex and elusive moment, each accommodating an idiosyncratic device of carnality. Like the Joy Rio, Williams's theater comprises a double spectacle, one (the "heterosexual") occurring on a bright screen while the other (the "homosexual," the more vibrant and productive of the two) takes place in the gloomy, subtextual, private galleries, onto which the glare from the cowboy pictures and other sensational and sentimental narratives is reflected. His is a theater of unexpected liaisons, of a hand suddenly brushing across a knee, of little scenes of panic aggravated or allayed, of mistakes of gender repeated so frequently that it is sometimes difficult to know which gender is to be paired with which. It is a theater punctuated by acts of violence, by rapes and murders, toward which the playwright displays sometimes revulsion, sometimes an attitude of surprising nonchalance. Strangely, it is as much a theater that privileges the senses of touch and hearing and smell, and requires an almost uncanny intimacy between subjects, as it is a theater of specularity (devoted, like Miller's, to the pleasures of exhibitionism and voyeurism). It is a theater of fetishism, in which the phallic object of desire is perenially dis- and misplaced, lost and found, and lost and found again. It is a theater in which the individual subjects, arrayed among the string of boxes, are barely perceptible and are always demurring to a collective subject on the verge of being produced, one that, despite—or, perhaps, because of—the persistent gloom, resists the prohibitions imposed on it by a desperate and increasingly archaic bourgeois morality. It is a theater of metaphor and metonymy, in which images and objects and words are continually and unexpectedly discovered to be similar to and contiguous with each other, a surrealist theater of extravagant and polymorphous desires.

The Personal Is the Political

Despite Tennessee Williams's commitment to a theater of resistance, he was never—in contrast to Arthur Miller—a political activist. He was never associated with the American Communist party, never called before the House Committee on Un-American Activities, and never especially troubled by Elia Kazan's naming names, and he never considered his political views "of particular importance in his work" as an artist.[2]

However, unlike Miller, who (at least in testimony before the House Committee) renounced his former leftist associations, Williams, in his *Memoirs* and in interviews dating from 1940 until the end of his life, insisted on his continued commitment to radical political change: "I was a socialist from the time I started working for a shoe company [1931–34]."[3] His letters to Donald Windham from the early 1940s bear out both his determined opposition to capitalism and his early (if inchoate) sympathy for communism.[4] In 1945, in answer to an interviewer's question about "the human situation," he declared that the "problem" is "not something mystical," but "social and economic." He went on to emphasize that there can be no "equity in American life until at least 90 percent of our population are living under different circumstances."[5] Throughout his life, Williams eschewed the kind of abstract and (falsely) universalizing rhetoric so characteristic of Miller's utterances in favor of an extremely specific and concrete mode of discourse. Insistently, he underscored the broadly social foundation for the personal tragedies with which so many of his plays are concerned, pointing out that the individual subject is not an isolated monad but a component of a "society" that insistently "rapes the individual."[6] Time and again he stated his fierce opposition to social and political tyranny, to the Vietnam War, to racism, and to the persecution of homosexuals. In his *Memoirs*, he several times describes himself as a revolutionary in both "personal" and "artistic" terms.[7] In a 1976 interview he went even further, insisting that all of his plays and, indeed, that "all good art is essentially revolutionary."[8]

This characterization of Williams as a revolutionary is at odds with the portraits offered by Williams's critics. Most ignore the political implications and resonances of his plays as decidedly as they ignore his homosexuality, preferring to deal only with questions of characterization and theme, and hypostatizing character psychology to a stultifying degree. For these critics, Williams is the quintessential modern dramatist of desire and sexuality, obsessed with and absorbed by the most deeply private aspects of life. Benjamin Nelson, for example, considers "the loneliness of human existence" to be "the dominant theme" in Williams's plays.[9] Robert Heilman, meanwhile, ascribes his characters' "troubles" to their "faulty neurological mechanisms," while Roger Boxill considers him "an elegiac writer, a poet of nostalgia."[10] Even Raymond Williams sees Williams's plays as an instance of bourgeois art at its most solipsistic, as the very essence of what he calls private tragedy, a drama peopled by "isolated beings who desire and eat and fight alone," whose emblem is the "animal struggle of sex and death."[11] In contrast, C. W. E. Bigsby provides the most incisive and historically rigorous portrait of Williams,

one of the very few that addresses the social implications of a character's deterioration and credits the "subversive" quality of sexuality in
Williams's early plays. Yet even Bigsby contends that Williams's radicalism is "not very" deep and that there "seems little in the way of an
ideological conviction in his work." He characterizes the playwright as
a nostalgic rebel and argues that Williams's "was not a political rejection
of capitalism but a romantic's reaction against the modern."[12]

Although Bigsby is certainly correct to note this strain of romantic
rebellion in Williams's work, I believe that his radicalism is far more
complex and vigorous than Bigsby makes it out to be, and that it deeply,
if equivocally, destabilizes mid-century notions of gendered subjectivity
and dramatic form. Despite his cautious skepticism, Bigsby gets very close
to the heart of Williams's politics when he argues that the playwright's
radicalism, "lacking a political correlative, tends to be displaced into a
sexual subversiveness."[13] Unquestionably, there is in Williams's work an
almost constant movement back and forth between the political and the
sexual. However, to characterize this movement as a simple displacement
rigidifies the two categories, erecting a set of congruent binarisms that
(following Arthur Miller's example) opposes the political to the sexual,
public to private, center to margin. At the same time, Bigsby's conceptualization systematically privileges the first in each pair, granting it a
historical and epistemological primacy. Similarly, John M. Clum's analysis
of homophobic discourse in Williams, although one of the more carefully
considered studies of the textual implications of Williams's homosexuality,
is based on an analogous set of assumptions. Almost in echo of Bigsby,
Clum asserts that the basis for Williams's representation of homosexuality
is his "intense consciousness of the split between the public persona and
the private actor." In his view, this split, which is "central to Williams's
treatment of homosexuality," exacts a crippling cost for Williams the
writer, whose representations, Clum alleges, are determinedly, if reluctantly, homophobic.[14] Although Clum reverses the polarity of the oppositions (privileging the sexual, the private, and the marginal) found in
Bigsby, he does not challenge the binary structure itself.

Unlike Bigsby and Clum, I believe that the work of Tennessee Williams
offers an urgent challenge to the stubborn antitheses between the political
and the sexual, and between the public and the private, binarisms so
crucial for normative constructions of gender during the 1940s and 1950s.
Unlike Arthur Miller, who attempts tirelessly (and finally, to my mind,
unsuccessfully) to police these binarisms, Williams insistently delights
in their precariousness. Williams's destabilization of mid-century notions
of masculinity and femininity is accomplished, in part, by his ability

both to expose the often murderous violence that accompanies the exercise of male authority and to valorize female power and female sexual desire. In the same gesture, his work undermines the hegemonic and hierarchical structure of masculinity itself by disclosing the contradictions on which its normative formulation is based and by celebrating various subjugated masculinities. Finally, and perhaps most important, his plays redefine and reconfigure resistance so that it is less the prerogative of rebellious individuals than a potential always already at play within both social organization and dramatic structure.

Contradictions

While writing *The Glass Menagerie* (1944) during his 1943 southern California sojourn, the aspiring young playwright—and maddeningly frustrated screenwriter—wrote his friend, Donald Windham, about the "two things" upon which he and his Santa Monica landlady agreed:

> One of them is communism. The other is our most ardent point of agreement but we only discuss it in knowing smiles at each other and the shyly understanding exchange of drinks and tomatoes, Etc.[15]

Just as important—and as misunderstood—as Williams's political radicalism is the construction of his desire, his passion (like his landlady's) for "the wrestling champion of the Pacific coast" who stalks the halls of the house "in an electric blue satin robe clinging like a kiss to all the lines of his body."[16] Although Williams's private correspondence with his friend is wonderfully candid and sensual, his homosexuality, to his landlady's ears, at least, is strangely and tellingly mute, communicated only in a silent transaction, in intimate and "knowing smiles" and in a "shyly understanding exchange."

Even more insistently than Williams's "communism," his homosexuality is the site of manifold contradictions, articulated by the unstable and fluid difference between secrecy and disclosure, between his ability to write about his sexual desire to his gay friend and his inability to speak about it openly to his straight landlady (or, for many years, to the theatergoing public).[17] Throughout his life, it is Williams's more or less open secret, the one he neither advertised nor tried to hide by marrying or masquerading as a heterosexual—like many of his Broadway and Hollywood confreres. When Williams finally came out publicly on "The David Frost Show" in 1970 (just six months after the Stonewall riot), it was with a quip that neatly combines fear of courting disfavor with delight in startling a coy interrogator:

> FROST: What about things like the homosexuality and so on, does everybody live with that, too?

WILLIAMS: I think that everybody has some elements of homosexuality in him, even the most heterosexual of us.
FROST: That no one is all man or all woman, you mean?
WILLIAMS: Oh, in my experience, no. I don't want to be involved in some sort of a scandal, but I've covered the waterfront. [*Laughter and applause*][18]

Given Williams's gaily euphemistic disposition, it should hardly be surprising that his work, like his behavior, covers the waterfront, configuring homosexuality in extremely conflicted ways, as a locus of desire and scandal, "freedom" and "crime."[19] Insistently, he renders it both natural and unnatural, allowing it, in Harold Beaver's words, "the dual distinction (and penalty) of simultaneously contravening both 'nature' and 'culture,' fertility and the law."[20] In his many interviews and his *Memoirs*, he provides a deeply conflicted portrait of himself as a homosexual: he is the former "sissy" who later disdains the "'obvious' types" and believes that "travesties of Mae West . . . make the whole homosexual thing seem ridiculous."[21] He is the one who, harboring "some quite dreadful or abominable secret," was "mortified" at its public revelation, yet who steadfastly maintains that he was "not . . . ever embarrassed particularly by it."[22] He is the one for whom "sex is so much an integral part" of his work that he must continually "talk about it," but who (at least until 1976) neither considered it "pertinent to the value of his work" nor found it "necessary" to write "a gay play."[23] He is the one who considers "gay lib" a "serious crusade," who insists that all "gay people" should support "legitimate revolutionary movements," who urges the consolidation of "the gay lib movement" with other "revolutionary" and "nonviolent" organizations, and yet who also maintains that he is "bored" with "movements" and that he finds the "gay libs' public displays . . . so vulgar they defeat their purpose."[24] And he is the one who so delights in all these inconsistencies and even provides two conflicting explanations for his adopted first name: "I *am* contradictory, baby."[25]

Like Williams's instinctive radicalism, his homosexuality is both ubiquitous and elusive, everywhere in his work and yet nearly impossible to pin down. It structures and informs all of his texts, yet rarely, especially in his plays, produces the unequivocally homosexual character that most critics look for in attempting to identify a homosexual text.[26] Instead, Williams's homosexuality is endlessly *refracted* in his work: translated, reflected, and transposed. Williams insisted, with some justification, that he could not stage his homosexuality directly or candidly during the 1940s and 1950s, believing that "there would be no producer for it" given the homophobic program of the Broadway theater of that period.[27] As a result, he developed a style with distinct similarities to that of his ideological and spiritual forebear, Hart Crane ("a tremendous yet fragile artist"), whose work is analyzed admirably by Thomas E. Yingling in his book, *Hart Crane and the Homosexual Text*.[28] Like Crane, Williams wrote (to borrow Yingling's phrase) "under a number of screens and covers" that would allow him to represent his homosexuality in other guises: as a valorization of eroticism generally and extramarital desire, in particular; as an endorsement of transgressive liaisons that cut across lines of social class, ethnicity, and race, and violate mid-century social prescriptions; and as a deep sympathy for the outsider and the disenfranchised, for "the fugitive kind."[29]

Throughout Williams's career—in his plays, short stories, and poetry—the "screens and covers" were constantly redefined and repositioned as a result of both changes in the public profile of the gay writer and the different visibilities accorded the different media he used. Although several of his short stories from the 1940s and 1950s are avowedly and almost jubilantly gay, such as "Two on a Party" (written 1951–52, published 1954), his pre-Stonewall plays and films, written for a much larger and more popular audience, are more cautious and, to use Williams's word, "oblique."[30] In their obliqueness, they embody the unresolved tension between Williams's assertions that he "never tried to disguise [his] homosexuality" and that he "never found it necessary to deal with [homosexuality] in [his] work."[31] Colonizing the contradictory ground between "never tried to disguise" and "never found it necessary to deal," Tennessee Williams consistently writes his desire as equivocally as he writes himself in a corpus of work in which "every word is autobiographical and no word is autobiographical."[32] Throughout his work for the theater of the 1940s and 1950s, homosexuality appears—ever obliquely—as a distinctive and elusive style, in every word and no word, as a play of signs and images, of text and subtext, of metaphorical elaboration and substitution, of disclosure and concealment—in short, as textuality itself. It is the unspoken secret that forces even Williams's most homophobic critics to disguise their attacks, upbraiding the playwright, in one carefully coded review, for his "obsessiveness of attitude," his "empurpling theatricalism," and his preoccupation with the "sordid," the "lurid," and the "lopsided."[33]

Most of Williams's more perspicuous and sympathetic critics attempt to explain the contradictions in his writing by sketching a portrait of Williams as a self-hating homosexual. Gore Vidal, for example, a friend of Williams for thirty-five years, suggests (in his distinctive terminology) that "at some deep level Tennessee truly believes that the homosexualist is wrong and that the heterosexualist is right."[34] Although Vidal's observation may well be accurate, the assumptions underlying his assertion—

like those of Clum and the other portraitists—bears careful examination. Vidal's statement seems to imply that a position radically different from Williams's is possible, that the product of a deeply homophobic culture can somehow avoid internalizing its values. I question whether one— even one as impudent and aristocratic as Gore Vidal—can so effortlessly assume the availability of a position beyond self-hatred and guilt. Is not the homosexual—or, dare I say, gay—subject of Williams's era necessarily split, alienated from its own desires, its guilt articulated by an inveterate (and, one hopes, increasingly obsolete) discourse of homophobia, while its desires rise in mutiny against that very discourse? Williams may well have been, "at some deep level," a self-hating homosexual, but this assertion is only the beginning, not the end, of an inquiry into his work.

Before Stonewall

Tennessee Williams's most productive years, the 1940s and 1950s, were extremely turbulent and trying decades for gay men and lesbians in America. Although the 1920s and 1930s had witnessed the growth of a gay and lesbian subculture in several major cities in the United States, the legal and ideological prohibitions were so stringent that an antihomophobic discursive counterpart was virtually inconceivable. In 1934 the Hollywood Production Code banned all representations of homosexuality in films.[35] And, as John D'Emilio notes, the proscription of homosexual works by the National Office for Decent Literature of the Catholic church impelled "publishers and newspaper editors" to practice "a form of self-censorship that kept homosexuality virtually out of print."[36] The massive social and demographic disruptions of World War II, meanwhile, allowed a greater possibility for sexual (but not written) expression by gay men and lesbians, both in and out of uniform. Although homosexuals remained officially banned from the military, Alan Berubé estimates that "possibly a million or more gay men" were accepted into the armed forces during the war.[37] Gay and lesbian bars may have flourished in the large cities for military and nonmilitary personnel, but this expansion of the gay subculture was accompanied by neither the development of a counter-hegemonic discourse nor the concerted—and, in Jeffrey Weeks's estimation, revolutionary—goal of "personal and sexual self-determination."[38]

When the war ended, gay men and lesbians were once again harassed and subjected—and even more brutally than they had been before—to "witch hunts, bar raids, arrests," which for many encouraged their "retreat to the closet."[39] The late 1940s and the 1950s were particularly trying, as the House Committee on Un-American Activities pursued a campaign against homosexuals almost as vigorous as its crusade against alleged

Communist "subversives." According to Senator Joseph McCarthy and his confederates, not only had Hollywood been invaded by Communists, but the very government and the armed forces of the United States had been infiltrated by homosexuals, whose presence, they insisted, posed grave security risks. According to the 1950 Republican national chairman, ninety-one employees of the State Department had been unmasked as "sexual perverts" and summarily fired, in the belief that they were excessively prone to blackmail.[40] During this same period, the job seekers who were refused government service and the military personnel who were dismissed as "undesirables" numbered in the thousands. The procedure used to purge the military was particularly insidious because, as D'Emilio notes, "defendents lacked the right to question or even to meet their accusers, and they had no access to the sources used against them."[41] By the end of the 1950s, the antihomosexual campaign had spread far beyond the government and the military. Fanatical vice squads arrested countless men and women in gay and lesbian bars, cruising areas, and even their homes, while local newspapers printed the names and addresses of these "perverts" (most notoriously in Boise, Idaho).[42] In 1958, a Florida legislator even succeeded in dismissing sixteen faculty and staff members from Florida State University in Gainesville on charges of homosexuality.[43]

For the first time in the United States, however, a crusade against homosexuals did not proceed unopposed. This period of intense persecution also marks the beginning of the modern homosexual rights movement, with the founding of the Mattachine Society in 1951 by Henry Hay, a former union organizer and political activist. From its inception, the society was dedicated to dispelling "the fears and antagonisms of the community," to lobbying for "progressive sexual legislation," and to making "common cause with other minorities in contributing to the reform of judicial, police and penal practices."[44] During the early 1950s, the Mattachine Society, composed of gay men and lesbians from across the political spectrum, established chapters in Los Angeles and the San Francisco Bay Area. In January 1953, several members of the society launched *ONE*, a magazine devoted to examining "homosexuality from the scientific, historical and critical point of view."[45] For the remainder of the decade, *ONE* provided a source of information for so-called homophiles, publishing news of government and police harassment, essays by psychiatrists and sociologists, fiction and reviews of reputedly gay fiction (including Tennessee Williams's book of short stories, *One Arm* [1948; reprinted 1954], which was greeted tepidly).[46] Although its staff included both men and women, most of the magazine's content was clearly addressed to male readers, whose "problems" and "neuroses" (two obsessively recurring terms) were almost invariably the subject of its feature articles. Its lesbian readers, meanwhile, were saluted dubiously with a column titled "The Feminine Viewpoint" buried in *ONE*'s final pages.

Given both the minuscule dimensions and the relative nonmilitancy of the homosexual rights movement in the early 1950s, plus the limited circulation of *ONE* and other, even smaller, magazines for gay men and lesbians, it is perhaps surprising that the forces of political reaction aimed their repressive artillery so determinedly at homosexuals. Zealots such as Senator McCarthy and Senator Kenneth Wherry, the Republican floor leader, insisted that there was an inevitable link between Communists and homosexuals, both of whom, in Wherry's estimation, were men "of low morality" and menaces to the American government.[47] Throughout the 1950s, these charges of political subversion were reiterated with a force that too often matched the fury displayed by the virile usher in "The Mysteries of the Joy Rio," or by Senator Wherry, whose "harangues," in columnist Max Lerner's words, were "so violent as to make me think he would explode."[48] This explosive anger, however, was extremely productive for the Cold War hegemony insofar as it rationalized the exercise of containment on the domestic front. Homophobic panic authorized an unprecedented level of surveillance of social and sexual practices and of political organizations, all in the name of safeguarding the American family and the American way. Even more effectively than allegations of a Communist insurgency, a hunt for homosexuals empowered Congress to police the most private corners of persons' lives and "to regain social control in a world tending towards disorder."[49]

Despite the radical pasts of Henry Hay and some of the readers of *ONE*, the contents of the magazine exemplify an oddly contradictory collection of texts in which the "homophile" is represented as conflicted and embattled, more an object of social proscriptions than a site of active resistance. The magazine's very statement of purpose betrays an equivocal attitude: on the one hand, announcing its dedication to "educational programs, lectures and concerts," and on the other, drawing attention to the "problems of variation" and calling for "the integration into society of such persons whose behavior and inclinations vary from current moral and social standards."[50] Rather than represent homosexuality as a positivity or call for a radical reconfiguration of the social body, most of the writers for *ONE* speak the language of *remorse*, eschewing revolutionary rhetoric in favor of a guilty appeal for tolerance from the heterosexual majority and for the liberalization of oppressive restrictions. (Hay noted in later years that the Mattachine Society, at least from 1953 until 1969, was dominated by the doctrine, "All we want to do is to have a little law changed, and otherwise we are exactly the same as everybody else, except in bed.")[51]

What is most striking about the editorial content of *ONE* during the 1950s is the difficulty in distinguishing between a residual discourse of homophobia, with its roots in the "sexology" of the late nineteenth century, and an emergent discourse of gay resistance and liberation that did not really begin to thrive until the late 1960s. Rather than forge a language in which a newly defined—or even provisionally liberated— homosexual subject could be articulated, *ONE* tended to appropriate the vocabulary (while adjusting the attitude) of those mid-century sociological and psychological texts in which homosexual behavior was characterized, in a series of negative definitions, as deviant and neurotic, and the homosexual subject as regressive, incomplete, and guilty.[52] Consider, for example, a character analysis from a 1958 issue of *ONE*, about one of the "tragic types" (much like the fictional Pablo Gonzales or the historical Roy Cohn) who

> looked like an "auntie" though barely thirty, but was quick to express his hatred of "queers." With sordid monotony, he made a nightly search of public "cans" for the most impersonal forms of sex contact. . . . Should we look for *causes* in rejection—loss of self-respect? Did he despise himself too much for affinity with another human being?[53]

Like the official texts of the burgeoning homosexual rights movement, most American plays of the 1940s and 1950s, even those considered at the time sympathetic to the "problem" of homosexuality, were written in the language of remorse. The New York theater, like Hollywood, was subject to strict legislative censorship that worked in complicity with the severe ideological constraints of the period. Dating back to the passage of the so-called Wales Padlock Law in 1927, plays that "depict[ed] or deal[t] with, the subject of sex degeneracy, or sex perversion" were prohibited from the New York stage.[54] During the first postwar years, the theater practiced a notable self-discipline, faithfully administering this repressive legislation by the homophobic dictates of Lee Shubert, who directed the Shubert monopoly until his death in 1954, and by the eager collusion of the press, particularly the Hearst newspapers.

Although intended as "the first sympathetic dramatic consideration of the homosexual's predicament," Ruth and Augustus Goetz's free adaptation of André Gide's *The Immoralist* (1954) recycles the shopworn homophobic conventions.[55] Homosexuality is still the crime that dares not speak its name. The play never uses the word *homosexual* and characterizes the protagonist's "sin of the flesh" as a vile and infectious condition endemic not to cultivated Europeans but to "lying and deceitful

and bad" Arabs who are promiscuous and dangerous, "like farm ani-
mals."[56] The play ends with the protagonist's flight from Algeria and its
Orientalist peril and his retreat back into the closet:

> There is no place on earth where those who are like me will not seek
> me out. Only here in this house where I was raised, can I shut them
> out.[57]

The most popular play of the 1950s to focus on homosexuality, Robert
Anderson's *Tea and Sympathy* (1953), registers a more conflicted, if
sympathetic, view of its subject than *The Immoralist*. It is a deeply
confused work (and, as a result, more instructive), inveighing against
homosexuality yet clearly revealing the glaring contradictions that inhere
within a homophobic, masculinist ideology. Even more explicitly than
Miller's works, it dramatizes the extraordinary level of anxiety—and
emotional disarray—that coalesces around the constitution of the male
homosocial bond, which Anderson characterizes as both a shield against
and a symptom of homosexual desire. As is so frequently the case with
popular treatments of "social problems," the ending of the play does not
attempt to resolve this contradiction, but buries it in a flurry of heterosexual passion and sentiment.

Only in the context of *ONE*, *The Immoralist*, and *Tea and Sympathy*
can one begin to understand the politics of Tennessee Williams's work
of the 1940s and 1950s and the extent to which his writing mocks his
own later insistence that an artist's "politics" and "sexual predilections
or deviations are not usually pertinent to the value of his work."[58] I
believe that Williams's plays offer far more than the minor adjustment
to the rhetoric of homophobia tentatively negotiated by the work of
most of his contemporaries. By impugning the sovereignty of the well-
made play and of theatrical naturalism, by mobilizing a surrealistic scenic
poetry, by reconfiguring bourgeois subjectivity, by undermining con-
ventionalized presentations of sexuality and gender, they offer a radical—
if incompletely realized—challenge to Cold War hegemony, and bestow
an inheritance that a progressive theater of the 1990s can ill afford to
ignore.

Beyond Liberal Tragedy

> The bird that I hope to catch in the net of this play is not the solution
> of one man's psychological problem. I'm trying to catch the true quality
> of experience in a group of people, that cloudy, flickering, evanescent—
> fiercely charged!—interplay of live human beings in the thundercloud of
> a common crisis.
>
> —*Cat on a Hot Tin Roof* (1955), act 2 stage directions

While Arthur Miller appropriates liberal tragedy, with its fixation on the opposition between disaffected subject and destructive society, to repress and conceal divisions within male subjectivity, Tennessee Williams develops a far more fluid and complex dramatic form capable of articulating a far more fluid and variegated subject. Turning to the plays of Anton Chekhov for a structural model, Williams time and again writes the spectacle of a dying culture in which all share the experience of discontinuity between a meaningful and integrative past and a commodified present, and all suffer the social atomization that inevitably accompanies that commodification. The civilization in collapse is, of course, the American South, which in the 1940s and 1950s was undergoing a profound economic, social, and political reorientation, as Williams, who was raised in Mississippi and Missouri, so well understood:

> The South once had a way of life that I am just old enough to remember—a culture that had grace, elegance . . . and inbred culture . . . not a society based on money, as in the North. I write out of a regret for that.[59]

In the years following World War II, the South was quickly transformed from a predominantly agricultural society (two-thirds of the population was classified as rural by the Census Bureau in 1940) to an urban and industrialized culture. In 1945 an unparalleled economic boom began as the war industries of the South were converted for peacetime manufacturing and the discriminatory rail rates that favored industry in the North were abolished. Between 1939 and 1972, the number of workers engaged in manufacturing in the South increased by 215 percent, almost twice the national rate, while the value of Southern products grew from 13 percent to 22 percent of the national total. The formerly stable demographics of the region were severely disrupted as vast numbers of workers migrated from the country to the fast-growing cities, many African-Americans left the region altogether, and what had been a rigidly hierarchized culture was replaced by a more flexible and mobile ordering of social classes that better served the interest of industrial capitalism, or, in Williams's brusque phrase, "a society based on money."[60]

Among Williams's works, the film *Baby Doll* (1956), directed by Elia Kazan, perhaps most graphically dramatizes the deterioration of the South. The antebellum mansion in and around which most of the action takes place serves as the emblem of a crumbling culture: a large and decrepit house, its grandeur derided by its formerly white columns strewn on the ground, its porch disintegrating, its wooden siding peeling and falling off, its plaster walls crumbling and riddled with holes (the better for Archie Lee Meighan's voyeuristic pleasures). Set on a huge withered field (once a lawn), littered with garbage, surrounded by chickens and pigs, the house is a vivid metaphor for a civilization whose decaying framework still stands, albeit unsteadily, while the spatial and social boundaries between inside and outside (which the house is designed to safeguard) are violated and ridiculed by its unhinged doors and the rotting furniture scattered across the yard. The film's action, as well, embodies the social and economic changes taking place in the South as Archie Lee, the small-time independent farmer and producer, is supplanted both sexually and economically by the Sicilian immigrant, Silva Vacarro, flaunting his potent masculinity as determinedly as the efficiency of his Syndicate Cotton Gin.

Like Chekhov, faced with the similarly unprecedented decay of the mansion of preindustrial culture, Williams eschews the binary structure of liberal tragedy that (in Raymond Williams's words) sets "an actively liberating individual" against the many who embody "the frustration and stagnation of available forms of social life." Instead, Williams's plays, like Chekhov's, dramatize that cultural moment when "the desire for liberation has passed into the group as whole," but when that desire has, "at the same time . . . become hopeless, inward-looking."[61] In Williams, the meticulously polarized *dramatis personae* of liberal tragedy is to a large extent replaced by a society both more minutely fragmented and more conscious of its deterioration. Yet there are also significant differences between Williams and Chekhov. The Williams protagonist is more independent and disaffected, more degraded by its frustrated desires, and conflicted, having internalized oppressive and self-destructive values more decidedly than its Chekhovian counterpart. Moreover, the Williams plot is usually more linear and relies more heavily on sustained and intensifying conflict (this explains why *The Seagull* was his favorite among Chekhov's plays, rather than *The Three Sisters* or *The Cherry Orchard*). In Williams, ideologies and desires collide in a more flagrant and concentrated way than in late Chekhov. Yet despite Williams's reliance on more traditional modes of dramatic conflict, his plays, even his most popular ones, move toward endings as inconclusive as those that close any Chekhov play. Suspending rather than resolving contradictions, the final moments of *Cat on a Hot Tin Roof* and *A Streetcar Named Desire* (1947) ironically (and without comment) juxtapose the different ends of different characters and thereby exemplify a surprisingly fluid, open-ended, and provisional teleology.

Following Chekhov's lead, Williams avoids postulating the overarching protagonist that so dominates liberal drama. He does not attempt, like Miller, to center the action on a heroic male subject (who is provided with an illusory stability and substantiality) or to define its movement as the gradual revelation of this exemplum of bourgeois individualism. Instead, Williams develops a much more deeply dialectical dramatic form that attempts to grasp and project, in the words of Williams's oft-quoted stage direction in *Cat on a Hot Tin Roof*, the "true quality of experience in a group of people" caught "in the thundercloud of a common crisis." The complex interactions among these more or less equally weighed subjects produce the dramatic action, "that cloudy, flickering, evanescent— fiercely charged!—interplay," that characteristically resists being reduced to a single linear narrative.[62] The action of all of Williams's plays is almost aggressively plural and indeterminate, as "cloudy, flickering, [and] evanescent" as the volatile desires and wills of his characters. Insistently, the latter form brief and tenuous alliances, then clash, then inevitably regroup and clash again. As a result, the social body is constantly being redrawn and reconfigured in unexpected ways, with the collective subject always at the horizon of possibility.

Like Chekhov, Williams engineers most of his plots so that they describe a carefully supervised ironic reversal, or a series of them, as characters' positions are gradually reversed: the victim becomes the victimizer; the innocent, the corrupted; the would-be destroyer, the savior; and the injured one, the transgressor. This ironic reversal is inevitably accompanied by numerous disclosures (rather than the single pivotal disclosure on which the well-made play characteristically depends). Thus, for example, although act 2 of *Cat on a Hot Tin Roof* pivots around the release of information about numerous situations, including Big Daddy's slightly queer patrimony and his intestinal cancer (two properties that so often accompany each other in Williams), the character of Brick's relationship with Skipper remains ambiguous. One reviewer's complaint, that the play "never quite defines itself as chiefly a play about a marriage, about a family, or about a man," ironically provides an extremely apt resumé of Williams's avowedly contrapuntal dramatic form.[63] *The Glass Menagerie*, meanwhile, reveals the secrets of Amanda, Laura, and Jim, while leaving Tom's nocturnal activities conspicuously in the dark. Unlike Miller's plays, each of which moves toward a climactic moment of apparently complete disclosure, Williams's—to the dismay of many critics— always imply far more than they speak, leaving certain characters and events shrouded in uncertainty.

This habit of constructing plot upon a "guilty secret" that is never entirely divulged certainly encodes Williams's own "guilty secret" and the impossibility of its revelation during the 1940s and 1950s as anything other than an "ugly truth."[64] Even more important, this practice acts both to ratify and subvert a psychoanalytical model of personality, for in the same gesture that directs the spectator's hermeneutical gaze toward the withheld secret, it seems to deny the primacy and intelligibility of that traumatic memory, both emphasizing and calling into question the determination of the present by a moment in the past. By so disrupting the relationship between past and present, Williams's plays tend to undermine the purely linear and irreversible temporal progression on which Miller's plays, and American realism in general, depends. By (almost) dislodging the present moment from the flux of time and causality, Williams's plays produce the possibility of a profound—and revolutionary—discontinuity between the present and the future. Like Chekhov's plays, Williams's seem to inscribe and look forward to that utopian (or messianic) moment that will, in Walter Benjamin's words, "blast open the continuum of history" and produce a new social and political order.[65] It is perhaps in this context that one should read Williams's most startling pronouncement about Chekhov, that he "was probably gay."[66] This assertion—for which there is little documentary evidence—reveals far less about Chekhov than about Williams himself and marks, I believe, Williams's own tacit recognition of the utopian (or desubjectifying) potential of his homosexuality, of the different attitude toward and stake in the past that it authorizes, and of the revolutionary social vision that it affords.

Williams's freewheeling adaptation of the Chekhovian and Freudian paradigms has far-reaching implications that locate the Williams play at the impossible intersection of two incompatible and contradictory forms: the one linear, liberal, and realist, and the other, episodic, protosocialist, and hallucinatory. The Williams character that colonizes this unthinkable site, meanwhile, is poised between the fractured, guilty, liberal subject and a collective, revolutionary subject not yet (capable of being) fully articulated. Williams's more popular plays, especially A Streetcar Named Desire and Cat on a Hot Tin Roof, tend to focus on the liberal problematic more intensively than those works usually judged by audiences and critics as overly difficult, including The Rose Tattoo (1950), Camino Real (1953), and many of his neglected later plays (such as The Red Devil Battery Sign, 1976, and Clothes for a Summer Hotel, 1980). All of Williams's drama, however, hovers uneasily between the two conventions, insistently destabilizing the liberal, while not yet quite able to formulate a structure that could be called, for lack of a better term, socialist.

Williams's repudiation of liberal tragedy also entails a rejection of the expressionist-realist hybrid associated with it on the American stage since at least the 1920s. In opposition, Williams develops a theater that is most properly labeled, I believe, surrealist. His is the "new plastic theatre" he writes of in the "Production Notes" to The Glass Menagerie, that will "take the place of the exhausted theatre of realistic conventions."[67] His plays abound in incidents and scenic elements that shatter the conventions of domestic realism and challenge the notion of the spectacle as an empirical replica. *Camino Real* is perhaps the most vivid example, a hallucinatory pageant set in a tropical seaport of diverse geographical identities, in which appropriated literary characters together play out (or against) the disparate stories from which they derive, and in which Kilroy, the all-American, dies and is resurrected only to steal his own solid-gold heart. *The Rose Tattoo* is also set in a locale with a fantastic interior: a dressmaker's shop strewn about with "at least seven" life-size dummies who compose a kind of grotesque and silent chorus, and whose "purpose," Williams insists, is "not realistic."[68] Even *The Glass Menagerie*, perhaps Williams's most lyrical and subtly integrated play, calls for an elaborate sequence of "projected magic-lantern slides" that disrupts and decenters the single thread of Tom's narrative (p. 8).

In his "Production Notes" to *The Glass Menagerie*, Williams writes approvingly of the use of "expressionism and all other unconventional techniques" on the stage (p. 7). Most critics have taken Williams at his word and have granted a priority to the one "unconventional technique" he specifies: expressionism. Thus, Mary Ann Corrigan, for example, classifies Williams as a kind of expressionist manqué and then proceeds to describe all of Williams's nonrealistic devices as expressionistic (while never providing a definition of expressionism that differentiates it from the other modernist avant-garde movements). Considered from her point of view, the plays that most obviously exploit these devices are conspicuous failures. She objects strenuously that "Laura's trauma is trivialized" by Williams's projections and that the characters' "illusions" seem "ridiculous when concretized in images." She particularly denounces *Camino Real* because Kilroy "lacks the depth of a good dramatic character," because the play's dialogue "is neither believable nor consistent," and because the action evinces "no sense of development." She even cites Williams's reference to De Chirico's protosurrealist *Conversation among the Ruins* in the stage directions for *Summer and Smoke* (1947), yet insists that his appropriation reveals his expressionist intentions.[69]

Williams's plays insistently challenge the expressionist model (as used so brazenly in *After the Fall*) for the simple reason that none of them stages the psychodynamics of a single, centrifugal consciousness projecting its thoughts, emotions, and desires onto characters, actions, and locale. Even a self-proclaimed "memory play" (p. 7) such as *The Glass Menagerie* does not center on Tom (as *After the Fall* does on Quentin). Instead, Tom remains, in Williams's words, "in the background," constantly deferring to the "leading characters," Amanda and Laura, the two figures in the play who undergo demonstrable transformations.[70] Indeed, of all the characters, Tom remains by far the most elusive, the most in shadow—never the spotlit and omniscient central consciousness of expressionism. Furthermore, Williams uses the slides to undercut the presumption that both the stage picture and the action contained within it are mere projections of that elusive consciousness. Throughout the play, Williams runs an almost closed system—the interpersonal dynamics among the four characters—against images on a screen that do not maintain a constant and stable distance from or attitude toward it. The images themselves shift restlessly between icons and words, so their dramatic function remains in constant flux. Sometimes a phrase spelled out on the screen provides a Brechtian distance from the action ("Plans and Provisions"; p. 52). More frequently, however, a word or phrase is used to specify a character's private response ("Terror!"; p. 74) or to comment unceremoniously and wryly on the action ("This is my sister: Celebrate her with strings!"; p. 71).

The projected icons Williams specifies in the script work in an even more complex way than the lines of text. Sometimes they are visualizations of a single character's thoughts or memories ("Amanda as a girl"; p. 81). More often, they evoke an interwoven series of memories and associations in several characters. Most striking and most complex is the picture of "blue roses" (pp. 29, 35), which becomes an emblem for Laura, not because she resembles a blue rose (although she does radiate a certain anomalous beauty), but because the two words that name the image are the malapropism coined by Laura's "gentleman caller" years before to describe her ailment: pleurosis. Screened initially at the opening of scene 2, this audiovisual pun obliquely links Laura with her gentleman caller, her infirmity with her beauty. At the same time, "blue roses" reaches outside the text, connecting Laura to Williams's own sister Rose, who underwent a prefrontal lobotomy in 1937 and was avowedly the model for Laura. A self-contradicting icon—simultaneously natural and unnatural, beautiful and grotesque, picture and spoken text—it does not belong to any one subject but, as a kind of collective hallucination, hovers above subjectivity and, indeed, above private property.

Williams's use of "magic-lantern slides" in *The Glass Menagerie* has little in common with the projections and distortions of individual experience and subjectivity that constitute expressionist drama. Rather, it seems far more closely allied to the techniques of surrealism as developed in France in the 1920s and 1930s. During these extraordinarily turbulent years, the surrealists attempted to foment ontological, erotic, and political revolution by launching an assault on logic, grammar, and the pieties and conventions of bourgeois culture and art. Under the leadership of André Breton, they made *amour fou*, mad love, into a transcendent principle that would shatter the deadening routine imposed by society, family, and work. They buoyantly declared their independence from the institution of literature and preached revolt, hoping that "revolutions, wars, and colonial insurrections will annihilate this Western civilization."[71] Capitalizing on the innovations of the symbolists, they forged a concrete and convulsive poetic language and glorified the decontextualized image. In the hope of unshackling the unconscious, they practiced, in C. W. E. Bigsby's words, the "ascription of uncommon properties to common objects, the confrontation of apparently unrelated objects, ideas, or words, and the wilful dislocation of object and context."[72] In their (post-)romantic quest for absolute presence, the surrealists believed that the use of images from dreams would resolve contradictory states of consciousness and coax into being an "absolute reality, a *surreality*."[73]

In Walter Benjamin's extraordinary essay on surrealism (a crucial document on the relationship between artistic and political revolution), he points out that the movement, like "an inspiring dream wave," aimed to integrate "everything with which it came into contact" and to push "the 'poetic life' to the utmost limits of possibility"—to political revolution.[74] Between 1927 and 1935, the surrealists formed a somewhat uneasy alliance with the French Communist party (not unlike the relationship between the American New Left and the counterculture during the 1960s) and committed themselves to materialist revolution. Yet, by their own account, hostile to "the traditional strategy of revolutionary movements," they resolutely insisted on the deployment of "new" political tactics.[75] In Benjamin's estimation, these tactics were focused on the "loosening of the self by intoxication" and by dreaming ("dream loosens individuality like a bad tooth," to quote his startling metaphor).[76] In an attempt to undermine romantic notions of expressivity and to extricate the artistic text from the dominion of the individual producer/owner, the surrealists experimented with automatic writing and collective compositions (the most celebrated being the jointly produced poem, "Le Cadavre exquis": "The exquisite corpse will drink new wine"). In so doing, they aimed "to win the energies of intoxication" for a "revolution" that Benjamin sees as a deeply conflicted political project, one much closer, arguably, to anarchism than to historical communism.[77]

The political questions raised by surrealism are, moreover, redoubled by its debilitating problems with gender and sexuality. Although eroticism was central to its reconfiguration of bourgeois subjectivity (Breton: "All the regenerative possibilities of the world lie in human love"),[78] for most of the circle this meant strictly heterosexualized eroticism. Despite their championing of Rimbaud and Sade, the surrealists remained viciously homophobic (Breton: "I accuse pederasts of proposing to human tolerance a mental and moral deficit which . . . would paralyze all enter-prises that I respect").[79] And, as is usually the case in a militantly homophobic milieu, women were consistently objectified and fetishized in surrealist art and literature—even more violently than in bourgeois culture—and virtually excluded from participation in its circle, except as wives and mistresses.[80]

Although conceived in much less brutally heterosexist terms, eroticism remained as pivotal to Williams as to the surrealists: the source of a transgressive and liberating energy that could shatter the individual sub-ject, and the most likely site for the reconciliation of contrarieties. More-over, Williams often set forth his own "wild and unrestricted" project in language very similar to that of the surrealists. In the foreword to *Camino Real*, for example, he honors the "great vocabulary of images" that dwells "in our conscious and unconscious minds," and insists that both "human communication" and "our dreams" are "based on these images." He defends his exorbitant use of symbols in the play by claiming that they "are nothing but the natural speech of drama."[81] And he echoes the surrealists' insistence that the unconscious be explored less for the sake of individual enlightenment than for the (revolutionary) transfig-uration of those readers or spectators who participate in the process. Although Williams's plays are more plainly linear and mimetic than most surrealist texts, his work consistently aims, like that of his surrealist brethren, to arouse his audience, "to give people a jolt, get them fully alive."[82]

To draw a comparison between a radical—and homophobic—faction of the European avant-garde of the 1920s and 1930s and an American playwright who stretched the parameters of realism during the 1940s and 1950s may seem unhistorical and mere formalist whimsy. However, surrealism was surprisingly belated in its arrival on American shores (unlike expressionism, which had a tremendous impact in the United States during the 1920s). Although there were several minor exhibitions of work by surrealists in New York during the early 1930s, it was not until 1936 that a show at the Museum of Modern Art, Fantastic Art, Dada, and Surrealism, provided a large-scale (and controversial) display of surrealist art. Even so, it was not until the early 1940s, with the massive wartime displacement of European artists and intellectuals, that surrealism began to have a major impact on American artists. In 1941, the Museum of Modern Art produced an exhibition of works by Joan Miró and Salvador Dalí. The next year, a New York gallery hosted First Papers of Surrealism, a major exhibition that for the first time included the work of American artists associated with the movement: Robert Motherwell, William Baziotes, and others. In 1943 Jackson Pollock (with whom Williams would become acquainted the next year in Provincetown) was invited to participate in a group show with Motherwell and Baziotes. For the remainder of the 1940s, many of the American artists who would shortly become leading abstract expressionists (including Adolph Gottlieb and Mark Rothko) were associated with the American offshoot of surrealism.[83]

Perhaps an even more important and useful context for Williams's surrealist theater than the early canvases of Pollock and Motherwell is the work of George Platt Lynes, who produced a remarkable series of homoerotic surrealist photographs from the 1930s until his death in 1955. In his nudes and mythological compositions that place the male figure in highly stylized, abstracted, and sometimes hallucinatory settings, Lynes used the formality of the "Art" photograph variously to heighten, aestheticize, or disguise the homoerotic content of his work. This ironic juxtaposition of the eroticized male form and the props and fixtures of the artist's studio allowed Lynes, in Allen Ellenzweig's estimation, to deploy both the conventions and the "psychological boundaries" of surrealism and to create "ambiguous allegorical dramas that display . . . marginal sexualities amid self-conscious surfaces."[84] Like Lynes, Williams transformed European surrealism into a distinctly American idiom, often accentuating the root word (*real*) at the expense of its overreaching prefix and incorporating indigenous inspirations such as the poetry of Hart Crane, whose verbal dislocations bear more than a passing similarity to those of the European avant-gardists. Williams's emphasis on the *real* in surrealism—his mobilization of a momentous yet comprehensible gap between text and subtext, the spoken and the concealed—also, in part, explains the relative ease with which his work is accommodated by most American Method actors. In most of his plays, particularly the ones from the 1940s and 1950s, his surrealism is inflected less by a disturbance in the relationships between characters than by the incongruity between environment and action, or, to borrow Kenneth Burke's terminology, by a disruption of the scene-act ratio.[85] This discrepancy between container and the thing contained, between the projections in *The Glass Menagerie* and the gentle contours of memory, between the delapidated cottage in *The Rose Tattoo* (its colorful interior overrun with mannequins) and the scenes of mourning and sexual passion played out within it, encodes a deep disruption in the relationship between the individual subject and the culture of which it is a part. In Williams's later plays, such as *In the Bar of a Tokyo Hotel* (1969), these surrealistic incongruities operate on so many levels, and so thoroughly colonize interpersonal relationships, that the latter become, like much of the play's dialogue, wild, stuttering, and fragmentary (and, I expect, rather more resistant to the analysis of Method actors).

During the 1940s and 1950s Williams maintained a strangely equivocal attitude toward the very devices he mobilized to fracture the apparent seamlessness of realism. In his notes to *The Glass Menagerie*, for example, he observes that the "extraordinary power" of Laurette Taylor's performance made him "not regret the omission" of the projections in the original production (p. 8). And photographs of his early successes suggest a scenic and directorial fluidity quite different from the suggestions of his, at times, tortuously detailed stage directions. For the first two decades of his career, Williams seems to have largely deferred his most revolutionary hopes, and his 1944 pronouncement in regard to the newly finished *The Glass Menagerie* could stand as an epigraph to all of his most popular works: "It is the *last* play I will write for the *now* existing theatre."[86] Until the 1960s, his full-length plays, almost all of them written for production on Broadway, practice a deep-seated yet extremely cautious reconfiguration of the styles, languages, and stereotypes prevailing in the commercial theater. Perhaps only now, in the 1990s, is the American theater (having incorporated some of the innovations of the American experimentalists of the late 1960s and the 1970s) prepared to accommodate a Tennessee Williams who is not simply an eccentric realist. Only in the wake of Robert Wilson, Richard Foreman, Mabou Mines, and the Wooster Group (among others) can one begin to understand not just Williams's deep antipathy to theatrical realism, but also his status as a postmodernist *avant la lettre*. In his fragmentation of narrative and of the subject, his questioning of universalist claims, his subversion of the antitheses between high and low art, philosophy and kitsch, he seems to have anticipated many of the theatrical practices that now pass as postmodernist.[87] Unquestionably, these remain crucial to Williams's (often lonely) advancement of a surrealist theater that does not aim, unlike Miller's hybrid of realism and expressionism, merely to dis- and reassemble the heroic male subject—the one who owns his memories, associations, and dreams the way he owns his house, car, wife, and children. Unlike this still imposing figure, the never quite whole subject that commandeers Williams's work is unable to claim the position of "hero" or even "protagonist." Instead, it is constantly decentered and dispossessed, stumbling through a dramatic structure that is similarly decentered and unstable. This structure, like a surrealist text, is adamantly plural, strewn with multivalent symbols, and reluctant to provide the interpreter with a master perspective or code. Rather than granting the reader or spectator a single locus of empathic identification, it offers multiple, and sometimes contradictory, points of interpellation. Like

Chekhov, his diabolically comic predecessor and adoptive "gay" father, Williams seems to delight in keeping his interpreters, like his characters, deliciously off balance, never quite sure how to respond to a situation or where to position themselves.

Homosexuality and the American Classic

Only once did either Tennessee Williams or Arthur Miller offer a sustained critique of the other's work. In a speech delivered to the New Dramatists' Committee during the 1956–57 season (and published in a revised version in 1958), Arthur Miller provided a fascinating analysis of Williams's then most recent play, *Cat on a Hot Tin Roof*. Not surprisingly, Miller attempts to remake it as liberal tragedy, discovering problems and contradictions in it that provide a gauge both to the limits of Miller's dramatic and ideological vision and to the crucial distance between the play that Williams calls his "most realistic" and the liberal vernacular of the commercial stage.[88] From the very beginning of his analysis, Miller tries to turn the play into one of his own. Since a female protagonist is unimaginable for him, he describes it as "a play seen from the viewpoint of Brick," whom he alleges to be the protagonist. He then proceeds to adapt it to the conventional liberal paradigm by refashioning Brick as the young rebel, "sensitized to injustice," who is fighting against a depraved and materialistic society embodied by Big Daddy. For Miller, the play's crucial question is "the right of society to renew itself when it is, in fact, unworthy," when it "senselessly reproduc[es] itself through ugly children." He astutely notes the play's apparent variance with itself, that although Brick and Maggie despise the hypocritical society around them, they accede to its continuation at the end of the play by the lie that Maggie hopes to make true—her pregnancy. The polemical Miller seems most disturbed, however, by what he sees as ethical indecision on Williams's part:

> There is a moral judgement hanging over this play which never quite comes down. A tempting analogy would be that of a Hamlet who takes up his sword and neither fights nor refuses to fight but marries an Ophelia who does not die.[89]

Despite the play's almost neoclassical adherence to the unities of time and place and its clear resemblance to the well-made play, *Cat on a Hot Tin Roof* is, in fact, neither neoclassical nor well made. Among the *dramatis personae*, at least three—Maggie, Brick, and Big Daddy—bear the intense desire and undergo the kind of transformations usually associated with protagonists. To grant a privilege to any one character's point of view is to misread the designs of interdependence and complicity that Williams so painstakingly constructs as solitary enterprises. At the same time, although *Cat* relies on the timely release of withheld information, it produces an array of secrets—among them the quintessential "guilty secret" during the 1950s—each of which defies the convention that it remain the hidden property of one character only. What appears as the originary event, the possibly homosexual relationship between Brick and Skipper, is secret insofar as it remains unspoken, and yet barely concealed, since most of the characters know at least part of the story and several have played an active role in its construction. Furthermore, as is so characteristic of Williams, the exact nature of this open secret is never completely disclosed, nor is the intrigue that it spawns resolved. Brick's relationship with his friend, Maggie's (nearly) adulterous liaison with Skipper, and the erotic connections of Big Daddy's youth remain, to some extent, shrouded in the "mystery" that, Williams avers, "should be left in the revelation of character" (p. 85). As a result, a single event in the past is granted neither the legibility nor the deterministic power with which a playwright such as Miller usually endows it.

Miller's most crucial insight into the workings of the play, however, remains his focus on the dynamics of inheritance and, by implication, on the constitution and filiation of patriarchy. Like *The Cherry Orchard*, *Cat on a Hot Tin Roof* focuses on the death throes of an old regime and dramatizes the conflict between two generations and two social classes for the ownership of a rich estate. The very setting of the play foregrounds the question of inheritance by commemorating the birth of the plantation: the bed-sitting-room once occupied by "a pair of old bachelors," Jack Straw and Peter Ochello, and "haunted" by the "tenderness" they shared, "which was uncommon" (p. xiii). When Big Daddy inherited the estate from them, he turned it into "th' biggest an' finest plantation in the Delta," the booty for which the dying patriarch's progeny are now competing (p. 41). Yet what is most striking about this pattern of estate ownership is less its conspicuously patrilineal nature than the homosexuality that stands at its imputed origin and so determinedly "haunts" its development. For not only has Big Daddy inherited the plantation from Straw and Ochello, he has also inadvertently passed along the possibility of arousing homosexual desire to his younger son, Brick, a man driven to despair (and alcohol) over the death of his friend Skipper and married to a woman he "can't stand" (p. 47).

Structurally, Big Daddy functions as the carrier of homosexuality— the heir to the estate, engineered "by hook or crook," and the man who confesses to having "knocked around in [his] time" (pp. 61, 85). But Big Daddy is paying a terrible price for his youthful prodigality (a price that would not be out of line in *The Immoralist*). He is dying of bowel cancer, which, as in "The Mysteries of the Joy Rio," becomes the currency of mortal debt in Williams's homosexual economy. For Big Daddy, bowel cancer seems to be the wages of sodomy (or, at least, of "knocking around"). Yet Brick, the heir to his estate (if not to his sexual practices), must also endure the effects of homosexuality. Unlike his father, he suffers from vicious self-hatred, a less life-threatening reward for a less tangible crime: the experience of—or incitement of another to—homosexual desire.

In *Cat on a Hot Tin Roof*, however, homosexuality is not just self-destructive and cancerous. Williams's most original move in the play is to turn Big Daddy, despite—or because of?—the taint of homosexuality, into the play's exemplar of normative masculinity. In the words of Arthur Miller, who has a particularly keen eye for such things, Big Daddy is "the very image of power, of materiality, of authority," the very model of a promiscuous—and misogynist—heterosexuality.[90] With his "lech" for Maggie and his deathbed longing for a young, "choice" mistress, his contempt for Big Mama's "fat old body," for her "sound" and "smell," yet his dutiful service to her ("*laid* her . . . regular as a piston"), he seems to epitomize the orthodox heterosexualized masculinity of the 1950s that simultaneously desires and degrades women (pp. 19, 72, 58, 80). Unlike Willy and Biff Loman, for whom masculinity is forever just out of reach, stowed securely in the *imaginaire*, Big Daddy need not fantasize about the acquisition of charismatic power, sovereignty, wealth, and expertise. He already possesses them.

Masculinity in *Cat on a Hot Tin Roof*, as in *Death of a Salesman*, is a site of division and instability. Yet, unlike Miller, who attempts desperately to conceal these rifts, Williams flaunts and magnifies the contradictions on which masculinity, and patriarchal relations generally, are founded. Homosexual desire is cast not as masculinity's anathema but as that which always already inheres inside the male subject (like a cancer). Homosexuality and homosociality are no longer represented as unmediated opposites, but as fluid and complicitous states of desire. While inscribing Big Daddy's viscera with a malignancy that is unmistakably the sign of his homosexual inheritance, Williams simultaneously provides him with this cancer's benign opposite: an antihomophobic position from which to preach "*tolerance!*" in an attempt to neutralize Brick's self-hatred and forfend his "queer" bashing (pp. 88–89). Furthermore, this progressive stance is coupled with an unusual sensitivity to economic injustice, whether to the plight of naked Spanish children "beggin' like starvin' dogs with howls and screeches" or to the child prostitutes of Marrakech (pp. 65–66). Alone among the play's characters,

Big Daddy understands the implacable logic of the commodity that decrees that "the human animal . . . buys and buys and buys" in its attempt to fend off death, hoping against hope that "one of [its] purchases will be life everlasting!" (p. 67). In his schizoid glory, Big Daddy, the revolutionary patriarch, epitomizes the analogy that runs throughout Williams's work between the commodity (which represents both life and death, which attracts yet never satisfies) and male homosexuality (which both cures and kills, which attracts and repels with a dismally lurid radiance).

Unlike *Death of a Salesman*, which attempts almost ritualistically to purify patriarchal relations of any taint of the homosexual, *Cat on a Hot Tin Roof* reveals—in what is one of the boldest moves in all of Williams's drama—the hom(m)o-sexuality that is always already inscribed within a patrilineal economy. The very room represented on stage, the imputed center and origin of the plantation, continually evokes the homosexual coupling whose progeny fill the play. Yet, as is so characteristic of Williams, the characters who recolonize this delivery room exhibit deeply conflicted attitudes toward their progenitors and the activities in which they delighted. As constituted in the play, homosexuality is both a materially and emotionally productive practice and yet the source of cancer and guilt; the foundation for empire, (self-)hatred and suicide; the "pure an' true" axis of desire (p. 90) and simultaneously the obstacle that must be overcome if the greed and ugliness embodied by Gooper and Mae are to be forestalled and Brick and Maggie conceive a child in the very bed once occupied by Jack Straw and Peter Ochello. By refusing to camouflage these contradictions, Williams ensures that the moral judgment Miller sees "hanging over this play" can never quite come down and thereby makes it impossible to resolve the play's action. By constructing a plot that is, to quote Eric Bentley, "fatally incomplete," Williams adopts a formal (i.e., rhetorical) strategy much like the one Brecht uses at the end of *The Good Person of Szechwan*, quietly insisting that the action of the play cannot be disentangled until those watching or reading it resolve the material contradictions that structure the culture in which they live.[91]

Mapping the Closet

Although taking Arthur Miller as a guide to *Cat on a Hot Tin Roof* provides a useful index to the differences between the strategies of the two playwrights, it does not illuminate the most elusive, resonant, and radical elements of Williams's dramaturgy. Miller's analysis assumes a measure of internal coherence and comprehensibility of character and of unity and, indeed, concentration of the dramatic action that, I believe, the play subtly yet assiduously belies. The more closely one examines the construction of subjectivity in *Cat on a Hot Tin Roof,* the less securely it seems to conform to the orthodox patterns dictated by liberal tragedy or liberal sociology. The more closely one examines the printed text (either the original or the Broadway version), the more eccentric it seems, its exorbitant stage directions swarming with philosophical reflections, almost microscopically specific character descriptions, and vividly pictorial metaphors.

The practice of writing extensive stage directions in dramatic texts dates from the mid-nineteenth century and parallels the development of realism. From Ibsen to Shaw to Miller, the realistic playwright uses stage directions in an attempt to consolidate his or her almost monopolistic control over the interpretation of the printed text in the face of several challenges to the authorial prerogative: the modern stage director, the development of competing styles of acting and scenic design, and the gradual elimination of lines of business. In addition to providing pointers to characterization and markers of subtext for actor and director, however, stage directions also serve as a guide for the nonprofessional reader, as a device to link a series of discrete speech acts into an apparently seamless movement. In most realistic plays, these supplementary—that is, absolutely crucial—jottings play a key role in constituting the dramatic characters as coherent subjects for whom the gap between spoken and unspoken, or action and desire, can be analyzed according to (various) psychological principles and thereby successfully negotiated. By producing ostensibly whole characters and an almost novelistic sense of continuity, they carefully regulate the operation of empathic identification and, as a result, play a vital role in supervising the reader's interpellation in the text.

Although Williams often uses stage directions in the manner of the orthodox realist, his texts also allow these authorial interjections to perform a very different function. Tellingly, it is not a patently surrealistic play such as *Camino Real* that most challenges their traditional use, but Williams at his "most realistic," as in *Cat on a Hot Tin Roof.* The elaborate stage directions in that play provide perhaps the most revealing example of Williams's practice of fracturing the coherence of both the realistic text and the ostensibly stable subject that takes up residence within it. From the very beginning of the play, the private interactions of Maggie and Brick (in act 1) and Brick and Big Daddy (in act 2) are almost continually invaded or interrupted by the various comings and goings, the screaming, songs, and laughter of Big Mama, Mae, Gooper, and the "no-neck monsters." With anarchic precision, these private scenes are broken by wildly incongruous sonic disruptions, by the "children shriek[ing] downstairs"; by their "loud but uncertain" singing; by a child "burst[ing] into the room, . . . firing a cap pistol . . . and shouting: 'Bang, bang, bang!'"; by the "blast" of "a Wagnerian opera or a Beethoven symphony"; by a "hideous . . . bawling"; by a "scat song"; and finally by Big Daddy's offstage wail, his "long drawn cry of agony and rage" (pp. 16, 31, 46, 49, 95, 120).

These interruptions—which are predictably softened and quieted by those directors for whom Williams is merely a slightly aberrant realist— work in complex ways not only to fracture dramatic continuity but also to decenter the scenic representation.[92] The force and violence of these intrusions and noises from elsewhere create the impression that the scenes enacted on stage, despite their dramatic urgency, are just a tiny part of a much more extensive and extravagant series of actions that constantly exceeds the bounds of theatrical representation. One way of conceptualizing the room that is represented on stage, the bed-sitting-room of Jack Straw and Peter Ochello, is as a modern analogue to what Roland Barthes calls the Racinian Antechamber: a space between, a room in which one waits, a "site of language," of debate, that stands in opposition to the turbulence outside.[93] It is at once a refuge from the world and from action, a private—indeed, erotic—chamber, and yet one whose privacy is always being violated, and whose inhabitants are constantly being monitored by curious and greedy persons looking for an opportunity to bring disgrace and ruin upon them. When described in this way, however, the bed-sitting-room seems less a neoclassical preserve than the space of the *closet*, of the open secret, a chamber in which the reign of hom(m)o-sexual patriarchy was conceived and delivered, and over which an almost constant surveillance seems to be posted, with spies always lurking just outside its closed doors or always attempting to eavesdrop through its fragile walls. It is a permeable space, only minimally distinct from the upstairs gallery that borders it and lies just beyond its "two pairs of very wide doors," containing a bathroom whose contents are barely discernible to the audience. It is dominated by two pieces of furniture, a "big double bed which staging should make a functional part of the set as often as suitable," and a "monumental monstrosity peculiar to our times, a *huge* console" containing radio-phonograph, television, and liquor cabinet. According to the stage directions, this console is itself a kind of miniature closet, or a closet-within, "a very complete and compact little shrine to virtually all the comforts and illusions behind which we hide" (pp. xiii–xiv).

Throughout Williams's work, the closet (this "monumental monstrosity peculiar to our times") is the subject of innumerable metaphoric and metonymic transformations, a constantly shifting site of concealment and disclosure, speech and silence. In *Cat on a Hot Tin Roof*, the closet is represented by the bed-sitting-room; in *The Glass Menagerie*, by the movie theater to which Tom makes a nightly pilgrimage; in *A Streetcar Named Desire*, by that chamber that Blanche discovers inadvertently "by coming suddenly into a room that I thought was empty—which wasn't empty, but had two people in it." It is a place of darkness and violence, a place whose mysterious geography and proscribed contents are articulated by the almost surrealistic juxtaposition of the verbal and the visual, by the strangely understated lucidity of Blanche's diction in the speech just quoted (figuratively) colliding with a stage direction, *"the headlight"* of a locomotive that, immediately after Blanche's revelation, suddenly *"glares into the room as it thunders past."*[94] It is a fantasmatic site that is crucial for the definition of private space and private persons in a homophobic culture, "centrally representative," in Eve Kosofsky Sedgwick's words, of the culture's "motivating passions and contradictions, even while marginalized by its orthodoxies."[95] It is the primal scene of Williams's drama, the culturally (rather than individually) produced inner sanctum usually relegated to an offstage position, the empty/not empty room in which the homosexual subject is constituted.

In *Cat on a Hot Tin Roof*, the characters occupying the closet/bed-sitting-room wrestle with guilty secrets and agonize over questions of disclosure. In conversation with both Maggie and Big Daddy, Brick debates the identity and status of his own sexuality as well as that of the man to whom he is scandalously linked, Skipper. Simultaneously, Brick, Maggie, Gooper, and Mae are faced with the need of divulging the secret of Big Daddy's cancer, a diagnosis that cannot be decisively separated from the patriarch's own ambiguous sexual history. For the others, as well, the room is a space of confession, the site in which Big Daddy speaks the proximity between sexual intimacy and economic abjection (as emblematized by the child prostitute, or procuress, of Marrakech) and in which he preaches an antihomophobic sermon to his own homophobic son. It is the site in which Big Mama confesses to the love of Brick, her *"only son,"* effectively disinheriting Gooper and securing an unimpeachable position for Brick and Maggie within the hom(m)osexual economy.

The constitution of the subjects that inhabit Williams's closet/bed-sitting-room in *Cat on a Hot Tin Roof* is even more startling than the latter's geography and permeability. As Sedgwick notes, "In this century . . . homosexual definition . . . is organized around a radical and irreducible incoherence."[96] Throughout the play, this incoherence is encoded not only in the relative instability of both male and female subject positions (Maggie is not the only character who scampers and bounds through the action like a cat on a hot tin roof), but also in the way that the text—especially its voluminous stage directions—figures forth the bodies of the *dramatis personae*. Insistently, Williams destabilizes and ruptures the coherence of the self-identical subject, turning all of the characters into subhuman creatures or human beings so radically fragmented, diseased, or wounded as to be barely recognizable as human. The more peripheral, greedy, and hateful figures are transformed into animalistic grotesques. They range from the "no-neck monsters" with "dawgs' names" (pp. 15, 29) to the hissing and grimacing Mae (p. 119) to the more sympathetic, yet strangely protean, Big Mama, whose dress bears "large irregular patterns" resembling "the markings of some massive animal," and whose "fat old body" alternates in appearance between that of an "old bulldog" and a "charging rhino" (pp. 50, 57, 33, 49).

The three principals are not, however, decisively contrasted (as unified subjects) with these embodiments of a gross and literally inhuman materialism. Like his wife, Big Daddy is constructed as a large animal who "wheezes and pants and sniffs" and who is, of course, being destroyed from within by cancer (p. 64). The incarnation of patriarchal authority, his body stages the contradictions inherent in the commodity: the impossible intersection of desire and disgust, of homosexual and heterosexual generation, of misogynist and antihomophobic discourse, and of his struggle against the social uremia that results from "the failure of the body to eliminate its poisons" (p. 113). Brick, meanwhile, is fashioned with a similar physical disequilibrium. He is an alcoholic who is "still slim and firm as a boy" only because "his liquor hasn't started tearing him down outside" (p. 17). He is a man who is physically crippled, whose ankle "is broken, plastered and bound," and yet who retains the aloof air of a "godlike being" (pp. 17, 43). Of the three, Maggie, a "pretty young woman," is the most subtly and yet the most radically fragmented, produced discursively as a collection of disarticulated corporeal details, an assemblage of body parts, a strange construction that *"giggles with a hand fluttering at her throat and her breast and her long throat arched"* (pp. 15, 20). Throughout act 1, Williams's stage directions teem with Maggie's parts: arms, armpits, eyelash (p. 17); hand, throat, breast (p. 20); fist, mouth (p. 32); head, brows (p. 36); shoulders, arms, fists, eyes, head, throat (p. 37)—with never a whole body in sight.

This peculiar fragmentation is connected, I believe, to Maggie's status as the play's primary desiring subject, the one "consumed with envy an' eaten up with longing," not only for Brick, but also for the "beautiful, ideal . . . noble" and "clean" relationship between Brick and Skipper from which she feels utterly excluded (pp. 30, 43–44). When she attempts to force her way into this relationship (that decisively unsettles the distinction between homosocial and homosexual desire), making love to Skipper, it is because "it made both of us feel a little bit closer to [Brick]," the common object of desire (pp. 42–43). Since her liaison with Skipper, Brick's repudiation of him, and Skipper's quasi-suicide, Maggie has become the inheritor, the mediator in a now-immobilized erotic triangle between the living and the dead, the woman who desires to be a partner in an impossible and belated erotic fascination, the woman who, in coveting Brick's aloofness, desires his very refusal to desire her. Likewise, in Brick's imagination, Maggie takes up a similarly contradictory position, representing both obstacle and goal, both the barrier to the fulfillment of his desire and the symbolic repository of his own sexuality. It is perhaps as the latter, as the locus of an impossible and proscribed desire, that Maggie's body comes into focus as being not only fragmented, but fetishized. Like the "no-neck monsters" she vilifies in the very first line of the play, she is constituted distinctively by the body part she lacks. In the case of her young in-laws, the absence of necks epitomizes their monstrosity. In her case, however, the absent Phallus becomes reinscribed in her body and so allows her to be produced as the one who "is" the Phallus. In her act 1 narrative, her liaison with Skipper— in which he proved impotent—is figured as a ritual of castration, the appropriation (or theft) of the other's Phallus that reimprints it metonymically in every limb and recess of her body, so turning her into an object of erotic fascination for the writer of the stage directions, if not for Brick.[97]

Maggie's status as a fetishized object, a phallic woman, the sign of both erotic desire and castration, is not, however, simply a benign transfiguration of this "pretty young woman." Rather, she becomes the play's prime example of what Lacan designates as the "imagos of the fragmented body," the images of "castration, mutilation, dismemberment, dislocation, evisceration, devouring, bursting open of the body" that "represent the elective vectors of aggressive intentions."[98] Although, throughout *Cat on a Hot Tin Roof,* these aggressive intentions are aimed in many different directions, at many different subjects (producing both Big Daddy's cancer and Brick's broken ankle), they are directed with particular (because almost subliminal) violence against women. They motivate Brick's brutal swipe at Maggie with his crutch that "shatters the gemlike lamp on the table" and seem to provoke Big Daddy's vicious threat to Mae: "I'll have your bones pulverized for fertilizer!" (pp. 45, 55).

While Arthur Miller's plays incessantly configure a dangerous female body constantly in danger of overflowing its corporeal limits, Williams's—like the work of so many surrealists—seem to cast the female body as a collection of dismembered fragments, constantly in danger of disintegrating. While Miller painstakingly opposes the transgressive female body to the unyielding male body, Williams radically destabilizes this binarism by producing male bodies that are as fragmented (if in a different way) as female bodies. The intensity of the violence directed against women by no means requires that Williams's men be left physically intact and integral, as Miller's are. In *Cat*, Brick is also rendered a fetishistic object, his distinctive status marked by the elongated white sheath wrapped around his leg, his cast, rather than, like Maggie, by the dismembering yet silent violence of the stage directions. Like the eponymous hustler, murderer, and ex-boxer of the story "One Arm" (written 1942–45, published 1948), whose absent limb commemorates his desirability—and his abjection—Brick's plastered leg is the sign of his status as a commodity, as an object of devotion, as one who both "has" (not) and "is" (not) the Phallus, as a castrated man (more object than subject of desire, neither fully hetero- nor homosexual) whose phallic insignia is silently and, in this case, metaphorically reinscribed elsewhere.

The different modes of corporeality in *Cat on a Hot Tin Roof*, the fragmentation of the body or the fetishistic encasement of a limb in plaster, are the visible signs of guilt and eroticism, anxiety and power, confinement and freedom, secrecy and disclosure—in short, all the emotional equivocations that characterize the inhabitants of the closet. In their dual and interdependent figuration as fetishized bodies, Brick and Maggie, the castrated man and the phallic woman, cut diagonally across the culturally produced antitheses between subject and object, masculinity and femininity, homosexuality and heterosexuality, or, more exactly, expose the arbitrary and provisional nature of these binarisms. They do so by installing in their place unstable sets of sheer difference that resist being conceptualized as polar opposites: desire and sterility, the Phallus and its multiple displacements, metonymy and metaphor, the scenic and the textual, spoken dialogue and (silent) stage directions. In *Cat on a Hot Tin Roof*, as throughout Williams's work, genders and sexualities are not set in opposition but are dispersed and plural, constantly in circulation, like the rose tattoo (in the play of the same name), constantly reappearing in unexpected places, on unexpected bodies. The nomadic subjects produced by this process are much like those Williams labels "make-shift arrangements" in an extraordinary letter to Donald Windham. During one of his "periodic neuroses," or "blue devils," as he called them, the young playwright reflected:

> Naturally we have very little integrity, if any at all. Naturally the innermost "I" or "You" is lost in a sea of other disintegrated elements, things that can't fit together and that make an eternal war in our

natures. . . . We all bob only momently above the bubbling, boiling
surface of the torrent of lies and distortions we are borne along.[99]

In *Cat on a Hot Tin Roof*, Williams radically redefines both the self
and the Other, the "I" and the "You" that are "lost in a sea" of "dis-
integrated elements," and cunningly destabilizes normative constructions
of sexuality. This destabilization is rendered particularly vividly by
Maggie's final and peripetous confession, her invented pregnancy, which,
ironically, becomes a testament not to the "naturalness" of heterosexuality, but to the impossibility of erasing male homosexual desire, and
to Skipper's irrevocable position in the erotic triangle. For even if Brick
were to accede to Maggie's demand and agree to "make the lie true" (in
Maggie's words), he would not resolve the question of his own sexual
identity, nor confirm the primacy of heterosexual desire, not an iota of
which he displays (p. 123). His successful impregnation of his wife in
the bed of Jack Straw and Peter Ochello would ironically attest less to
the sudden and timely triumph of a "natural" heterosexuality than to
the perpetuation of a homosexual economy and to the force of Maggie's
fetishistic appropriation of Skipper's sexuality. (It is in this sense that
Brick's act of making the lie of Maggie's pregnancy true would also make
true the "lie" about Brick and Skipper.)

Although *Cat on a Hot Tin Roof* reveals many of the contradictions
inscribed in homophobic ideologies and practices, it simultaneously bears
witness to the (at times) painfully oblique discourse that must be spoken
in and around the closet during the 1950s. It attests distressingly to the
level of aggression that may be unleashed against its occupants: the
violence that dismembers, maims, ravages—and eroticizes—the inhabitants of the empty/not empty room. At the same time, the play ironically proves how crucial this site is for the construction of a theory of
patrilinearity during the triumphalist display of containment in the 1950s.
It demonstrates that the closet, like the "glass box" in which Brick had
worked as a sports announcer and from which he had watched the games,
is both a means of concealment and a privileged perspective on both
the dominant culture and what it seeks to police and contain: those very
adventures for which Brick is no longer deemed "fit," the tumultuous
athletic—and sexual—contests in which men are engrossed in "sweating
out their disgust and confusion" (p. 84).

By the end of this widely acclaimed and, indeed, Pulitzer Prize-
winning play, Williams begins cautiously to redefine the male homosexual subject, by conceiving of him less as a positivity than as a kind
of absent (offstage) presence—like Skipper, or Jack Straw and Peter
Ochello, or the Phallus inscribed in Maggie's dismembered body. In 1955

Williams was able to protect this homosexual subject from "the torrent of lies and distortions" that overwhelms him on the commercial stage only by displacing him, or by not allowing him to speak, since the only language he was permitted to speak was the very one that ensured his abjection and his marginalization. By appropriating the language of convention (and subtly turning it against itself), and by absenting the homosexual subject (and drawing attention to his absence), another homosexual subject, Tennessee Williams, is allowed not only to speak, but virtually to reign over the commercial theater of the 1940s and 1950s. Long before Stonewall, and during a period of brutal and murderous homophobia, Williams's "most realistic" play practices a cautious sleight of hand, simultaneously articulating a potentially revolutionary site of resistance and reducing the language of homophobia to a barely comprehensible babble.

Three

Tennessee Williams II
"'Revolutionary' is a misunderstood word"

There are only two times in this world when I am happy and selfless and pure. One is when I jack off on paper and the other when I empty all the fretfulness of desire on a young male body. There must be a third occasion for happiness in the world. What is it and where?

—Tennessee Williams, letter to Donald Windham (1943)

Homosexuality is an historic occasion to re-open affective and relational virtualities, not so much through the intrinsic qualities of the homosexual, but due to the biases against the position he occupies; in a certain sense diagonal lines that he can trace in the social fabric permit him to make these virtualities visible.

—Interview with Michel Foucault (1981)

One of Tennessee Williams's most elusive short stories, "Hard Candy" (written 1949–53), which was published in the 1954 collection of the same name, provides an intriguing variation on another story that first appeared in the same volume, "The Mysteries of the Joy Rio" (1941).[1] Like so many Williams texts, the two form a linked pair of variations on a common theme, narrative structure, group of characters, locale, or even mood. Despite the decade or so separating the composition of these two works, however, they are not related as sketch to finished product, or outline to realization, but rather compose a "diptych," in the words of one critic, in which the one more or less radically reconceptualizes the other.[2] As the stories "The Night of the Iguana" (1948) and "Kingdom of Earth" (1954) are to the later plays that bear the same names, these two brief narratives are linked metonymically, sharing the same setting, following an analogous narrative spine, and foregrounding characters whose names are clearly permutations of each other. Although Williams's diptychs are often written in different media, these two texts almost certainly remained short stories, in part, because their subject matter would have prohibited their production as plays during the 1950s.[3]

Like "The Mysteries of the Joy Rio," "Hard Candy" traces the peregrinations of an aging, ailing, furtive homosexual to the darkness of the balcony of the Joy Rio movie theater, where he initiates one final erotic adventure and dies. Here the protagonist is Mr. Krupper (a variation on the name of Pablo Gonzales's late protector, Emiel Kroger), the retired owner of a candy store and a man afflicted with a diseased heart and that perennial mark of male homosexuality in Williams: "unhealthy intestines."[4] Like Mr. Gonzales, Mr. Krupper is made a scapegoat by others, this time by a distant cousin and his contemptuous family who had bought the "small sweetshop" and who "conveniently adopt the old man as their incarnate image" for all of their own "little sorrows and resentments," despite the fact that they know nothing of his sexual practices (pp. 353, 355). Thrice weekly, Mr. Krupper makes a pilgrimage to the sweetshop and then to the "third-rate cinema," which specializes in cowboy movies, where he cruises young men and remunerates them for their sexual favors with six tinkling quarters and as many hard candies as they can consume. On the afternoon in question, Mr. Krupper wends his way to the balcony, where he encounters a "shadowy youth" with "dark and lustrous" hair, whose "odor is captivating" (pp. 360, 361). As a western reaches its triumphant conclusion on the screen and "the cowboy hero"—that icon of normative masculinity—is "galloping into a sunset," the "fat and ugly" Mr. Krupper, "shameful and despicable even to those who tolerate his caresses," offers the bag of candies to his hungry prey and then makes a "bold move," jingling the quarters between his fingers, hoping to bribe the youth to accept a more affectionate proposition (p. 363). The young man acquiesces, "the coins descend, softly, . . . and Mr. Krupper knows that the contract is sealed between them" (p. 364). The narration then politely breaks off, and in the vacant line between two paragraphs, the old man performs fellatio on his young prize.

When the theater lights come up again and the narrative resumes, Mr. Krupper is discovered dead, "with his knees on the floor and his ponderous torso wedged between two wobbly gilt chairs as if he had expired in an attitude of prayer." Ignoring this piquant detail, the obituary in the local newspaper testifies only that the old man had died "of thrombosis at a cowboy thriller with a split bag of hard candies in his pocket and the floor about him littered with sticky wrappers, some of which even adhered to the shoulder and sleeves of his jacket" (p. 364). Mr. Krupper's relatives, however, are positively delighted by the old man's death. At sighting this "astonishingly agreeable" announcement, the family boils "with excitement and glory," while the little daughter exclaims credulously, *"Just think, Papa, the old man choked to death on our hard candy!"* (pp. 364-65).

Williams's quaintly wicked story is, I believe, far less simple and far less homophobic—or rather, much more deeply conflicted about the homophobic attitudes and guilty practices it depicts—than most of

Williams's critics make it out to be.[5] One can quickly and easily tabulate the many adjectives in the text that mark Mr. Krupper as degenerate and diseased: gross, unattractive, sick, detested, yellow-toothed, dangerous, sad, unhealthy, terrible, shameful, despicable, and so on. And yet the force of this list is ingeniously undercut by two factors: first, the narrator's wonderfully wry tone, and second, a curious and elaborate metanarrative intrusion near the beginning of the story. Immediately after setting the scene and introducing the major players, the narrator interrupts the action with this stern warning:

> In the course of this story, and very soon now, it will be necessary to make some disclosures about Mr. Krupper of a nature too coarse to be dealt with very directly in a work of such brevity. The grossly naturalistic details of a life, contained in the enormously wide context of that life, are softened and qualified by it, but when you attempt to set those details down in a tale, some measure of obscurity or indirection is called for to provide the same, or even approximate, softening effect that existence in time gives to those gross elements in the life itself. When I say that there was a certain mystery in the life of Mr. Krupper, I am beginning to approach those things in the only way possible without a head-on violence that would disgust and destroy and which would actually falsify the story. (p. 355)

The narrator's appeal here to the reader's sense of decorum and propriety is almost ludicrously out of place in the context of Williams's narrative fiction of the 1940s and 1950s. Unlike his plays of the same period, which intensively deploy measures of "obscurity" and "indirection," both *One Arm* (1948) and *Hard Candy* are so filled with stories that are explicitly and even graphically homoerotic that it is difficult not to read Williams's petition parodistically—as an indictment of those obfuscating habits of writing and reading that belie "the grossly naturalistic details of a life" in favor of literary (or theatrical) decorum. In "Hard Candy," the information allegedly "too coarse to be dealt with very directly" happens to be absolutely pivotal to the story, and is, in fact, communicated by a series of almost startlingly "naturalistic" visual and odoriferous details. Even the quality of the sexual act itself, which passes in the silence of the ellipsis, is specified quite exactly (to all but the most naive or obtuse reader) by the placement of Mr. Krupper's adoring corpse.

To read "Hard Candy" as a story—or even the parody of a story—about the pathetic demise of a guilty homosexual is to reduce the complexity of the work and to underestimate the subtlety of Williams's strategies as a writer. I believe, instead, that this story should be understood as providing a guide to the possible ways of reading a Williams text and, more specifically, to the way that homosexuality, that "certain mystery in the life of Mr. Krupper," is coded and decoded in his writing for that most public of literary arenas, the theater. Williams has carefully sequestered the paragraph quoted above from the rest of the narrative in order to draw attention to and comment on the conventions of reading and writing. Furthermore, the import of the story, and the pivotal function of its last line (which operates much like a punch line), depends entirely upon the reader's recognition of the different ways in which the position of the old man's body can be interpreted, that is, upon the incongruity between his or her own enterprising reading and the two rather more naive ones offered by characters in the text. For the writer of the obituary, Mr. Krupper's death signifies (in Clum's elegant phraseology) "the sentimental extinction of a man with a sweet tooth and a love for westerns."[6] For the hateful little girl and her family, his demise exemplifies the poetic justice incurred for his pilfering their stock of hard candies. For the perspicacious reader, meanwhile, who is able to read quite literally between the lines, the old man's passing acquires a rather different meaning, becoming perhaps a pathetic exemplum of a perverse, impersonal, and deathly eros; or perhaps a kind of *liebestod*, an almost mystical love-death; or perhaps an illustration of a desubjectification, the dissolving away ("in an attitude of prayer") of an individual subjectivity, and a life, as deliciously as the hard candies with which Mr. Krupper has been so prodigally generous.

Much more unambiguously than "The Mysteries of the Joy Rio," "Hard Candy" is structured as an act of disclosure, an unwrapping of a mysterious sweet, as it were. And yet Williams's admonitory paragraph draws attention to those conventions of decorum during the 1950s that prevented a full disclosure, demanding that discourse, when homosexuality is the "gross element" in question, must proceed by "some measure of obscurity or indirection." Like all narratives of disclosure (and like the well-made play), "Hard Candy" moves toward the discovery of a secret. In this case, however, the secret that is revealed is the near impossibility of reading the secret, or rather, the fact that this secret has already been so decisively marked by the very "head-on violence" that the narrator would at all cost avoid (believing that it will not simply "disgust and destroy," but "actually falsify the story") that it can be apprehended only as a falsehood. In other words, in its determined polyvocality, in its analysis of the different codes of reading and writing, "Hard Candy" testifies to the "violence" that almost inevitably marks all sexual representations in a squeamish and censorious culture intent on policing sexuality, and to the unfortunate fact that within this system, even the unmistakable evidence of one's eyes will be consistently misrecognized, truth will become falsehood, sex will become sentiment, and spilled semen will become sweetly transformed into melted glucose.

Transvestite Poetics

Interpreting the "gross elements" in Williams's most public texts of the 1940s and 1950s, and the various devices he uses to provide a "softening effect" on them, has been a sometimes daunting problem for the critic, the theater professional, and the lay reader. Beginning in the late 1950s, with an increasing public suspicion (or awareness) of Williams's homosexuality, a species of criticism emerged that attempted cunningly to decipher the language of "obscurity" and "indirection" in Williams's plays by translating his heroines into homosexual men in drag and, as a result, turning many of his heterosexual couplings into homosexual liaisons in disguise. This particular maneuver dates back to a 1958 essay by Stanley Edgar Hyman in which he decries a "somewhat unattractive" trend that, he alleges, enfeebles the American "tradition" and compromises its most "virile" achievements. The "Albertine strategy," as he calls it (commemorating Proust's "Albert-made-Albertine," whom he believes to be the "godfather" of all such transpositions), entails "metamorphosizing a boy with whom the male protagonist is involved into a girl," and characterizes, he claims, both Williams's novel *The Roman Spring of Mrs. Stone* (1950) and *A Streetcar Named Desire*.[7] This particular line of argument has been appropriated by many of Williams's scholarly critics. Stephen S. Stanton, for example, cites approvingly Hyman's "perceptive discussion of the homosexual element" in Williams's work and insists that his plays are "frequently transvestite."[8] Nancy M. Tischler, meanwhile, asserts that "the puritanical, idealistic, confused females" throughout Williams's work "are really only female impersonators."[9] Even Edward A. Sklepowich, in his pioneering essay on homosexual characters in Williams, makes no attempt to critique the assumptions underlying Hyman's charges.[10]

Hyman's line of argument raises some very difficult questions about Williams's use of "obscurity" and "indirection" in his representations of gender and sexuality, about different ways of reading and performing his texts, and about the relationship between a writer's work and his or her sexual practices. In recent scholarship on Proust, J. E. Rivers and Eve Kosofsky Sedgwick attack this "transvestite criticism" (from very different positions) and demonstrate the violence the "Albertine strategy" inflicts on the Proustian text by recklessly transposing both gender and sexuality and producing an unintelligible clutter whose only coherence becomes the ill-concealed homosexuality of its author.[11] In the case of Williams, as well, the metamorphosis of Blanche from heterosexual female to homosexual male makes nonsense of Bianche's panic at discovering the homosexuality of her late husband, of Stanley's brutally normative masculinity, and of the carefully gendered specificity of sexual violence. Even more alarmingly, the postures of Hyman and Stanton betray a crude (and homophobic) essentialism that opposes the presumedly natural and comprehensive character of heterosexuality to the eccentricity and perversity of homosexuality (Stanton: "In drawing on his private experience, [Williams] has universalized it").[12] They assume that the gay writer, who allegedly produces only more of his own gender and his own sexuality, is in essence unlike the straight writer, who, it would seem, can construct characters who are authentically either heterosexual or homosexual (they would never dream of suggesting that the suspected homosexual liaison in Robert Anderson's *Tea and Sympathy* is, in fact, a furtive heterosexual coupling in disguise!). They also seem to hearken back to the nineteenth-century figuration of homosexuality as "sexual inversion," as the trapping of the soul of one gender in the body of its "opposite."[13] Williams himself strenuously and angrily denied that his female characters are transvestite, insisting on several occasions that the allegations are "preposterous" and "very dangerous."[14]

The virtual ubiquity of the "Albertine strategy" as a guide to interpreting Williams is a sign that the problems attending his representations of gender, and more generally, by the profusion of "screens and covers" in his work, are very difficult to assess and answer. Although Hyman's and Stanton's assessments are demonstrably heterosexist, it does not necessarily follow that all readings that ferret out gender transpositions will be homophobic. In chapter 2, I argued that Williams's plays disrupt orthodox modes of genderization by cutting diagonally across the binary oppositions between masculinity and femininity, heterosexuality and homosexuality. Although throughout his career Williams reiterates this destabilization in complex and subtle ways, the widespread popularity of transvestite readings seems to indicate that there is another level of intelligibility—or narrative thread, or principle of genderization—in his works that tends simply to reverse the polarities of these binarisms. In fact, one of the texts that Hyman singles out, *The Roman Spring of Mrs. Stone*, a novel about the sexual awakening of a rich, middle-aged widow, is so riddled with signs of gender inversion that Williams seems almost to be daring the reader to transpose its male and female characters. Thus, for example, in the very beginning, the narrator wryly characterizes Karen Stone's lesbian friend, Meg Bishop, as having a "shockingly transvestite appearance, almost as though the burly commander of a gunboat had presented himself in the disguise of a wealthy clubwoman."[15] Later, "the fabulously wealthy Jewish Baron Waldheim," on the prowl for a young paramour, is described as being called "the Baroness" by all his confidants and "talked of exactly as if he were a woman" (p. 28). Mrs. Stone herself is characterized as having been a "tomboy" in her youth (p. 100) while Paolo, her more or less heterosexual gigolo, is identified by a feminine Italian noun, as a "marchetta," which may be translated as either (female) prostitute or (male) homosexual (p. 51).

The most striking and complex instance of gender transposition, however, is a description halfway through the novel of a hasty and impulsive sexual encounter between Karen Stone and a young actor playing opposite her in a touring production of *As You Like It*. The narrator carefully describes how she invades his dressing room, interrupting his "Narcissean gaze" into the mirror, and then proceeds to "envelop" him in a "violent embrace,"

> in a manner which was more like a man's with a girl, and to which he submitted in a way that also suggested a reversal of gender—although finally, at the necessary moment in the embrace, she had changed to the woman's more natural pose of acceptance and he had managed to assume the (fairly well-acted) role of the aggressor.

Although this may seem an apparently straightforward representation of a simple "reversal of gender," the scene is rendered almost exquisitely enigmatic when one elaborates its context. Williams carefully specifies that this "violent embrace" occurs not before or after the performance, but during "the interval," that is, while Karen Stone, as Rosalind, is disguised in male attire. In other words, Williams here illustrates a scene in which an actress, who plays a female character pretending to be a boy named Ganymede (a virtual synonym for "sodomite" during the Renaissance and a role that would originally have been acted by a boy playing a woman playing a boy), seduces a young actor of a "Narcissean" disposition, "whose good looks and lyric style were in serious competition with her own" and whose adoption of the "role of aggressor" was itself only an impersonation, albeit one that was "fairly well-acted" (pp. 82–83).[16]

Williams's almost ludicrously baroque characterization of this "violent embrace" between two theatricalized, "Narcissean" doubles, his vertiginous piling up of masquerade upon masquerade, gender upon gender, and sexuality upon sexuality, effects far more than the simple transposition detected by those critics who seem to think that a "transvestite reading" cagily deciphers Williams's own homosexuality. This passage from *The Roman Spring of Mrs. Stone* demonstrates how difficult it is to read the complexly gendered network that Williams painstakingly weaves, for the convolutions of the cited passage are exacerbated by Williams's omission from the narrative of two crucial details. He neither specifies that Karen Stone is dressed as Ganymede nor hints at the performance conventions of the Elizabethan theater. These details are communicated silently, that is, either not at all (to those either unaware of the Shakespearean references or intent on noticing only the simple "reversal of gender") or with a knowing wink of the eye (to others intent on reading a much more complex and unstable distribution of genders and sexualities). As a result, Williams is able to reverse the imputed binary opposition between masculine and feminine and simultaneously to unsettle, subtly and brilliantly, this same binarism.

Throughout *The Roman Spring of Mrs. Stone* and, indeed, throughout almost all of Williams's more public and popular works of the 1940s and 1950s (that is, his plays), Williams seems to practice a kind of double writing that, in turn, encourages a double reading analogous to the one so elegantly dramatized in "Hard Candy." The difference between these two modes of writing—between the "gross" and the "indirect" detail—corresponds to the distinction between a naive reading and a more knowing or perspicacious one. Another way of conceiving the difference between these modes of writing and reading is to borrow Susan Sontag's nomenclature and label the former "straight" and the latter "camp." As formulated in Sontag's 1964 essay, "camp" (much like Sue-Ellen Case's "butch-femme aesthetic") is a "way of seeing the world as an aesthetic phenomenon," a celebration of artifice and extravagance, an epicene style whose theatricalization of social roles "doesn't reverse things" but instead offers "a different—a supplementary—set of standards."[17] According to this strategy, a "camp" reading of Williams will not simply "reverse" gender because it will be based on the assumption that genders and sexualities are not produced in opposition and therefore cannot be "simply" reversed. Rather, a "camp" reading will pay particular attention to problems of coding and language, to innuendo and gossip; it will make elaborate substitutions and delight in the capriciousness of spoken and performative languages. It will also frequently and pointedly transpose genders, producing transvestite subjects based on its recognition that all gender is masquerade and all costume is a form of drag.

The allegedly transvestite subject in Williams's work is also produced, I believe, as a result of a functional similarity between the cultural position of the independent woman (like Blanche, Mrs. Stone, or Maxine) who is ambitious both occupationally and sexually, and that of the comfortably middle-class homosexual male (like the Baron de Charlus, Billy in "Two on a Party," or Tennessee Williams himself) whose gender, during the domestic revival, grants him a significant measure of economic and social power and yet whose sexuality guarantees he will remain marginal to its cultural norms. This symmetry between the independent woman and the homosexual man, however, is severely disrupted by Williams's representation of the androgyne, the "effeminate" man who, in Zelditch's unforgettably evocative words, "has too much fat on the inner side of his thigh."[18] Despite Williams's apparent—if tacit—recognition of the historical linkage between misogyny and homophobia, the "effeminate," androgynous, or transvestite male, in his very few appearances in Williams's work, provokes considerable anxiety both for the other characters and for the writer of the stage directions.

Among Williams's published plays, only *Kingdom of Earth* (1968) features a transvestite male, Lot, whose quasi-tragic passion is rather different from the "camp" ludicrousness of "the Baroness" in *Mrs. Stone*. In the final scene of the play, Lot enacts his death scene wearing his mother's summer dress, slowly descending the staircase of the family manse. Struggling and gasping for breath, he is *"bizarre and beautiful,"* the very exemplum of *"the sexless passion of the transvestite."* Like the phrase used to describe the hapless Lot, the transvestite in Williams is an oxymoron, the embodiment of an overdetermined "sexless passion" that both elides "sexuality" with "gender" (at the zero degree) and attempts carefully to separate the two by marking the male transvestite's sex(lessness) as heterosexual. In the epicene—but not gay—Lot, *"a frail, delicately—you might say exotically—pretty youth,"* Williams equates androgyny with impotence while attempting carefully to detach effeminacy from homosexuality (p. 127). By this gesture, Williams reveals perhaps his most crucial acquiescence to the conventions of Cold War sexual orthodoxy, his practice of championing—and often romanticizing—a powerful and phallic masculinity (as embodied by Lot's half-brother, Chicken) and of deriding and disdaining the "swish" and the "camp."[19]

Yet Williams's contempt for the transvestite and for transvestite readings of his own plays by no means invalidates those interpretations of his work by directors or actors who transpose gender. Drag need not simply invert the polarities of gender; as Sue-Ellen Case points out, it may also function to denaturalize gender, to make "all gender roles appear fictitious," and, in so doing, to underscore the strain in Williams's work that does not simply reverse but rather deconstructs the sex-gender system.[20] For Williams's critics, as well, a "transvestite reading" of *The Roman Spring of Mrs. Stone* or *A Streetcar Named Desire* is not by definition regressive and homophobic. However, for it to be effective in teasing out the contradictions in Williams's work that accumulate around gender (rather than simply reinscribing despotic binarisms), the interpretation must recognize the coexistence—and even codependency—of different modes of writing and reading, of the "gross" and the "indirect," of the "camp" and the "straight," of the reversal and radical subversion of gender. For the knowing reader, it is less a question of choosing among the different modes than of noting how these various strategies play themselves out simultaneously in Williams's plays, and what contradictions they engender. In particular, how is the desiring subject articulated? What are the narratives by means of which he or she is produced? Which sets of difference are eroticized in these narratives? How does Williams negotiate the "head-on violence" that always seems to be a part of his mode of representation? And, finally, why are the most revolutionary and utopian aspects of desire in his work produced according to a scenario that is far more subtle and enigmatic than the reductive formulas of Hyman and Stanton could possibly detect?

Masculinity, Narrative, and Racial Difference

BABY DOLL: Wait, please!—I want to—
She starts to come running down the stairs, her hair wild, panting, sweating, smeared with attic dust. Then halfway down she stops....
BABY DOLL: *(Now stealing towards [Silva Vacarro])* I want to—
But she can't remember what she "wants to." He waits quizzically with his cocky grin for her to complete her sentence but she doesn't. Instead she looks up and down him and her eyelids flutter as if the image could not be quietly contained.

—*Baby Doll*

Even before *Baby Doll* opened at movie theaters in December 1956, it had become the subject of an intense and heated dispute. Two days before its premiere, Francis Cardinal Spellman made one of his rare forays into the pulpit of St. Patrick's Cathedral to denounce the film as "immoral" and "revolting," "a contemptuous defiance of the natural law," a "corrupting influence" and a stimulant to "immorality and crime." Although he had not seen the movie, he bemoaned its certification by the Motion Picture Association of America as an "astonishing and deplorable" feat and forbade Roman Catholics to see it.[21] The Catholic National League of Decency, meanwhile, labeled it "salacious" and gave it a "C" rating, for "Condemned."[22] Both screenwriter Tennessee Williams and director Elia Kazan took strong exception to Spellman's judgment, and over the next month newspapers and magazines buzzed with the controversy. As is usually the case when accusations of salaciousness are hurled so liberally, the film did extremely good business initially, amassing revenues its first week that *Variety* called "HUGE, SOCK, WHOPPING," and "TERRIF."[23] It received generally positive, if cautious, reviews, with *Time*, predictably, leading the denunciations, calling it "just possibly the dirtiest American-made motion picture that has ever been legally exhibited," and opining that Williams's "language" and "subject matter" seem "to have been borrowed from one of the more carelessly written pornographic pulps."[24]

Watching the film years after the dispute, most critics of Williams and Kazan agree that it is difficult to understand why the film provoked such an acrimonious response (in Kazan's words, "It's so mild that you wonder what in hell all the fuss was about").[25] Certainly, in comparison with the frank treatment of sexuality in American films of the late 1960s and the 1970s, *Baby Doll* seems extremely restrained and "almost quaint," in one critics's words, hardly deserving Spellman's personal intervention.[26] Like the leader of the current crusade against counterhegemonic art, Senator Jesse Helms, the cardinal seems impossibly obtuse as a critic, incapable of recognizing irony, of understanding the film's formal strategies, or of grasping its ethical project, one that even *Time* called "almost puritanically moral."[27] However, as with the controversy over the Robert Mapplethorpe show, The Perfect Moment, in Washington and Cincinnati in 1989 and 1990, the furor over *Baby Doll* was not the result of a lone individual's fulminations over the exhibition of transgressive sexualities. Letters of protest deluged Warner Brothers. A censored version of the film was screened in Providence, Rhode Island, while in Memphis and Atlanta it was banned altogether. Several persons among a presumptively random assortment of moviegoers questioned by *Life* magazine found the film "trashy" and "immoral." One Memphis-born man declared "it will hurt the South," while an African-American woman "did not like" the scene in which Archie Lee orders Baby Doll away from the cotton gin simply "because Negroes are there."[28] If these rejoinders—by persons who had at least seen the movie—are less easily dismissed than those of Spellman, it is perhaps because they are indicative of the film's ability to arouse a cluster of anxieties (much as the Mapplethorpe show did) that circulate around two subjects that were not, however, broached in criticism of the film: sexual violence and racial difference.

Baby Doll is adapted from two Williams one-act plays written before 1946, *27 Wagons Full of Cotton* (which is, in turn, based on the 1935 short story of the same name) and *The Long Stay Cut Short, or, The Unsatisfactory Supper*. Like *27 Wagons*, *Baby Doll* dramatizes the revenge of "a handsome, cocky young Italian," Silva Vacarro (Eli Wallach), on an impoverished cotton gin owner, Archie Lee Meighan (Karl Malden) for the fire Meighan set to destroy the Syndicate gin (over which Vacarro had been superintendent).[29] Vacarro accomplishes this by his dexterous seduction of Archie Lee's still virginal young wife,

Baby Doll (Carroll Baker). As Sy Kahn points out, the film clearly dramatizes a social crisis: "the impact of the new industrialism on the Old South," the collapse of small estates and family farms in the face of the corporate power and economic leverage of the menacingly generic Syndicate Plantation.[30] As is so frequently the case in Williams's work, this confrontation is figured as a sexual contest over a woman between a virile young man and a weak or effete older man. This triangle is perhaps the most durable characterological pattern in Williams's work and remains the nucleus of many plays, most notably *Kingdom of Earth* (1968), which restages the struggle with an almost uncanny similarity. Over the fifty-year course of Williams's career, it is incessantly adjusted and reconfigured. Sometimes, as in *The Roman Spring of Mrs. Stone* or the diptych *Battle of Angels* (1940) and *Orpheus Descending* (1957), one partner in the triangle (usually the older man) is relegated to a mysterious and ominous position, waiting somewhere offstage, somewhere in the wings. Sometimes, as in *In the Bar of a Tokyo Hotel* (1969), the young man fades into the background after the first scene. At other times, as in *A Streetcar Named Desire*, this older man is less an individual subject than an entire past life or the expiring culture with which the subject in question is associated. Or sometimes, as in *The Glass Menagerie*, the eroticism of one side of the triangle is concealed beneath an apparently asexual, fraternal relationship.

In *Baby Doll*, as in these aforementioned plays, a young, charismatic man, the embodiment of power and virility, disrupts a woman's life and her affiliations, inaugurates a sexual encounter tinged with violence, and effects her transfiguration (either her ambiguous deliverance from the older man or her less ambiguous destruction). Like the illegitimate Chicken (of *Kingdom of Earth*), whose body is a paradigm of "power and male grace"; or the "fresh and primitive" Val Xavier, with his "virile grace and freedom of body"; or the Japanese Barman who resembles an *"Oriental idol"*; or that "gaudy seed-bearer," Stanley Kowalski, for whom "pleasure with women" is the "center of his life" (p. 29); or the dynamic Jim O'Connor, the champion of the three principles upon which "democracy" is built—knowledge, money, and power (p. 100); Silva Vacarro unmistakably "has" the Phallus and all that it symbolizes.[31] These six characters (along with John Buchanan, Alvaro Mangiocavallo, Chance Wayne, and many others) are (hetero)sexually vital young men who epitomize what Kazan describes as "the virility that will rejuvenate," the force that can suddenly and almost magically awaken sexual desire and transform a woman like Baby Doll (along with Myrtle, Myra/Lady Torrance, Miriam, Blanche, Stella, and so many others) from a state of real or feigned innocence to a wary yet vigorous adulthood.[32]

In its practice of foregrounding a phallic male, *Baby Doll* (like most of Williams's plays) appears to (re)construct masculinity by appealing to the same mythical narrative as the plays of Arthur Miller. In so many respects, Silva Vacarro epitomizes the conqueror, that lone hero who, in the words of Teresa De Lauretis, "crosses the boundary and penetrates the other space," overcoming feminized obstacles, like Archie Lee, in order to subdue and win—in a burst of phallic power—a distinctively feminine prize.[33] Although Williams appropriates this narrative time and time again, he in fact radically transforms it by decentering this heroic male figure, almost invariably constructing this subject not as the magisterial self of Miller's *imaginaire*, but as distinctively and unmistakably *Other*, not just the Other of Williams's own slightly faded, middle-class, queer, white Anglo-Saxon self, but also as the Other of a culture whose emblem is the industrious, paternal breadwinner epitomized by Zelditch, "the 'capable,' 'competent,' 'go-getting' male."[34]

What is most remarkable about the phallic male in Williams is his striking divergence in terms of social class, ethnicity, and temperament from the white Protestant bourgeois paradigm so feverishly promoted in theater, film, and television during the domestic revival (and so clearly embodied by the authoritative fathers of "The Adventures of Ozzie and Harriet," "The Donna Reed Show," and "Father Knows Best"—those sterling exemplars of "self-possession, probity and sound judgement").[35] Throughout Williams's work, this normative paternal figure is never portrayed as the "hero"; instead he is usually redrawn as an ineffectual or impotent older man, like *Baby Doll's* Archie Lee, who becomes the obstacle to the project of the younger, more vital, phallic male. Silva Vacarro is carefully differentiated from Archie Lee by his relative economic and sexual prosperity, as well as by his Sicilian ancestry, which makes him "natcherally dark" and, to the others' xenophobic imaginations, a "foreign wop" (pp. 56, 32). Like the "dark-complected" and "foreign"-looking Chicken (who is economically and culturally abject in relation to his half brother, Lot), Vacarro's ethnicity and dusky skin are the signs of his power, of his charismatic efficiency as businessman and seducer.

Unlike most other producers of popular masculine icons during the 1950s, however, Williams almost always presents this phallic male as a relatively nonempathic figure in comparison to a more richly sympathetic and humane woman, such as Baby Doll, Myrtle, Miriam, or Blanche. This latter is given a more extensive and enigmatic history than the male's, one that makes her unmistakably the site of emotional conflict and the subject of (male) speculation. She is also more unequivocally a desiring subject than the phallic and, to some extent, self-sufficient male, harboring desires that are far more expansive and restless. In being constituted as the primary desiring subject, Williams's heroine is also far more nuanced, complex, and sympathetic than the female characters produced by most of his contemporaries. Williams's often noted precept that he finds it "much easier, much more interesting to write about women" accounts in part for the substantial empathic investment in these characters on the part of the playwright and, consequently, of so many actors, readers, and spectators (these are certainly among the most superbly actable female roles in the American theater).[36] More unambiguously than the phallic male, who is always already Other, an object of scopophiliac and fetishistic desire, the Williams heroine functions much like the hero of classic narrative, the one who endures "a passage, a crossing, an actively experienced transformation."[37] Although her pivotal structural position no doubt encourages the "transvestite readings" of some of Williams's critics—those unaccustomed to such a richly textured female subject—I do not believe it produces a "simple" inversion of gender, a kind of negative image of classic narrative, with female protagonist and male object of desire.

Rather, Williams's transposition of gender effects a destabilization of classic narrative, producing a female character who is both an actively striving subject and an object of the desire of others. Because of her position in the narrative structure, she *must* desire, but because of various social (i.e., contextual) proscriptions, she is not allowed to act on her desires authoritatively or to articulate them completely. In *Baby Doll*, for example, the desires of the title character are far more difficult to compass and express than those of either Vacarro or Archie Lee, which are "simply" economic and libidinous. For Baby Doll, as for most Williams heroines, need is given a metaphysical dimension; it is intransitive; it is expressed not as the quantifiable, but rather as a figure of inexpressibility. Unquestionably, the pivotal moment for this desiring subject takes place immediately after Vacarro has violently forced her to sign the affidavit accusing her husband of arson. She suddenly runs down the stairs to him and implores, "Wait, please!—I want to—," but is unable to complete her sentence (p. 105). The ellipsis that follows is the privileged figure of female desire in Williams and a remarkable instance of the convergence of Baby Doll's modesty, the strictures of the Hollywood Production Code, and the fact that the language ("of obscurity or indirection") that Baby Doll has at her disposal is by definition incapable of carrying the freight of her desire. In the context of Williams's other works of the 1940s and 1950s, it is precisely this inability to articulate that marks her desire as being symmetrical with "homosexual" desire, that is, always exceeding representation. The ellipsis in the text functions much like the crucial ellipsis in "Hard Candy," which authorizes multiple readings while speaking the impossibility of speaking the sexual. The disparity between the written direction that elucidates the ellipsis and the filmed sequence provides yet another example of the same double strategy, both belying desire and representing the impossibility of its representation. Although the text of Williams's screenplay asserts that her silence is the result of Baby Doll's failure to *"remember what she 'wants to,'"* the silent yet sexually charged exchange in the film suggests that the ellipsis is less the sign of amnesia than of an inadmissible desire, one that can no more be accommodated by the desiring subject than the *"image"* of Vacarro can *"be quietly contained"* by Baby Doll's gaze (p. 105).

In *Baby Doll*, as in all of Williams's works, desire is bred in the distance between the desiring subject and the "image" that cannot be "contained." Despite the different media and the diversity of subjects, however, the laws governing the production of desire are surprisingly stable and durable. With a remarkable consistency, desire is provoked by differences in race, ethnicity, social class, and age. Almost inevitably, subject and object are configured as antitheses that are congruent with a series of binary oppositions—white/black, wealthy/poor, old/young. Almost inevitably, the first in the pair is granted the priority of the desiring subject, while the second is objectified and exoticized, and thereby endowed with the power to arouse sexual desire: the white craves the black; the Anglo-Saxon, the Italian; the well-to-do, the street urchin; and the old, the young. (In this sense, desire in Williams is never strictly "homosexual"—of same, for same—but always cuts across economic and cultural boundaries.) In Williams's most popular works, gender is added to this catalog of differences, and male and female, like the "almost identical spinsters" Shannon describes in *The Night of the Iguana*, are conveniently reconfigured as "the opposite sexes."[38] In so doing, Williams ensures the palatability of these desires for a culture ill at ease with the blurring of the lines of demarcation between races and social classes.

Throughout Williams's career, differences in ethnicity and race prove to be almost unfailingly the most potent, inflexible, and explosive sources of desire, the necessary spark to sexual liaisons in countless short stories, in *The Roman Spring of Mrs. Stone* and *Moise and the World of Reason* (1975), in *Summer and Smoke*, *The Rose Tattoo*, and *Kingdom of Earth*. Furthermore, as a rule, the greater the difference in skin color, the more violent the sexual encounter. The extreme example is the notorious story "Desire and the Black Masseur" (written 1942–46, published 1948), which features sadomasochism, murder, and cannibalism. But two other stories, "Big Black: A Mississippi Idyll" (1931–32) and "Rubio y Morena" (1948), also foreground racial difference together with a libidinous intensity and a fury not easily distinguishable from sexual violence. In each of these stories, as in *Baby Doll*, physical brutality is the sign of the impossibility of discourse to contain and express desire. Insistently, it is the cost of the estrangement of desire from speech: as the former grows fiercer, the latter becomes increasingly unthinkable. Both the ever-pliant Anthony Burns and his black masseur refrain altogether from speaking about their intimacies, while Big Black, who nearly rapes a young white woman, is utterly "inarticulate," his characteristic utterance not spoken language at all, but an ear-splitting, "savage, booming cry."[39] In "Rubio y Morena," the novelist Kamrowski's turbulent relationship with the Mexican woman, Amada, stimulates his writing but renders him so completely silent with her that "the words would not come off his tongue, not even in the intimacies of the night."[40] In stories and plays, the inability to speak—but not to write—is symptomatic of a desire that is so violent that it can be expressed only by the pen(is) of the narrator or the whir of the stage directions (in a narrative ellipsis or a scene break). Consistently, sexual desire in Williams exceeds the representational machinery of the mid-century commercial theater.

Given the censorship of the 1940s and 1950s, and Williams's more or less conscious internalization of these prohibitions, his plays and films of this period characteristically translate these inexpressible desires into subtext and/or transform them into an interethnic heterosexuality that remains provocatively at odds with hegemonic social values. In being so foregrounded, this transgressive eroticism seems to work in concert with a manifestly antiracist thematic that runs through many of Williams's plays. Frequently, for example, the older, inadequate white man, the one who is the embodiment of the law and the obstacle to the sexual fulfillment of a young wife or daughter, is plainly characterized as a racist. In *Battle of Angels*, for example, the sheriff and his men harass the fugitive, Val Xavier, for rescuing "that nigger," Loon, with the taunt, "Pack 'em all off togethuh, Jews, and radicals, and niggers! Ship 'em all back to *Rooshuh!*"[41] And Val's saving of Loon is clearly one of the primary factors that motivates his gruesome murder at the end of the play. In *Sweet Bird of Youth* (1956), perhaps the most despicable character in Williams's work, Boss Finley, is epitomized by his fanatical and vicious racism, by his declaration of "the threat of desegregation to white women's chastity" and fulmination against "blood pollution."[42] On many occasions, Williams himself spoke out against racism, as in a 1974 interview, for example, declaring it "the most horrible thing" and noting that

"White people in America . . . have exercised the most dreadful injustices, historically."[43] Yet for all of Williams's no doubt sincerely held notions of social justice and equality, his work almost unfailingly objectifies and exoticizes the dark Other and, in that respect, clearly exemplifies a contradiction inherent within a certain liberal egalitarianism. Following liberalism's lead, many of Williams's works attempt to combat hierarchizing strategies less by unpacking the principle of hierarchy than by *inverting* the scale and romanticizing an oppressed group, in this case "the Blacks" whom Williams describes in the same 1974 interview as one of his two "favorite people."[44] In Williams's short stories especially, the black male is presented as being startlingly congruent with one of the most durable racist formulations that, in Calvin C. Hernton's words, conceives "of the Negro male predominantly in genital terms—that is, as a 'bull' or as some kind of 'walking phallus.'"[45] The "exotic" and "not completely Caucasian" Mr. Jones in "Miss Coynte of Greene" (1973), for example, has as his most distinguishing feature, in Miss Coynte's coy expression, his "member," which at her touch (the narrator confides) "was erect and pulsing riotously in her fingers."[46] Elsewhere, black men—there are no black women in Williams except servants or menials—are always conceived as objects of fetishistic fascination and paradigms of masculinity.

Although Williams's plays and films are far more restrained, "obscure," and "indirect" than his narrative fiction, their structure almost unfailingly demands the charismatic masculinity of the dark-skinned male who "has" the Phallus. In *Baby Doll*, Silva Vacarro's dusky complexion is unmistakably the mark of his desirability, his status as object, as Other, as an almost exotic species of man. Moreover, throughout the film, in his spirited antagonism to the feckless (and very pale) Archie Lee, he is pointedly identified with the nonwhite characters on the film's margins who always seem to be ridiculing Archie Lee: the Asian-Americans outside the pharmacy delighting in the spectacle of the humiliated husband waiting impatiently while his "succulent" virgin bride licks an ice cream cone, or the African-Americans lurking around the plantation and the cotton gin, "laughing unfeelingly" at the sight of the desperate landowner outwitted and outflanked by Baby Doll and her Sicilian protector.[47]

Although never broached in contemporary reviews, this identification between the swarthy Vacarro and the film's dark-skinned others represents, I believe, a major source of anxiety in 1956 for many of the affronted viewers of this "strong-smelling piece of photographic realism."[48] While virtually all reviews and articles focus on the question of sexual explicitness, the *Life* magazine story also foregrounds racial differences in its (somewhat sensationalized) portraits of the film's characters:

> slatternly Baby Doll, her lusting husband, the sexually wise Sicilian who tempts Baby Doll, scorned and scornful Negroes and small-souled whites.

Further, *Life* reports (quite correctly) that the film's "whites are a poor and prejudiced lot" and, judging from the disposition of photographs in the opening spread, seems to conceive the film's conflict in racial terms. The layout features five photographs, reading from left to right: a large picture of Baby Doll, two smaller ones of Archie Lee and Vacarro, and the two smallest of a white and a black townsperson. The captions underscore the symmetry between, on the one hand, the "mean white" and the "mocking Negro," and on the other, the "small-town Southerner" and the "conniving Sicilian."[49]

The undercurrent of anxiety in regard to racial differences both in the film and in the discourse surrounding the film becomes much clearer and more unmistakable when one places *Baby Doll* in a historical context. As is well known, in the years after World War II, African-Americans remained an intensively subjugated and, particularly in the South, legally segregated racial group. In 1949, the median income of southern blacks was only one-half that of their white counterparts. President Truman's 1948 executive order banning racial segregation in the military and federal government agencies did little to undermine the strict segregation (read: inequity) that ruled in every other area of daily life. In particular, the "separate but equal" educational system heavily favored white populations. In 1954, for example, in Mississippi (the state in which *Baby Doll* takes place and in which the film was shot), the expenditure for each black student was only one-fourth the amount spent on each white student.[50] In May of that year, the U.S. Supreme Court issued its landmark *Brown* v. *Board of Education* ruling, which ordered school desegregation and which, Charles P. Roland asserts, "may ultimately be considered the most momentous judicial decision of the nation's entire history."[51] A year later, when the Court issued a detailed plan for desegregation, most southern states passed legislation in the hope of blocking its implementation. Even more alarmingly, the *Brown* decision sparked an aggressive and often violent resistance movement among many whites who were convinced that desegregation was a Communist plot and that, in fact, "Communists dominated not only the NAACP, but the federal government and the Supreme Court of the United States." In every state organizations were formed whose racist programs were clearly identified by their names: National Association for the Preservation of the White Race, White Citizens' Council, Pond Hollow Segregation Club. The Ku Klux Klan, which had been dormant for almost a generation, resurged, standing "not only for 'womanhood' and white supremacy, but for Protestant Christianity and 'pure Americanism.'" African-Americans and those whites suspected of favoring integration were shot, beaten, and murdered; their homes, schools, and churches were incinerated and bombed.[52] In the fall of 1956, when black pupils were finally admitted to formerly all-white schools in Kentucky, Tennessee, Texas, and North Carolina, violence erupted and the National Guard had to be called in to quell the disturbances.[53]

When *Baby Doll* was released in December 1956, much of the United States was outraged over the prospect of mixed-race schools (the film's premiere also followed by a mere month the Supreme Court's unanimous ruling that segregated buses were unconstitutional). The reasons behind white opposition to desegregation were manifold and complex, but it is clear from the pamphlets and pronouncements of the most vociferous segregationists that "the most insistent single ingredient in Southern hostility to the desegregation ruling" was the fear that integrated schools would lead to interracial marriages. According to the appalling assessment of one federal judge from Mississippi, the *Brown* decision was calculated to help "the Negro . . . to breed up his inferior intellect and whiten his skin and 'blow out the light' in the white man's brain and muddy his skin."[54] In this charged context, *Baby Doll* would hardly assuage the almost pathological fear of miscegenation that this rhetoric betrays, for the "seduction scene" between a dark "seducer" and his blond "victim," the scene about which Cardinal Spellman and all of the reviews buzzed, is unmistakably and crucially interethnic.[55] Furthermore, the oddly chaste outcome of the scene apparently did little to calm the uneasiness of a number of viewers. The scene ends shortly after Baby Doll's truncated plea "I want to—" as Vacarro, at Baby Doll's invitation, settles down (fully clothed) in her crib for a nap as she sits on the floor by his side. There is a cut to a short sequence with Archie Lee and then another cut back to the nursery (implying that some time has elapsed), which finds the two characters in the same position they were in previously. Although it is thus made explicit in the film—and this is corroborated by Kazan's statements—that there is no sexual contact between Vacarro and Baby Doll, not all the critics read the scene as being so innocent.[56] The *Time* critic interpreted the ellipsis rather differently and judged that Vacarro "apparently ends up with her in the crib," an appraisal that seems to reveal more about the reviewer's determination to damn the film as a "prurient peep" than it does the content of the film itself.[57] Spellman's more sweeping judgment, meanwhile, that *Baby Doll* represents "a contemptuous defiance of the natural law" could conveniently cover a multitude of sins, including, for many Americans in 1956, either interracial or interethnic sexual relations (not until 1967 did the U.S. Supreme Court rule that antimiscegenation laws were unconstitutional).[58]

When considered in the context of the extraordinary sensitivity to the nuances of race relations in the wake of the *Brown* decision, *Baby Doll* becomes a very difficult film to decode. On the one hand, given the storm of discourse around racial purity the decision unleashed, *Baby Doll* seems a flagrantly transgressive text that not only taunts those "poor and prejudiced whites" who fall within its purview (as when the African-American waitress, when asked by the sheriff to sing, complies by intoning "I Shall Not Be Moved"), but also eroticizes interethnic relations and delights in inverting—rather than deconstructing—racial hierarchies. On the other hand, the presentation of Vacarro as a "conniving" and darkly exotic sexual being, who is (particularly in Williams's screenplay) almost as much an object of voyeuristic pleasure as Baby Doll herself, coupled with the starkly objectifying representations of leering African-American men, seems to vindicate at least some of the fears of segregationists.[59] In my view, this undecidability, both for mid-century audiences and for the contemporary spectator or reader of Williams, is inescapably bound to the question of the relationship between race and masculinity. In *Baby Doll*, as throughout Williams's work, the normative masculine male is never characterized as a self-possessed, paternalistic, and empathic subject, but as a volatile, dangerous, and alien species, whose otherness is eroticized and whose dusky skin makes him unusually susceptible to the caressing gaze of camera, spectator, or reader. In opposition to dominant cultural conventions, he is epitomized not by the cowboy hero galloping off into the sunset (that trailblazer for American imperialism and collaborator in the extermination of an indigenous people), but by one much closer in character to the cowboy's human prey: an ethnically marked, dark-skinned, and exotic Other. Like the "reversal of gender" with which Williams so often flirts, this reconfiguration of masculinity and inversion of racial hierarchies function in complex and contradictory ways, both to subvert and to reinscribe the binarisms on which these constructions are founded historically. In its equivocations, in its capacity to arouse the disgust and indignation of millions, *Baby Doll* seems to have been a particularly sensitive barometer to the anxieties circulating around questions of race, eroticism, and masculinity during the 1950s. In that sense, Thelma Fox, the African-American college student questioned by *Life* magazine about

Baby Doll, is certainly correct in voicing an uneasiness in regard to the film's representation of "Negroes," but, after all, in conceding that the movie "in general . . . seems pretty accurate."[60]

Criticism and Homophobia

> MARK: When I say that I'm terrified of the new canvasses, you think I'm exaggerating.
> MIRIAM: Not at all in the least.
> MARK: No separation between myself and.
> MIRIAM: Don't keep repeating it to me. Saying a thing once to me is enough, you know. Sometimes a thing doesn't even have to be said to me. I'm able to guess it.
> MARK: It's something that.
> MIRIAM: I said, "Don't discuss it." Not outside the office of a.
> MARK: In the beginning, a new style of work can be stronger than you, but you learn to control it. It has to be controlled. You learn to control it.
>
> —*In the Bar of a Tokyo Hotel*, part I

When C. W. E. Bigsby notes that "Williams's reputation declined sharply in his later years," he is being extremely charitable.[61] Williams's late plays—indeed, all those written after *The Night of the Iguana* (1961)—were damned almost unanimously by the press when first produced, and few of his scholarly critics have attempted a substantive reevaluation of these late works since the playwright's death. Both Bigsby himself and Ruby Cohn have credited the startling imaginative and theatrical power of some of these plays (both single out *The Two-Character Play*, 1967–75; *Vieux Carre*, 1977; and *Clothes for a Summer Hotel*, 1980, for muted praise).[62] But most critical narratives of Williams's last twenty-two years read like dirges, bemoaning the decline and fall of a great prodigy whose writings—tragically or pathetically, depending on the interpreter—document his own disintegration. The publication of the *Memoirs* in 1975 was read by many as an invitation to attack Williams on account of his sexual practices and to link his alleged sharp decline as a writer to a moral decadence that intensified after the death of Williams's longtime lover and companion, Frank Merlo, in 1963 (the gay imitation of a heterosexual marriage is apparently far less threatening to many readers than the cruising for sex documented by the *Memoirs*).

In the most melodramatic—and viciously homophobic—account of Williams's "collapse," Signi Falk complains in particular about the *Memoirs*, noting that "the sexual excesses described . . . disturb many who recall" Williams's characters for the stage. The section of her monograph titled "Preoccupation with Sex," meanwhile, observes Williams's supposed dotage almost with relish, noting that "the old men, gallery habitues in 'Hard Candy' and 'Mysteries of the Joy Rio,' and the ancient who pursues the writer in *Moise* [and who is unmistakably a self-portrait], are pitifully depraved figures." (Falk, incidentally, does not even credit the emotional significance of Williams's relationship with Merlo, referring to him stonily as the playwright's "paid secretary-companion.") In Falk's feverish imagination, Williams's "collapse" represents the wages of "sexual abnormality," just retribution for his perverted practices.[63] In her view, his sexuality destroyed his writing, leading him in his late plays to have woefully "overloaded" his "experience with abstract forms and complicated symbols." As a result, these works "reveal an even greater tortured state of mind" than his early ones, and are mitigated only by the playwright's "dogged determination to continue in the face of despair."[64] Although the most moralistic and condemnatory, Falk's narrative is echoed by virtually every other critic of Williams, from whose pages the words "maudlin," "strident," "fear of age," "fear of death," "neurosis," "mannerism," "self-pity," "sentimentality," and "decadence" ring out dolefully and repeatedly.[65]

Williams's post-*Iguana* plays represent an extremely disparate lot. Most of them have tortuous performance histories (on both sides of the Atlantic), often involving extensive revisions. Many, such as *The Two-Character Play/Outcry*, have been published in two versions. Others, such as *This Is (An Entertainment)* (1976) or *Something Cloudy, Something Clear* (1981) have not been published at all. In many respects, it is even more difficult to generalize about the idiosyncratic structures, characters, and themes of these plays than about those of the playwright's earlier works. Vividly, the post-*Iguana* plays document both Williams's keen response to the social and political crises of a tumultuous era and his restless experimentation, his almost systematic attempt to push style, dramatic form, and language to their limits (in none of these later works does Williams try to imitate the style of his previous successes). Simultaneously, they attest to a change in arena for Williams, from Broadway to Off Broadway (although this shift began, in fact, in the late 1950s), where innovation was not just more acceptable but expected. And while I would not claim the post-*Iguana* plays to be an uninterrupted string of brilliant experiments, I believe that they must be read in relation to what is unmistakably a concerted attempt by critics to police the consolidation of the canon by scuttling Williams's most radical works. To dismiss them, as Frank Rich does in the woefully shortsighted "Appreciation" that accompanied Williams's obituary in the *New York Times*, as "poorly crafted and sometimes self-parodying" is to reclaim Williams for the liberal-humanist theater that appalled him, with its masking of historical difference behind that most pernicious of deceptions (which, not surprisingly, forms the basis for so many of Rich's own reviews): "the ontological chaos that is man's universal plight."[66]

The Incomplete Sentence

When *In the Bar of a Tokyo Hotel* opened Off Broadway in May 1969, at the very height of the Vietnam War and just one month before the Stonewall riot, it was greeted with a combination of skepticism and wariness by the critics. Most did not know what to make of a play radically different from Williams's immediately preceding work. Unlike *The Milk Train Doesn't Stop Here Anymore* (1962) or *Kingdom of Earth* (1968), both sprawling and digressive works, *Tokyo Hotel* is extremely concentrated and concise, its plot focusing on the physical and emotional disintegration and death of a "ravaged" painter, Mark, and his less than compassionate wife, Miriam (p. 13). Unlike *Slapstick Tragedy* (1966), it almost completely eschews extravagant rhetoric and imagery in favor of a dramatic style and tonality that is intensely, if grotesquely, naturalistic. In the *New York Times*, Clive Barnes confessed to finding the play "strange" and being both "repelled" and "fascinated" by it. While conceding that "there are more flashes of genius here than in any of his later plays," he lamented that the play's "human insights" are "regrettably obvious and shallow."[67] Plainly aware of Williams's stature, critics for both *Time* and *Newsweek* cautiously assailed the play, while Harold Clurman penned a more forthright and philosophical evaluation in *The Nation*.[68] Among reviewers, only Stefan Kanfer in *Life* attacked both play and playwright, excoriating the former's *dramatis personae* drawn (he alleged) from a "deviate zoo" and the "ritual stasis" of its plot, and viciously lamenting Williams's "infantile regression" and the "extinction" of his talent.[69]

Despite the range of critical opinion, almost every review singled out for disapprobation a technique that Williams uses more prodigally in this play than in any other: the fragmentary or incomplete sentence. On average, three or four times per page (or, in performance, about every fifteen to twenty-five seconds) characters are unable or unwilling to finish a statement and their words simply come to an abrupt halt, followed in the text by an end stop. Sometimes another character will finish the sentence or, after an interruption, the original speaker will continue. Most of the time, however, the words are simply left dangling on the page, or in the air, as fragments. Consider the following exchange between husband and wife:

MARK [Slowly.]: I've always approached my work with a feeling of frightened timidity because the possibilities are.
MIRIAM: You are making an effort to explain a mystery that I.
MARK: The possibilities of a canvas that presents itself for.
MIRIAM: The assault of a madman. You're destroying.
MARK: I suppose I might say it's.
MIRIAM: Crock.
MARK: *Adventure.*
MARK: I'll.
MIRIAM: You'll stay here with your work.
MARK: —It could be a fantasy that I'm.
MIRIAM: Shattering a frontier? (pp. 27–28)

In 1969 this technique was itself "shattering" a dramaturgical "frontier," being virtually without precedent on the American stage and the source of more than a little uneasiness for Williams's critics. Among them, only Clurman admitted that he was "puzzled" by its use.[70] Others tried to explain it as an unsatisfactory alternative to "eloquence," or as an example of the work's unfortunate status as a "too indirect, too inconclusive" experimental play.[71] More recent critics share the discomfiture. George Niesen judges the play "strange," "difficult to follow," and "an aberration perhaps, . . . without Williams' usual sure sense of language."[72] Roger Boxill reasons that because Miriam and Mark are bound in "a symbiotic relationship," they are not obliged to finish sentences (this exegesis blithely ignores the fact that *all* the characters speak in fragments).[73] Writing from a more theoretically sophisticated perspective, Bigsby sees the device as being primarily an expression not of marital harmony but of "a series of relationships which are so fractured that even language is made to bear the impress of a certain hysteria." But he, too, complains of incoherence, insisting that because ("confusingly") all of the characters speak in incomplete sentences, the "trauma" that generates these utterances cannot be "an expression of character" but must lie "outside the text."[74]

Yet *In the Bar of a Tokyo Hotel* is not the only one of Williams's later works to be constructed of discursive fragments. Most of his works of the 1970s and 1980s use the device, in particular the novel *Moise and the World of Reason*, in which he even dispenses with the end stops, and the one-act plays, *Now the Cats with Jewelled Claws* (1969) and *The Demolition Downtown* (1971), which, like *Tokyo Hotel*, distribute the incomplete sentences democratically among the *dramatis personae*. Even his late essay "The Misunderstandings and Fears of an Artist's Revolt" (1978) makes use of false starts and stops, assorted shards of discourse, and emphatically circles (or dances) around ideas rather than presenting them seamlessly and syllogistically. Indeed, the most striking characteristic of Williams's late writings, beginning with *Tokyo Hotel*, is, I believe, an insistent and radical fragmentation of discourse, character, and plot that is far more aggressive and overt than that which marks even the most surrealistic of his earlier plays. Many of these late works, such as *The Red Devil Battery Sign* (1976), virtually atomize dramatic action (even more radically than late Chekhov), substituting for linear plot the accumulation of laconic and often enigmatic scenes that lead (almost by chance) to a grandly surrealistic apotheosis. The indigent and rootless characters that populate these plays are often as mysterious as the action, deeply split or radically fragmented subjects for whom consistency is meaningless and the law of cause and effect, a delusion. Not surprisingly, the languages these characters speak do not cohere any more than their subjectivities do. Often, as in *The Red Devil Battery Sign*, they converse in hallucinatory fragments and apparent non sequiturs or, as in *The Demolition Downtown*, in polite clichés that are utterly incapable of compassing emotional distress or, as in *Clothes for a Summer Hotel*, find their attempts at communication drowned out by the sound of the wind.

In its status as the most distinctive emblem of Williams's late plays, the incomplete sentence is an almost grotesquely overdetermined phenomenon. Its meanings change insistently from scene to scene and play to play, now inviting one interpretation, now a very different one. Unquestionably, in most of its applications, it is symptomatic, as Bigsby suggests, of a deep disruption in personal relationships, an almost staggering inability either to communicate or to share any kind of emotional experience ("They seemed like— . . . Strangers, complete strangers, to me," a woman in *The Demolition Downtown* says of her own daughters).[75] It also exposes a radical split within the subject, who, like Mark in *Tokyo Hotel*, is no longer able to frame or articulate thoughts and feelings, let alone impart them to another. In Williams's works of the late 1960s, the sentence fragment is the mark of rebellion, the allegorization of the civil disturbances then being ignited on the streets of major U.S. cities and on so many college campuses. It is the sign of a political violence that consistently exceeds the grasp of the individual subject, who, as in *The Demolition Downtown*, can respond only by spouting slogans or muttering incoherencies. Because the completed sentence is, as Roland Barthes has observed, so profoundly "hierarchical," implying "subjections, subordinations, internal reactions," the incomplete sentence in Williams also betrays his sympathy with the rebels, by its overthrow of both hierarchy and subjection and its questioning of the mastery granted "someone who finishes his [sic] sentences."[76] At the same time, in all of these plays, the incomplete sentence seems to mark an intensification of the same ellipsis that betrays Baby Doll's desire, and thereby to bear the imprint of a longing so inadmissible and unfathomable that it can be represented only by an absence of discourse.

Yet Bigsby's remark that "the trauma" (of which the incomplete sentence is a mark) "seems to lie as much outside the text as within it" seems to me a crucial observation. To some extent, Williams's critics are correct in linking the use of this device to the medley of drugs and alcohol the playwright consumed during the late 1960s (in what Williams brazenly refers to as his "Stoned Age"), which ended with his breakdown in September 1969 and three-month internment in the psychiatric wing of a St. Louis hospital (or, in Williams's inimitable words, in the "Friggins Division of Barnacle Hospital in the city of St. Pollution").[77] Despite the temptation (particularly during the "Just Say No" era) to link linguistic degeneration to the use of psychoactive substances, I find it patently unsatisfactory to ascribe Williams's calculated and adept usage of a complex theatrical and literary design ("a new style of work" that is rigorously "controlled"; p. 21) solely to chemical dependency. Rather, I would like to propose that the fragmentation and incoherence that mark most of Williams's texts from the late 1960s until his death are also the result of a pivotal change in his public status: his coming out. Although his "official" emergence from the closet was not to take place until eight months after the opening of *Tokyo Hotel*, his homosexuality was neither the monumental secret that it had been during the 1940s and 1950s nor the subject of strict proscription on the commercial stage. In two prominent articles (that sparked considerable debate) in the *New York Times* in 1966, Stanley Kauffmann examined "homosexual drama and its disguises" and asserted, without naming names, that "three of the most successful American playwrights of the last twenty years are (reputed) homosexuals."[78] (It did not take much ingenuity on the part of readers to fill in the names of Tennessee Williams, William Inge, and Edward Albee.) In the same year, a British import with lesbian protagonists, Frank Marcus's *The Killing of Sister George*, was produced on Broadway. Two years later, Charles Dyer's *Staircase* was given a brief run in New York, and Mart Crowley's *The Boys in the Band* opened Off Broadway and played for more than two years.

Although all three of these plays are written in a comfortably realistic idiom and plainly (if grudgingly) perpetuate negative lesbian and gay stereotypes, they unquestionably represent a watershed in the American theater. For the first time, the love that dared not speak its name could colloquize—and at great length. With these productions, and with an increasing public awareness of and dialogue about "homosexual drama,"

Williams found himself suddenly outflanked. The language of "obscurity" and "indirection" on which he had relied for thirty years was abruptly outmoded. For the first time, Williams was able to speak openly in the theater about his sexual practices. Yet the theatrical language at his disposal was no more capable of articulating his subjectivity and his desire than the idiom of *Tea and Sympathy* had been almost twenty years before. Suddenly allowed to discourse about all that had been forbidden, Williams's much-praised "eloquence" ground to a halt. No longer able to rely on the outdated codes and obliquities he had used for so many years, he had to devise a way of canceling or scratching out his own ability to speak. He had to invent a new language of "obscurity or indirection," a new discourse of concealment and disclosure that simultaneously could bear the imprint, even in the revolutionary climate of the late 1960s, of the difficulty of articulating the most revolutionary of desires. Finally empowered to speak directly after so many years of (self-)censorship, he could only stutter, only hammer out a broken and lacerated speech.

The Magic of Misrepresentation

In the Bar of a Tokyo Hotel is a death-of-the-artist play with a difference. Like two of Ibsen's late dramas, *The Master Builder* and (especially) *When We Dead Awaken*, it focuses on the stormy relationship between an eminent artist during the last days of his life and his exploited yet resistant wife. With an almost clinical detachment and precision, it charts, in its brief compass, the passion, madness, and collapse of Mark Conley, a celebrated American painter, in an unnamed Tokyo hotel and the inability—or refusal—of his wife, Miriam, to intervene in his (self-) destruction. Although literally foregrounded, this marital dyad does not provide the principal itinerary of the play's plot. Rather, it is structurally subordinated to the fluid and seductively combative relationship between Miriam and the Japanese Barman, the two characters who remain on stage during the entire play. In part I, Williams sets the scene, "a small round table" in a hotel barroom "in a small area of intense light" (p. 3), and introduces the three principal characters: vigorous and promiscuous wife, inscrutably attractive and disputatious Barman, and monomaniacal husband. In contrast to Ibsen, Williams relegates the heroic artist to the margins of the drama and configures Miriam, whose desires are far more complex and volatile than those of her tormented husband, as the primary point for the reader or spectator's interpellation into the text. Steadfastly, he maintains the dramatic focus on Miriam's fiercely independent (sexual) desires and her apparent unconcern with

Mark's decay. In part II, one or several days later, as the flirtation continues between Miriam and the Barman, and Leonard (Mark's New York representative) arrives to take the ailing painter back to the States, the distracted artist suddenly staggers and dies. At the end of the play, after Mark's death, as the Barman looks on in silence, Miriam (who *"appears to see and feel nothing"*) explains that Mark expired because he "deliberately" stepped outside the protective "circle of light," an enterprise she carefully avoids (pp. 50, 53). Rather than credit her new independence, however, she seems to discover—like so many other American women before the rebirth of feminism in the 1960s—that even her (apparent) autonomy can be articulated only in relationship to her husband's desires and his presence. Finally unyoked from him, she finds that she has "no plans," has "nowhere to go" (p. 53), and even her relationship with the Barman remains unresolved, hanging in midair, like an incomplete sentence.

Like *When We Dead Awaken, Tokyo Hotel* is set (self-evidently) in a hotel, its aging artist and wife characterized as a pair of travelers. Unlike Ibsen's verdant lawn or commodious spa, however, Williams places his characters in an entirely artificial environment (one *not* described in any detail in the stage directions), a place of buying and selling, an Oriental(ist) bazaar in which a Barman is paid to serve his customers' various needs, a space of consumption in which the consciousness of the consumers is altered by the very beverages they imbibe. It is a space that pointedly undermines the distinction between public and private, a locale in which the most intimately personal and sexual exchanges take place (between Miriam and the three men) and yet in which a silent, strangely mythologized Hawaiian Lady wearing *"a dress printed with large flowers"* (p. 8) wanders in and out at whim, like the Fahrenkopfs in *The Night of the Iguana*, a sudden and jarring intrusion of an exotic decadence into an already exoticized locale. Unlike the bar in *Small Craft Warnings*, the *Tokyo Hotel* bar is not the site in which a preexistent community gathers, plays out its multifarious dramas, and departs, but the scene of chance encounters between natives and travelers, or between tourists marooned in a country and culture utterly unlike their own. Furthermore, Williams's East Asian watering hole has unmistakable historical resonances: a civilian outpost in America's most hotly contested imperialist arena, stretching from South Korea to South Vietnam. (Major military installations in Vietnam, Korea, Japan, Taiwan, and the Philippines were among the 2,300 bases that the United States maintained around the world in the late 1960s.) By 1968 the U.S. government had more than a million soldiers stationed abroad, more than half of them fighting an undeclared and disastrous war in Southeast

Asia that, by 1969, had killed or wounded at least 725,000 South Viet-namese civilians and displaced an estimated four million.[79]

Williams started work on *Tokyo Hotel* just months after the beginning of the Tet Offensive (31 January 1968) and finished it during a period in which intensive antiwar protests collided violently both with the military agenda and with the rhetorical flourish of then Vice President Hubert Humphrey, who had the audacity to proclaim to the U.S. embassy staff in Saigon: "This is our great adventure, and a wonderful one it is."[80] When, at the beginning of the play, Miriam explains to the Barman that "in America what we have is an explosion of vitality which is world-wide" (p. 3), her peculiar turn of phrase enacts the imperial project, the violent traversal of borders and cultures, the domination from afar, on which political, economic, and military intervention is founded. The "explosion" of which she speaks tellingly evokes the three million tons of bombs that had been dropped on Vietnam by October 1968 (nearly 50 percent more than the United States had discharged in Europe and Asia during all of World War II) far more concretely than any American "vitality."[81] It is the perfect metaphor for the imperialist adventure, being sited both "world-wide" and "in" America, wreaking havoc on indigenous cultures, undermining the distinction between inside and outside, and claiming the other as one's own.

In *Tokyo Hotel*, the primary agent of imperialism is not a soldier or businessman, but the most seemingly apolitical of men, a world-famous visual artist who has come to Tokyo and turned his hotel room into an impromptu studio in which he crawls about "naked over a huge nailed-down canvas," the paint from his "spray guns" penetrating the "several sheets of newspaper" placed carelessly beneath his work (pp. 17, 14). In his renunciation of the modest paintbrush and his monumental self-absorption, Mark unmistakably embodies the quintessential American postwar artist: the action painter, the abstract expressionist "gone through drip, fling, sopped, stained, saturated, scraped, ripped, cut, skeins of, mounds of heroically enduring color" (p. 41). He is hugely successful and widely respected, Leonard's "most lucrative property" (p. 11). Like a Jackson Pollock or a Willem de Kooning, Mark seems to epitomize the artist as self-styled hero, obsessively immersed in a deeply individualistic and solitary ordeal, the aesthetic analogue of the cowboy, who, at the opening of the play, is made to stand in for the entire American imperialist adventure: "Many cowboys exported?" the Barman asks Miriam (p. 3). Like the cowboy riding out heroically to vanquish and subdue the Native American, or the pilot of a B-52 who in 1969 was engaged in bombing Vietnam "back into the Stone Age" (to borrow General Curtis LeMay's picturesque turn of phrase), Mark disrupts the ongoing activity in the hotel in which he is a guest and devastates "the floor of the room" (p. 15) with his orgy of paint.[82] Tellingly, he even articulates his artistic project in explicitly imperialist terms, describing it as a process of "adventuring into a jungle country with wild men crouching in the bushes . . . with poison arrows" (p. 23), to conquer or to be destroyed.[83]

Williams's presentation of the American modernist *in extremis* is far more radically critical than Ibsen's portrait of the ornery and egotistical sculptor Rubek in *When We Dead Awaken*. Mark is wild and mad, a man "raging in the dark," suffering "a total collapse of the nervous system" (pp. 39, 11), and cutting a preposterously incongruous figure. In part I he enters with *"vivid paint stains on his unpressed suit"* (p. 13). In part II he turns up with a *"clean white suit"* that *"obviously . . . doesn't fit him"* (suggestive of the clean white canvasses on which he works), his newly shaven face covered *"with bloodied bits of tissue paper"* (p. 42). But these tokens of a veritable hachet job on the self are merely the physical insignias of his total immersion in a metaphysical crisis conceptualized entirely in spatial terms: "No separation between myself and" (p. 21). Exhilarated and aghast, incapable of maintaining a stable distance from his artwork, he is "terrified of the new canvasses" (p. 21). In his delirium, he has—or so he believes—broken through to the other side, penetrated the darkness, the Other, his mania encoded in a disruption of the relationship between subject and object (or between self and self) and in an almost total syntactic breakdown: "I've understood the *intimacy* that should, that has to exist between the, the—painter and the—I! It!" (p. 17). A nightmare version of the artist-as-hero (a General Westmoreland of the *atelier*), he attempts futilely to contain and master the Other, journeying into "jungle country" only to be slain by the invisible "poison arrows" he had hoped to elude. The deeply solipsistic nature and self-destructive power of this masculinist enterprise is not lost on Miriam, who scorns him and mockingly describes his new canvasses as "circus-colored mudpies" (p. 19). Much to her chagrin, her action-painter husband's heroic potency is expended not in an emotionally or sexually gratifying relationship with her, but narcissistically, in his rapport with his work, which is to say, with the image of his own egotism. In her eyes, his exploits with a spray gun are little more than a banal variation on the project of another artist in Leonard's stable who, less enrapt than Mark by the religiomystical dimension of art, simply "paints with his penis" (p. 40).

While clearly critiquing this cowboy of the canvas and offering a devastating assessment of the phallo-imperialist pretensions that underlie a variety of the high modernist project, Williams is careful not to allow Mark to overwhelm *In the Bar of a Tokyo Hotel*. Rather, he emphatically decenters this would-be protagonist by producing Miriam as the pivotal character, the one whose desires determine the shape of the play, the one who solicits the coy Barman, who makes intriguing "excursions at night," who carries around a suicide pill in a Regency snuffbox, a "woman burning," yet with "no inner resources of serenity" (pp. 4, 37). In many respects, she exemplifies the normative (female) desiring subject in Williams, the one whose sexual desires have become both inflamed and commodified, who at whim pursues either the cool Barman or a "desired stranger," who can consume a pagoda "at the most in five minutes" ("I look. I absorb. I go on."), and who prefers "to have someone living" for her than "dying" for her (pp. 37, 9, 45). Like so many Williams heroines, she is a woman torn between the abusive husband she can't abide and a dark stranger who fascinates her. Like Baby Doll or Lady Torrance, she is a character whose resistance to an oppressive status quo is figured in sexual terms, as a refusal to comply with the dictates of bourgeois morality or to abide in a state of monogamous self-sacrifice. (Harold Clurman, apparently far more beholden than Williams to the domestic revival's conjugal settlement, denounces her in his review as "a heartless woman," "a bitchy wife," and a "nymphomaniac who makes shameless passes at all available men.")[84]

Framing the play as emphatically as Miriam's sexual desires is her obsession with a "circle of light," the very domain of visibility in which the play's action takes place. At the beginning of part I, Miriam takes from her handbag a *"large mirror"* ("I like to see what is going on about me in the circle of light") with which she espies the Barman, and, in the process, presumably focuses the beams from the lighting instruments over the stage onto his person so that he, too, is surrounded by a circle of light (p. 4). After Mark's death, after characters have wandered in and out of the circle of light—only Miriam, seated at the table, remains at its center—she finally explains its significance in a flurry of incomplete sentences. For her, what is decisive about the circle of light is less its brightness than its edge, its limit.

> The circle is narrow. And protective. We have to stay inside.
>
> . . .
>
> This well-defined circle of light is our defense against. Outside of it there's dimness that increases to darkness: never my territory.
>
> . . .
>
> . . . The circle . . . attends us faithfully as long as our bodies don't betray us and our minds don't make excursions of a nature that's incompatible with the.
>
> . . .

> If I should say that the circle of light is the approving look of God it
> would be romantic which I refuse to be.
>
> . . .
>
> Mark . . . made the mistake of deliberately moving out of the.
>
> . . .
>
> He thought that he could create his own circle of light. (pp. 51–53)

According to Miriam, Mark was destroyed because of his (imperialist)
expedition outside the circle, across its border, into the dark "jungle
country" in which he perished. She, in contrast, is determined to stay
within the charmed circle and so recalls Blanche, who is horrified when
Mitch brutally tears the colored paper lantern off the light bulb (in an
act of rape that clearly anticipates Stanley's) and tells him: "I don't want
realism. I want magic. . . . I try to give that to people. I misrepresent
things to them" (p. 117). Like Blanche, Miriam wants to preserve the
power of fiction under the circle of light; she longs to supervise the
magic of misrepresentation. And in the last line of the play, she seems
to declare her determination to stay within the charmed circle: "I have
no plans. I have nowhere to go" (p. 53).

Yet, at the very end of *In the Bar of a Tokyo Hotel*, Williams re-
hearses the same kind of contradiction between (spoken) text and
(silent) stage direction that is so consequential in *Cat on a Hot Tin
Roof*. Miriam's final assertion is vehemently undercut by the action
described in the stage direction that immediately follows: *"With abrupt
violence, she wrenches the bracelets from her arms and flings them to
her feet"* (p. 53). Although Miriam's gesture, like so many in this
determinedly polyvalent play, resists a categorical interpretation, it can
be in part deciphered by appeal to one of her speeches to Leonard
near the beginning of part II. There she tells him of her own fear of
death and her knowledge that death

> would have to remove, wrench, tear!—the bracelets off my arms.
> Insignia of attraction still persisting. Then? In solitude, in a grove of
> afternoon trees or the bedroom of a hotel, the mortal pillbox. (p. 37)

In light of this pronouncement, Miriam's final gesture would seem to
signal her determination *not* to stay within the charmed circle but to
follow a pathway much like Mark's. Perhaps she, too, is slain by his
death and her gesture signals another extinction, that of her "attraction,"
her desire. Now that Mark is dead, she has "nowhere to go," except
(perhaps) to a "grove of afternoon trees" (so different from Mark's "jungle
country") or upstairs to her bedroom to take the contents of the "mortal
pillbox," as she (perhaps) irrevocably leaves the circle of light.

The suicidal import of Miriam's final gesture is not, however, totally unexpected. Although Miriam earlier insists that the "darkness" has "never been at all attractive" to her, her actions consistently belie this assertion (p. 51). Has she not, from the beginning of the play, been as fascinated by what lies outside the circle as her husband? Have not her midnight excursions, her sundry quests for the "desired stranger," her attempted seduction of the dusky Barman, been proof of her vigorous desire for what lies outside the circle (p. 37)? In this sense, she is explicitly presented, at a pivotal moment at the end of part I, as Mark's double (and this procedure handily distinguishes her from Baby Doll or Lady Torrance): "Are we two people, Mark, or are we . . . two sides of . . . one" (p. 30). Indeed, the problem of separation with which she wrestles— she several times declares her urgent need of "space" from him—seems to replicate the very crisis Mark faces in regard to his own work ("No separation between myself and"; pp. 39, 21). So, ironically, the dilemmas Miriam and Mark confront turn out to be symmetrical. Sexual appetite confronts artistic production across the divided self. Miriam's desires and fears echo Mark's. Her "desired stranger" mirrors his artwork: both are blank canvasses in which desire is simultaneously reflected and inscribed; both provide a mirror and an imaginary *telos* for a radically split subject that would remain in pieces even in a fantastic conjunction:

MIRIAM: An artist inhabiting the body of a compulsive—
MARK: Bitch! (p. 30)

This schizophrenic subject both longs for and is terrified of the dissolution of the polarities between subject and object and between one "side" and another "side of yourself" (p. 30), the twinned binary oppositions under whose aegis "misrepresentation"—and imperialism—reign. Neither the death of the artist-as-hero nor the ending of the play brings closure, and these differences remain unresolved, the rifts between subject and object and self and self protracted and monumentalized. Although Mark, in the end, is dissolved and swallowed up by his art (as surely as Mr. Krupper is in "Hard Candy"), Miriam makes an undecidable decision. She will live on/commit suicide; she will categorically remain within/leave the circle of light. Yet she little suspects that the theatrical apparatus, the very stage she inhabits, will precipitously foreclose her already impossible desire.

Miriam's final line and gesture are not, in fact, the end of the play. After she throws her bracelets to the floor, there remains one last sentence in the text: *"The stage darkens"* (p. 53). While this stage direction simply and conventionally describes the expected ending of the play, this fade-out must also, I believe, be read as a startling rejoinder to Miriam's final statement. While speaking her determination to remain within/leave the charmed circle of light, she is suddenly plunged into darkness. It is as if "the approving look of God" were abruptly withdrawn and, at the behest of the playwright (who, like Mitch in *Streetcar*, brutally destroys the illusion), Miriam, too, is forced to submit to death—the death of Mark, of desire, of "attraction," of the "circle of light," of "misrepresentation," of the theatrical performance itself. As a result, the action, like the desires that have driven it, is categorically suspended, and Miriam's final line and gesture hang in the darkness and the silence like Leonard's request, spoken earlier in part II, "Barman, I would like" (p. 38). (The implied parity between Miriam's petition and that of Leonard, the first male character in Williams who merely happens to be homosexual, is, I believe, more than coincidental: neither character is given a language in which to articulate desire fully.) Miriam's narrative, her sentence—in both the grammatical and juridical senses—is never finished. The darkness that descends, that closes off her circle of light, is the visual analogue of that silence that simultaneously consummates and cancels so many sentences, so many desires, in *In the Bar of a Tokyo Hotel* (and in Southest Asia beyond). "Barman, I would like." But the Barman never speaks again in the play, nor surrenders to the requests of Miriam or Leonard (except to help Leonard carry out Mark's body). He merely stands behind the bar in silence, a resistant subject, watching and waiting.

Revolution

WILLIAMS: All good art is essentially revolutionary, in the wide sense of revolutionary. "Revolutionary" is a misunderstood word.
WHITMORE: I'm trying to get a little more specific. If we're going to have a gay community that has a revolutionary thrust to it, should we be concentrating on agit-prop theatre—or propagandistic or street theater?
WILLIAMS: Well that is never art really, if it's strictly that. It has to be implicit; revolution is implicit; not explicit, but woven into the fabric of the work.

—*Gay Sunshine* Interview with Tennessee Williams (1976)

A Klee painting named "Angelus Novus" shows an angel looking as though he is about to move away from something he is fixedly contemplating. His eyes are staring, his mouth is open, his wings are spread. This is how one pictures the angel of history. His face is turned toward the past. Where we perceive a chain of events, he sees one single catastrophe which keeps piling wreckage upon wreckage and hurls it in front of his feet. The angel would like to stay, awaken the dead, and make whole what has been smashed. But a storm is blowing from Paradise; it has got caught in his wings with such violence that the angel can no longer close them. This storm irresistibly propels him into the future to which his back is turned, while the pile of debris before him grows skyward. This storm is what we call progress.

—Walter Benjamin, "Theses on the Philosophy of History" (1940)

Tennessee Williams's insistence on the revolutionary quality of his work, both in the 1976 *Gay Sunshine* interview and in his much ballyhooed *Memoirs* of the previous year, strikes most of Williams's critics as ingenuous. As I noted in chapter 2, Bigsby takes up the more or less widely accepted position that Williams's "radicalism" was not very "deep," and that his sympathies "with the outsider, the bohemian, the underclass" have nothing to do with any "revolutionary potential" these groups might represent.[85] Bigsby's unwillingness to credit Williams's radicalism results, I believe, from the extremely idiosyncratic nature of a politics that no more favors a traditional Marxist-Leninist notion of class struggle and proletarian revolution than the tenets of Cold War liberalism. But Williams's tacit repudiation of the principles and methods of the Old Left and the Popular Front does not in itself depoliticize his work. Rather than reject his declarations out of hand, I propose instead to conclude this book by taking Williams at his word and examining the revolution "implicit" in his work through an analysis of how *textual pleasure* is coupled with a process of *desubjectification*, an unbinding and deconstruction of the sovereign subject. By naming and delimiting this complicity, I hope to identify and credit a radical—and deeply utopian— potential that is so finely "woven into the fabric" of Williams's work that it too frequently passes undetected: a profligacy of words that disrupts traditional notions of narrative continuity and dramatic form, in company with its double, a profligacy of bodies that disrupts postwar moral and sexual norms. And finally, returning to consider the contours of material struggles, I will (re)situate both Williams's work and these two theoretical figurations in their historical contexts.

For a reader versed in the niceties of poststructuralist theory, the use of such terminology as *textual pleasure* and *desubjectification* will immediately evoke the names of Roland Barthes and Michel Foucault, two theorists whose late works are, I believe, indispensable for understanding the nearly contemporaneous late works of Tennessee Williams, an American writer with whom they had far more in common than their sexual orientation. I am not claiming that the homosexuality of Barthes and Foucault makes their work comparable to that of Williams, or of any other gay writer. I do believe, however, that their theoretical positions were in part determined by their sexuality, understood here not as an ahistorical essence (a universalized homosexuality), but as an ideology and a set of practices articulated in a contested cultural space, a site of social and political struggles, of diverse liberation movements, that were themselves the result of a worldwide economic realignment taking place during the 1960s. It is my intent not only to situate Williams's late work in relation to the various upheavals of the 1960s, to which they take up a complex and conflicted relationship, but also to ground the work of Barthes and Foucault in the geopolitics of a period that many have argued was the decisive moment for the development of late capitalism.

In "Periodizing the 60s," Fredric Jameson argues that the late 1960s (which, in fact, he identifies as the period from 1967 to about 1974) marked the end of a thirty- to fifty-year economic cycle that witnessed a fundamental transformation in the relationship between the First and Third Worlds. Jameson points out that although decolonization began in 1947 with the independence of India and gained extraordinary momentum following the independence of Ghana in 1957, it was followed almost immediately by the "neocolonialist transformation of the Third World," the (re)introduction of a colonial system even more insidiously violent than its predecessor. Under the auspices of the World Bank and the International Monetary Fund, "old-fashioned imperialist control" was superseded by a subtler "market penetration," a control of economic policy and the means of production by First World banks and government foreign aid programs. Jameson notes that this reconfiguration represents "a far more thoroughgoing form of penetration and colonization than the older colonial armies," and produces a Third World that is both more discreetly and more profoundly dependent on the First than it had been previously. The late 1960s were such crucial years because the last vestiges of precapitalism in the Third World were in the process of being wiped out just as the worldwide political and cultural superstructure was becoming mechanized, penetrated, and commodified by a culture industry (firmly under Western hegemony) and its propaganda arm, the media. Yet the Vietnam War and other colonial struggles testified that this new relation between base and superstructure, this "systemic restructuring," was by no means a peaceful or uncontested process. On the contrary, despite—or perhaps because of—this massive restructuring, the late 1960s was the last period to valorize the possibility of "a universal liberation," an "unbinding of social energies, a prodigious release of untheorized new forces," which Jameson sums up in a memorable phrase: "an immense and inflationary issuing of superstructural credit."[86]

In the First World, those who most took advantage of this sudden expansion of superstructural credit and borrowed most heavily from the system were unquestionably the New Left and its cultural adjunct, the so-called counterculture. In the United States, in particular, these political and social movements radically changed the face of the dominant social formation, ending the Cold War consensus and, in many respects, dislodging the ethos of the post-World War II settlement. And although the New Left as a political force was largely dissipated by the mid-1970s, its several cultural descendants—in particular the women's movement and the gay and lesbian liberation movements—continue to exert a powerful force on the American cultural scene. Despite the fact that Tennessee Williams was never actively involved in either the New Left or the gay liberation movement, his late work does provide, I believe, a remarkably sensitive gauge to the emergence of a new political culture far more compatible with his aesthetic, social, and sexual norms than the Cold War consensus. Williams's own declaration, meanwhile, in a 1966 interview, "I love what the young people of today are doing," barely hints at the degree to which *In the Bar of a Tokyo Hotel*, *The Demolition Downtown*, and *Moise and the World of Reason* were affected by a revolution whose goals and strategies must be examined in detail, not only because it is almost synonymous with the "revolution" that is so subtly "woven into the fabric" of Williams's late work, but also because it irrevocably changed the modality of progressive politics, both in the United States and worldwide.[87]

The New Left

During the 1960s, the New Left developed in the United States as an almost extravagantly plural and heterogeneous venture, composed of disparate social and political groups with diverse and often contradictory tactics and goals. As most historians recognize, the New Left had its roots squarely in the civil rights movement's crusade for racial equality and, at least until 1964, its nonviolent strategies: community activism, sit-ins, and demonstrations. In the early 1960s, a generation of university students, both black and white, placed their faith in the democratic system and, following the lead of the Student Non-Violent Coordinating Committee (SNCC), participated in the civil rights struggle as Freedom Riders and as workers in voter registration drives. When, in 1962, the Students for a Democratic Society (SDS), the most conspicuous and important political movement of the decade, issued its major document, the Port Huron Statement, it clearly drew on the principles and methods that had propelled SNCC. More than any other text, the Port Huron Statement set the agenda for the New Left, putting its emphasis, in Stanley Aronowitz's estimation, on *process* and signaling "an almost religious return to *experience* and a converse retreat from the abstractions of the red politics of yesterday."[88] Inspired by "the Southern struggle against racial bigotry," and reacting as much against traditional Marxist categories and rhetoric as against the Cold War and "the idolatrous worship of things by man," the Port Huron Statement called for "a participatory democracy" based on equality, nonviolence, and community.[89] It attempted to break decisively with the legacy of American radicalism and, indeed, as Paul Buhle points out, its principles were hardly radical at all "by the standards of the Old Left":

> It spoke for human relationships over the fragmentation blessed by the various existing social systems; it called for more freedom for the young (specifically on campus); it condemned the Cold War restriction of political debate even as it condemned existing Communism; and it urged a democratic, peaceful approach to world problems.[90]

The humanistic rhetoric and somewhat naive idealism of the Port Huron Statement did not, however, long dominate SDS. The increasing deployment of American troops and materiel in Southeast Asia came to preoccupy SDS and other leftist organizations (such as the Berkeley Free Speech Movement) more and more, and by 1965, the New Left coalesced as a loose confederation of political and social movements focused by their radical opposition to the Vietnam War. The escalation of hostilities in Vietnam profoundly changed the nature of SDS, radicalizing, in Buhle's words, "the student revolt at a dizzying rate while simultaneously investing it with profound public responsibilities for organizing opposition to the war."[91] Increasingly, SDS turned its attention to global concerns, transforming universities into centers of resistance to both the Vietnam War and the draft and provoking increasingly militant confrontations with university and civil authorities. At the same time, the civil rights struggle became more and more dominated by black power radicals who had little patience for the nonviolent tactics of the early 1960s. On both fronts, effecting meaningful political and economic change within the constitutional system began to seem impossible. During the summer of 1967, the impoverished, largely black ghettos of many major American cities erupted in riots. The most devastating, in Detroit, left forty-three persons dead and 7,200 arrested. H. Rap Brown, the new chairman of a transformed SNCC, described the riots as a "dress rehearsal for revolution."[92] Stokely Carmichael, meanwhile, recognizing the structural impediments to racial equality, called for a radical redistribution of economic and political power:

> Ultimately, the economic foundations of this country must be shaken if black people are to control their lives. The colonies of the United States—and this includes the black ghettoes within its borders, north

and south—must be liberated. For a century, this nation has been like an octopus of exploitation, its tentacles stretching from Mississippi and Harlem to South America, the Middle East, southern Africa, and Vietnam.[93]

During the mid-1960s, the black power movement and SDS were allied, in rhetoric at least, by their attention to American imperialism worldwide and by their acknowledgment that only revolutionary change could shake the "economic foundations" and "liberate" the oppressed. As Jameson notes, the New Left must be understood as a part of "the great movement of decolonization" under way during the 1960s. He points out that the "First World 60s owed much to Third-Worldism in terms of politico-cultural models, as in a symbolic Maoism, and, moreover, found its mission in resistance to wars aimed precisely at stemming the new revolutionary forces in the Third World."[94]

By 1969, however, the fragile coalition that had made up the New Left had come apart. The Black Panthers (founded in 1966) committed themselves to anticapitalist rebellion, combining, in Todd Gitlin's words, "the anarchist impulse" with a "Third World mystique, the aura of violence, and the thrust for revolutionary efficiency."[95] Despite (or perhaps because of) the Panthers' success in mobilizing black urban communities, their relationship with white radicals was uneasy and conflicted. The latter, meanwhile, had splintered into an array of often antagonistic groups, including the neo-Maoist Progressive Labor Party, the Revolutionary Youth Movement, the Yippies (or the Youth International Party), groups devoted to the women's liberation movement, the Gay Liberation Front, and the Weathermen. As James Weinstein points out, each of these factions conceived of itself as "the one true or key revolutionary agent," and thereby rejected both the valorization of local struggles and the broad-based consensus ("participatory democracy") that had been founding principles of the New Left.[96] Despite the continuation of the Vietnam War and of severe racial and economic oppression at home, the New Left had, in Buhle's words, "come to a crashing halt" by 1971, ending what had been the only genuinely popular revolutionary political movement in the United States since the Great Depression.[97]

Despite its failure to effect radical social and economic change, the polyglot New Left transformed both American progressive politics and the cultural dominant. Perhaps its most important contribution—and one that undoubtedly led to its decline and disintegration—was its rejection of a politics of class struggle and its embrace, in Jameson's words, of "new 'subjects of history' of a nonclass type (blacks, students, Third World peoples)."[98] Poverty, rediscovered by SDS in the early 1960s, came to supersede questions of class, and for the duration of the decade, an alliance between the impoverished urban and rural classes, the student activists and blue-collar workers, never materialized. On the contrary, the white working class remained, for the most part, among the most vehement opponents of both SDS and the black power movement. Buhle notes the contradictory implications of the New Left's eschewal of class politics, observing that the lack of "analytical (or ideological) roots in socialized labor, and in racial and ethnic community life" significantly attenuated the efficacy of the New Left's program, but, at the same time, unleashed "a powerful utopianism based, like the Civil Rights movement, on the American radical tradition" that stretched from Thoreau to Debs to W. E. B. Du Bois. Faced with the truculence of legislators and judges, the young revolutionaries promoted a politics of protest, intervention, and direct action; faced with the bureaucratic hierarchy, they advocated the dismantlement of "all authority structures in a society of anarchic freedom and abundance"; faced with the dominion of the nuclear family and the sober norms that had dominated postwar America, they offered cultural revolution.[99]

Despite its eminence during the 1960s, the New Left cannot be understood without reference to the social movement with which it enjoyed a deeply ambiguous and conflicted relationship: the counterculture. Inspired, in part, by the "wild ones" of the 1950s, by the growing popularity of folk music, rock and roll, and marijuana, by the free-form life-styles of the Beats, with their devotion to "principled poverty" and their "taste for sexual libertinism," a youth culture began to solidify in the early 1960s.[100] A historically contradictory phenomenon, this new adversarial culture represented a continuation and extension of the modernist avant-garde at the same time that it signaled the deterioration of the binary opposition between high and mass culture. As a result, it can be seen to mark both the limit and the end of the modernist insurgence. By 1966, as (hetero)sexual liberation surged in the wake of widespread distribution of "the pill," as LSD became the drug of choice, as Dylan went electric, and the Beatles and the Jefferson Airplane supplanted Peter, Paul and Mary and the Beach Boys, the counterculture blossomed in both San Francisco and New York's East Village and quickly spread to other major cities and university towns, supported by the triple pillar of sex, drugs, and rock and roll. Dedicated to a rejection of political organizations (whether on the right or the left) and to the creation of a new, ostensibly free subject in a new, ostensibly loving society—in short, to a revolution in consciousness—the counterculture carved out alternative communal spaces and produced an art and culture that was variously derisive of bourgeois norms, deeply utopian, and solemnly mystical. Ironically, however, at least through the mid 1960s, the cultural nationalism of American youth continued to enforce the separation of art from politics that had characterized the postwar settlement. Until the end of the decade, most of the counterculture carefully maintained its distance from the New Left, which it believed to be as enrapt in an illusory and dangerous realm as the cultural dominant (in the words of drug guru Timothy Leary: "Don't vote. Don't politic. Don't petition. You can't do *anything* about America politically.")[101] Rather than working toward political change, many, impelled by a deep nostalgia for a mythologized preindustrial society, urged retirement to a self-contained, romantic, agrarian world.

By 1967, however, when the Summer of Love coincided with a summer of race riots and a newly intensified wave of antiwar protests, the New Left and the counterculture began making tentative moves toward each other, despite their fundamental dissimilarities. The one, as Gitlin explains, was dedicated "with discipline, organization, commitment to results *out there*," while the other was devoted to the "idea of living life to the fullest, *right here*, for oneself, or for the part of the universe embodied in oneself, or for the community of the enlightened who were capable of loving one another."[102] The one was committed to the Marxian notion that material circumstances produce consciousness, while the other espoused the belief in a nearly autonomous consciousness that, if "expanded" (whether by sex, drugs, rock and roll, or mystical enlightenment) could change the world. Despite these irreducible differences, the late 1960s frequently bore witness to an improvised, albeit uneasy, alliance of the antiwar Left and the counterculture that was pledged to revolutionary social and cultural change.

Among radical groups, the anarchic Yippies seemed most closely to embody this impossible union, in their attempt at instituting a carnivalesque politics and fomenting a "revolutionary action-theater."[103] And in many respects, this "theater" was a crucial event for the antiwar Left—a "model" of total revolution, a hybrid of radical politics and aesthetics that made (and continues to make) the more orthodox Left a bit uneasy. This hybrid plainly epitomizes the Althusserian reconceptualization of politics and culture during the 1960s that authorized the ideological "superstructure" to be pried (almost) loose from the economic "base." Jameson sees this reconceptualization as a pivotal theoretical shift and identifies it with Althusser's notion of the "'semi-autonomy' of the levels of social life" that would license "a repudiation of old-fashioned class and party politics of a 'totalizing' kind." In so reconfiguring the association between politics and culture, the Yippies, like the Black Panthers, coincidentally aligned themselves with an American brand of

Maoism ("richest of all the great new ideologies of the '60s"), in which "the new binary opposite to the term 'bourgeois' [is] no longer . . . 'proletarian' but rather 'revolutionary,' and the new qualifications for political judgements" are made "in terms of personal life."[104] Jerry Rubin neatly summarized this populist cultural revolution in his equation, "Our lifestyle—acid, long hair, rock music, sex—is the revolution."[105] By so undermining the opposition between politics and life-style, between public and private revolution, the Yippies and their fellow travelers in the politicized counterculture helped, in Jameson's view, to open "a whole new political space, a space . . . articulated by the slogan 'the personal is the political,'" which would, during the 1970s, be colonized most conspicuously by the women's liberation movement and the Gay Liberation Front, and, in the process, would transform American culture.[106]

One of the most contentious and contradictory dimensions of the politicized counterculture was its instigation of sexual revolution. In his history/memoir, *The Sixties*, Gitlin provides a complex portrait of this revolution, emphasizing the importance of what he calls a "transpersonal libido" operating in SDS, a "circle of energy" that was "intellectual and moral, political and sexual at once."[107] As a generation of activists and hippies rebelled against the mores of their parents' generation, sexual liberation surged, becoming part of the same "over-arching transcending" rebellion: "Orgasm was the permanent revolution, . . . or was it that The Revolution was orgasm writ large?"[108] Yet, ironically, sexual liberation turned out in certain ways to be as conservative as the sexual ethos of the domestic revival. *The Sixties* testifies to the fact that radical politics and masculinity were as inseparable in the student movement as they had been in the Old Left. SDS was steeped in patriarchy and machismo. Its primary actors were almost exclusively heterosexual men, cowboys of the New Left, among whom were passed sexual appurtenances—women—who remained strictly subordinate to the male activists and constituted the "cement" that held SDS together. Gitlin quotes approvingly one woman's only "half-ironic" quip of 1962, that "the movement hangs together on the head of a penis," and in retrospect concedes "the homoerotic implication of male bonding" among the student activists that at the time was altogether inadmissible.[109] Not only were women often disadvantaged by being stripped of "the defenses available in bourgeois social relations," but most gay men and lesbians found it as necessary to conceal their homosexuality from their comrades-in-arms as from their families.[110] In a 1969 article in the *Berkeley Tribe*, Konstantin Berlandt vividly documents the homophobia of the National Students Association, as emblematized by one woman delegate who, although "pretty radical" in most areas, confessed to Berlandt, "I saw one man with his arm around another's leg and I freaked."[111]

The counterculture was, in many ways, as deeply misogynist and homophobic as the New Left. In most circles, "free love" meant strictly free heterosexual love, and the models of gender remained, for the most part, as rigorously normative as they had been during the 1950s. The masculine ideal of a wise and imperturbably autocratic guru (another omniscient Western subject in Eastern drag) was as much a permutation of the authoritarian father of the domestic revival as the feminine ideal, the bounteous Earth Mother (another intermediary between "nature" and "culture"), was of the organized, nurturing housewife.[112] By 1966, the women's liberation movement was challenging this polarization of genders and all that it sanctioned, calling, in Kate Millett's words, for "the attainment of the female sex to freedom and full human status," for a "re-examination of traits categorized into 'masculine' and 'feminine,'" and for an end of "the patriarchal proprietary family," sexual violence, and "enforced perverse heterosexuality."[113] The Gay Liberation Front (GLF) and the Gay Activist Alliance were founded in 1969 and 1970, respectively, both to extend and to critique a cultural revolution that was in many ways as misogynistic and homophobic as the culture against which it rebelled.

The gay and lesbian liberation movement that erupted after Stonewall and spread, in John D'Emilio's estimation, with "amazing rapidity" both within the United States and to Western Europe, was very clearly an outgrowth of both the New Left and the counterculture.[114] Like SDS, it comprised a social group that had hitherto not exercised its prerogative as a class; like the Black Panthers, it promoted cultural nationalism and pride ("Gay Is Good" is obviously a transformation of "Black Is Beautiful"); like the youth culture, it advocated a revolution in consciousness and the free expression of sexuality; like the Yippies, it emphasized lifestyle and self-representation through "revolutionary action-theater"; and like the women's movement, it carefully attended to the interconnection of economic, social, and political subjugation:

> We are a revolutionary group of men and women formed with the realization that complete sexual liberation for all people cannot come about unless existing social institutions are abolished. We reject society's attempt to impose sexual roles and definitions of our nature. . . . We are creating new social forms and relations . . . based upon brotherhood, cooperation, human love, and uninhibited sexuality. Babylon has forced us to commit ourselves to one thing—revolution![115]

Despite the fact that the GLF collapsed in 1971 and no more halted sexual oppression than SDS did American imperialism, the aggressive rhetoric and militant program of this declaration is indicative of the GLF's success in radically changing the complexion of gay and lesbian politics. Bolstered by the other liberation movements of the period, it made a decisive break with the cautious, reformist practices of the Mattachine Society and dedicated itself to full-scale revolution.

A 1973 collection of essays, poems, and cartoons, *The Gay Liberation Book*, testifies to the revolutionary fervor and practices the GLF left in its wake. Although this volume is a diverse and, at times, contradictory assortment of texts, its agenda is clearly cultural revolution. In the preface, the editors emphasize the importance of process ("gay liberation is ever changing, . . . ever growing"), of community, and of the status of the homosexual liberation movement as merely one part of a "total human liberation."[116] In his introduction, Dennis Altman sets forth a neo-Maoist program that attests to the dual focus of GLF, "attack[ing] social oppression while also altering the consciousness of gay people." He acknowledges "a whole generation which has ceased to accept . . . monogamous one-to-one relationships" and insists that gay liberation "means a release of genuine eroticism."[117] Elsewhere in the volume, writers attack sexism, the construction of fixed and repressive gender roles, the nuclear family, militarism, and other oppressive formations. Perhaps the most provocative essay, however, is one by Huey Newton, then supreme commander of the Black Panther Party, in which he cautiously criticizes homophobia among the Panthers and points out that both the Women's Liberation Front and the GLF are "potential allies" of the Panthers, reluctantly (and very progressively!) conceding that "maybe a homosexual could be the most revolutionary" of subjects.[118] Despite Newton's reservations, the enlistment of the support of the most prominent black revolutionary of the time is quite congruent with *The Gay Liberation Book*'s overall project. In its emphasis on the development of a gay "class consciousness," on full sexual liberation, on the "zap" as guerrilla operation (both a "political theater for educating the gay masses" and a form of militant resistance), and on the formation of gay and lesbian communes, it bears witness to a profoundly utopian spirit that underlies the notion of cultural revolution in the late 1960s and early 1970s.[119]

An Erotics of Writing

Among Tennessee Williams's late works, none seems closer to the new social, political, and sexual culture than his 1975 novel, *Moise and the World of Reason*, in many ways the fictional counterpart to the *Memoirs*, published later that same year. It is set in a Greenwich Village obviously transformed by gay liberation, in a subculture of sexual and artistic adventurers who bear more than a passing likeness to the circle surrounding Andy Warhol, with which Williams had become acquainted in 1972 (Candy Darling was then appearing in *Small Craft Warnings* at the Truck and Warehouse Theatre). As Edward Sklepowich points out, *Moise* is one of Williams's first works that takes homosexuality simply as a given.[120] (At the same time, Williams carefully foregrounds contemporary attitudes by featuring, at a pivotal moment in the novel, a scene of attempted—and resisted—"fag bashing" by two sadistic policemen.) The novel's narrator is a thirty-year-old southerner, a "distinguished failed writer" with an immoderate passion for "the fractured sentence."[121] Much like the Tennessee Williams of the 1970s interviews, he is "committed" to "the Gay Libs" and "all conceivable libs this side of My Lai and of child-molesters in public" (p. 139). Living with his new lover, Charlie, in an abandoned warehouse near the docks on West Eleventh Street, he is a self-proclaimed "sensualist" whose "undoing" as a writer is "an excess of sentiment" (pp. 11, 14). The plot, which takes place over a twenty-four-hour period, is organized around the very principle the warehouse embodies: abandonment. It is composed of three desertions: Charlie's, of the narrator for a young poet; the narrator's, of a "garrulous old" playwright with one clouded eye (who longs to seduce him), whose latest play is being performed at the Truck and Warehouse Theatre (and who is obviously a portrait of Williams); and that of Moise, a woman painter "committed to a spirit of revolution but waiting for God and time," who has decided to abandon "the world of reason" for more congenial and mystical climes (pp. 45, 188). (Although as fanatical as Mark in *Tokyo Hotel*, Moise is a very different species of artist, a visionary with a taste for anal intercourse and an aversion to the heroic *machismo* of the tortured abstract expressionist.) Only in the last three pages of the novel is this ubiquitous movement toward retirement countered by a precipitous reversal, a *deus ex machina*, in which the narrator suddenly discovers his next love, a young, blond photographer whose eyes contain "a very blue and open declaration of love" (p. 188).

Yet this résumé of the novel's principal actions does not describe its real subject, which is the act of writing. From the very beginning, the narrator stubbornly foregrounds his own activity: stringing words, events, and characters together by writing obsessively on shirt cardboards, on the back of rejection slips from countless literary magazines, and, most important, in his Blue Jay, a kind of "grade-school notebook which is approaching extinction like certain species of real birds" (p. 55). The narrative he weaves is as discontinuous as the

surfaces on which he writes, a metanarrative composed of descriptions
of the ongoing activity of writing; of encounters with Charlie, Moise,
and the "has-been playwright"; and of the narrator's memories of his
family, his Alabama hometown, and, most crucially, his one true love,
Lance, "the living nigger on ice" (yet another dusky and phallic object
of desire), who one day, on a drug overdose, skated "into the silent ice
world forever" (pp. 180, 13, 145).

Like Williams's *Memoirs*, *Moise* runs the present against the past,
writing against remembering. Using the vexatious "here and now" as a
framework, it repeatedly calls up a more idyllic "then," emphasizing the
difference between them, in form as well as content. The past is figured
in more or less coherent and self-contained stories and anecdotes; it
comes whole, precious, understood, filled with (mostly satisfied) desires.
The present, by way of contrast, is enunciated in fragments, false starts,
incomplete sentences, and metanarrative intrusions that document the
skittishness of creative energies (both those of the narrator and the
enigmatic Moise), skating back and forth between unfulfilled wishes and
fantasies. In the act of writing, the narrator self-consciously and self-
referentially articulates his sexual desires by figuring the present not as
a plenitude but as an always already depleted instant, as his pencil jumps
from rejection slip, to cardboard, to Blue Jay. Intensifying the sense of
the inexpressibility of desire that reaches back to the ellipsis in *Baby
Doll* and the emblematic incomplete sentence, "Barman, I would like,"
in *Tokyo Hotel*, the narrator's discursive stuttering becomes the very
figure of desire in Williams's late work. Unlike *Tokyo Hotel*, which uses
the fractured sentence (and an inconclusive closure) to commemorate the
undecidability, the open-endedness of desire, the narrator of *Moise* painstakingly dedicates all his fragments to the service of completion, fru-
ition, in the hope of recuperating an unbroken sentence or narrative, of
filling the final notebook. But until the last three deeply utopian pages,
in which the narrator completes the last Blue Jay with the (magical)
discovery of his next lover, he writes the present only to exhaust it, to
produce an inveterate lack, a restless state of desire. His imagination
and his pencil bound from Lance to Charlie, and from writing surface
to writing surface, and in so doing confirm one of the most persistent
and compelling linkages in Williams's work: the association of writing
with lovemaking.

In its figuration of desire, in its dual focus on texts and bodies, on
the defloration of Blue Jay and Lance, *Moise* posits, more explicitly than
any other Williams work, the symmetry of writing and sexuality, pencil
and penis, page and anus. Just as, with the help of "a bit of petroleum
jelly," the narrator takes Lance's "cherry," so does he ensure, by making

his written mark, that "the Blue Jay has been fucked by the pencil and is no longer bare beauty" (pp. 67, 84). Furthermore, the two activities are constantly intertwined in the narrator's (literally) feverishly erotic imagination, in the circularity of his reasoning that decrees that "the purest delight of living which is companionship" will be discovered "while doing that thing which you care about even more than love-making," writing (p. 72). Moreover, this symmetry between sexuality, or, more properly, homosexuality, and writing is an almost constant feature in Williams's work. It is the central equation in his luminous short story, "One Arm" (1945), in which the "torrent of letters" that Oliver receives from former sexual partners performs a "resurrection" of this condemned and mutilated man, waiting on death row, restoring his life and his (at least "autoerotic") desire. Transfigured by the love letters, Oliver goes to the electric chair carrying them like a fetish object, "as a child takes a doll," placing them, before the *coup mortal*, "in the fork of his thighs."[122] This crucial equivalency also evokes one of the most extraordinary of Williams's own letters, written some thirty years before *Moise*:

> There are only two times in this world when I am happy and selfless and pure. One is when I jack off on paper and the other is when I empty all the fretfulness of desire on a young male body.[123]

In its mutual configuration of sexuality and textuality, *Moise*, more clearly than any other of Williams's works, announces an erotics of writing and reading. Indeed, despite (or perhaps because of) the darkness of the novel's content, the almost interminable twenty-four-hour expanse of time and desire in which the action occurs, it seems an exemplary text of pleasure according to the (anti-)schematic established by Roland Barthes in one of the founding works of poststructuralism, *The Pleasure of the Text*, published in 1973 (just two years before *Moise*). In this slim, seductive volume, this exquisitely detailed guide to the delights of read-ing, Barthes simultaneously installs and undermines a distinction between textual pleasure (*plaisir*) and textual bliss (*jouissance*, which also means "orgasm"), positing the former, in clearly Adornian terms, as a char-acteristic of "a mass culture" and the latter as a form of "mandarin *praxis*."[124] Striking out against what he perceives as a deeply ascetic streak "on the left," Barthes champions a pleasure—or, sometimes, bliss— of the text that will replace the stolid bourgeois reader with a new ecstatic and polyglot reader who "abolishes within himself all barriers, all classes, all exclusions, . . . mixes every language, . . . silently accepts every charge of illogicality, of incongruity, . . . endures contradiction without shame" (p. 3). According to Barthes, this reader's pleasure does not proceed from a stable empathic investment in a stable text. Rather, it is always constructed as an overflow of the text: a "perversion" that "exceeds any (social) function and any (structural) functioning" and bears a closer relationship to "shock, disturbance, even loss" than to "euphoria, fulfillment, comfort" (pp. 52, 19).

In its emotional profligacy, rhetorical excess, and vibrant homoeroticism, *Moise and the World of Reason* can well serve as a paradigmatic text of pleasure. As Barthes points out, however, this latter is very different from "the text that recounts pleasures," and the erotic descriptions in *Moise* account, I believe, only for a small portion of this text's ability (to quote its narrator) "to excite with words" (p. 98). Rather, I find that the novel's juxtaposition of discrete discursive blocks, its mixing of anecdote and desire, its atomization of narrative, mark it most clearly as a text of bliss. And in this sense, it is surprisingly reminiscent of one of Williams's earliest and most surrealistic short stories, "Sand" (1936), a portrait of an old woman and her ailing spouse. In one section, as the woman remembers a day at the seashore with her husband from many years before, her memories (and the words that produce them) graphically reconfigure their aged bodies as glorious, fetishistic objects:

> She hears the sound of waves coming in and her eyes close slowly
> against the glitter of the sun. Prismatic colors flash through her tangled
> lashes. She hears his voice slow and caressing as the grains of trickling
> sand. Rose. Rose. Rose. Rose. He is trying to make her smile. But she
> will not smile. She keeps her lips drawn tightly together. The sand
> trickles slowly. Then more swiftly. Then slower. It is warm, so very
> warm against her bare skin. In spite of herself her lips begin to curl up
> at the corners. She laughs out loud. The earth rises and sways beneath
> her. Her body grows large. Immense. The moment is timeless.[125]

In its figuration of an ecstatic and "timeless" moment, this passage atomizes language, colors, bodies, words, an identity (a name) like grains of sand, or like the silent, dismembering stage directions of *Cat on a Hot Tin Roof*. It is a quintessential Barthesian text of pleasure, "reveal[ing] itself in the form of a body, split into fetish objects, into erotic sites" (p. 56). This correspondence, moreover, between these two texts of pleasure, between "Sand" and *Cat*, between a narrative and a set of stage directions that pulverize bodies, places them in signal opposition to Williams's use of the more coherent discourse of dramatic dialogue and provides an insight into what is perhaps the fundamental irony of Tennessee Williams's work. Beginning with his earliest writings, America's preeminent playwright has conceived the theater, and the drama that fills it, as a site of schism, of division, of falling away from utopia toward abjection and isolation, in opposition to diegetic prose, and to the rapturous act of writing of which it is the consequence and to which it provides almost unmediated access. And while this observation undeniably respects the widely held recognition that Williams's theater is primarily a tragic one, in contradistinction to his narrative fiction, which is far more inclined to a gaily comic mode, I am less concerned with distinguishing thematically or tonally between the two genres than between two radically different, yet contingent, notions of textuality, reading, and desire that they embody.

Perhaps the clearest presentation of the distinction between these two modes is found not in Williams's writing for the theater but in his narrative fiction. In what is surely his most notorious short story, "Desire and the Black Masseur," Williams recounts the chronicle of the timid Anthony Burns and his "instinct" for "things that swallowed him up," an instinct that leads finally to his death, dismemberment, and ingestion by his powerful black masseur/lover/destroyer. In the very first paragraph, Williams sets up his sadomasochistic story by describing Burns's single consuming appetite, his passion for movies. Watching a film, Burns would be soothed and relieved of all anxieties, but not, strangely, by being absorbed in the film's narrative, in what the characters "said or did." Burns "didn't follow the story on the screen but watched the figures . . . who warmed him as if they were cuddled right next to him in the dark picture house."[126] Thirty years later, Williams reiterates this pattern in *Moise*, in the narrator's remembrance that, as a youth at the movies, he "had been so entranced" by Gary Cooper's face on the screen that he'd "barely followed the story" (p. 109).

In both instances, Williams distinguishes between two different modes of address or interpellation. The first calls upon a spectator to be attentive to what characters "said or did," to plot, narrative continuity, and anecdote, to the larger structures of desire and meaning that impel Williams's theater. Like classic narrative cinema, the "cowboy pictures" showing at the Joy Rio, or the Gary Cooper movie referred to in *Moise* (or like *Baby Doll*, for that matter), it depends upon the patient unfolding of a conventionally linear (and sometimes melodramatic) narrative that articulates relatively orthodox and satisfiable longings on the part of a primary desiring subject within the action. The second mode of address, which is much more likely to be evoked through diegetic prose, stage directions, or visual images, is far more unstable and perilous. It is the force that pulverizes plot by drawing the reader or spectator's attention to a detail, an image, a metaphor, or a charged moment of silence. These disruptions, or moments of fascination that suspend time, produce a radically discontinuous narrative and simultaneously articulate inchoate and unspeakable desires that (as in the case of Anthony Burns) may be positively hazardous to the safety and integrity of the desiring subject of the narrative and to the reader who, enjoying danger, allows him- or herself to be interpellated into the text, "absorbed," like the hapless Burns, "like a particle of food dissolving in a big hot mouth."[127] (Although all of Williams's works rely on this second mode of address, the film *The Fugitive Kind*, 1960, based on *Orpheus Descending* and directed by Sidney Lumet, provides particularly vivid examples of the fiercely charged yet amazingly quiet interactions that simultaneously suspend and further the action, in its scenes between Val [Marlon Brando] and Lady, Carol, and Vee [played by three of Williams's favorite actors: Anna Magnani, Joanne Woodward, and Maureen Stapleton].)

For the sake of convenience, the first mode of address could be labeled "heterosexual," because of both its cultural orthodoxy and the way that it (en)genders erotic relationships. The operative mode of reading it encourages is, to borrow Susan Sontag's distinction again, a "straight" one. The second mode could be labeled "homosexual," not because all (or sometimes any) of the longings represented are same-sex desires, but because, in their penchant for transgression, for the suspension of norms, they function as a structural equivalent to homosexual desire. The second invites a "camp" mode of reading, which is to say, an oblique, supplementary, and slightly queer interpellation. The former mode hails the reader in the language (according to postwar standards) most appropriate to "opposite" sexes. The latter radically undermines the mobilization of these same rigorously gendered identifications. Taking up a metonymic, overlapping relationship with each other—rather than a polar opposition—the two modes of address coexist simultaneously in every Williams work. (If, while patronizing one, you stop and squint, or drift off for a moment, you may find yourself suddenly attending to the other.) And although one of the two modes usually dominates a given text, it is precisely the undecidability of the "heterosexual" and the "homosexual," the linear and the fragmentary, the real and surreal, the straight and the camp, the normative and the polymorphous, that is a constant source of structural and semantic tension and, yes, intense textual pleasure.[128] (If I privilege the erotics of the Williams text, the "homosexual" mode of address and the text of bliss to which it gives rise, it is because this mode has been systematically marginalized by those critics who would claim him as a safely canonical writer and those producers and directors who consider his plays respectable bourgeois entertainment.)

A stress on the "homosexual" mode of address in Williams provides access to what is, I believe, the most radical aspect of the Williams text: its surrealistic subversion of the liberal humanist subject, its tendency to dissolve both the imaginary integrity of the subjectivities in its midst

and those of the readers and spectators who are (knowingly or inadvertently) hailed into this text of bliss. Barthes again acts as a guide,
delighting, in his poststructuralist rapture, in a process that his terminology explicitly links to the self-annihilating thrill of orgasm (*jouissance*). As a (former) leftist, he notes responsibly that, under the aegis
of bliss, the search for "the materialist subject" can proceed by criticizing
the "illusions" of "the imaginary subject," acknowledging its "dizzying
schism," or by generalizing it. Yet, simultaneously, Barthes is careful to
distance this "materialist subject" from anything that smacks of traditional leftist rhetoric. He emphasizes that while pleasure is "not personal,"
it is still profoundly *"individual"* in its complexion, and that to
"generalize the subject . . . does not mean collectivize it" (pp. 61–62).
Barthes's refusal to conceive a pleasure that might go beyond individual
hedonism—that is, by associating it with a collective or transindividual
subject—is an unequivocal (and, to my mind, disturbing) repudiation
of the Left. Not only does it mark a vigorous rejection of the admittedly
orthodox and puritanical Leninism of the French Communist party during the 1960s, but it is also indicative of Barthes's apparent reluctance
to acknowledge the antihierarchical and libertarian French Maoism that
developed during the late 1960s and early 1970s and nurtured radical
collectives such as Vive la Revolution and the Front Homosexuel d'Action
Revolutionnaire.[129] Barthes's refusal to credit a pleasure-loving Left,
together with his notion of purely *individual* pleasure, ironically returns
bliss to the realm of bourgeois aesthetics from which he hoped to pry
it loose, and strips it of the "revolutionary" potential to which he gives
lip service (p. 23) and that it had indeed acquired both in France and
the United States during the heady days of 1968. Andreas Huyssen is
certainly correct to note Barthes's turn to the right (or, rather, to so-
called apoliticism) during the 1970s as an attempt to transform "the dung
of post–68 political disillusionment into the gold of aesthetic bliss."[130]

Barthes's near contemporary Michel Foucault reacted to "the events
of May" very differently. Rather than proceed further along the high
road of structuralism, as he had in *The Order of Things* (1966) and *The
Archeology of Knowledge* (1969), Foucault deliberately took up a radical political agenda, to which *Discipline and Punish* (1975), *The History
of Sexuality* (1976–84), and his later interviews attest. At the core of
Foucault's work is a theorization of the transition from a traditional,
feudal society to a modern, industrial one, accompanied by a rigorous
mapping of the new, self-disciplining subject produced under modern
capitalism. In detailing the emergence of this new subject, Foucault's
works of the 1970s and 1980s enunciate a widely influential—and controversial—poststructuralist (and post-Marxist) politics based upon a

reconceptualization of power. Rejecting a totalizing schema and widening the Althusserian fissures between (or the "semiautonomy" of) different means and arenas of production, Foucault turned his attention to local political practices (micropolitics) and to what he called "a non-economic analysis of power."[131] He reconceived it as *productive* rather than *repressive*, and broke with those orthodox Marxists whose theorization of power is dependent upon "a central point" (upon an irreducible economic determinism), defining it instead as "the multiplicity of force relations immanent in the sphere in which they operate." Noting, however, that power is never exercised unopposed, Foucault insisted that "points of resistance are present everywhere in the power network," or, to use his celebrated formulation, "Where there is power, there is resistance."[132] Despite the formidable (some would say disabling) political problems Foucault's work raises—the writing out of the Third World and the international division of labor, its scant attention to class domination or to questions of gender and female subjectivity—it has had an incalculable impact on feminist, gay and lesbian, and other minority studies.[133] With its rigorous articulation of a historical subject, inflected by material social struggles, it would seem extremely useful as a partial corrective to the almost wholly aestheticized pleasure that Barthes theorizes in *The Pleasure of the Text*.

An important interview with Foucault, conducted by Jean Le Bitoux in 1978 but not published until ten years later, provides a particularly rich source for those looking for a Foucauldian analysis of pleasure and its relationship to male homosexual practices. In this interview, he carefully distinguishes between "desire" and "pleasure," investing the latter with a political resonance and revolutionary capacity far more powerful than the Barthesian orgasm. He explains that he prefers the word, in part, because it lacks the psychoanalytical baggage of "desire" and characterizes it as

> an event "outside the subject," or at the limit of the subject; it is
> something neither of the body, nor the soul, neither interior, nor
> exterior; in short, it is an unassigned and unassignable notion.[134]

For Foucault, pleasure does not simply perform an ecstatic and quasi-mystical dissolution of subjectivity, as it does for Barthes. Rather, it is inextricably linked (like the mongoose to the cobra) to the modern subject whose sovereignty is potentially imperiled by its exercise. He emphasizes that the subject of humanism, whose profile Foucault defines as an interlocking set of "subjected sovereignties" (the soul, consciousness, the individual, and basic freedom), is not invulnerable. In 1971, rather more sanguine than he later became about the possibility of revolutionary change, he points out that because it stands "at the heart of humanism," this subject is susceptible to attack, either by

> a "desubjectification" of the will to power (that is, through political struggle in the context of class warfare) or by the destruction of the subject as a pseudosovereign (that is, an attack on "culture": the suppression of taboos and the limitations and divisions imposed upon the sexes; the setting up of communes; the loosening of inhibitions with regard to drugs; the breaking of all the prohibitions that form and guide the development of a normal individual).[135]

Like so many of his compeers during the early 1970s, Foucault conceives of revolution in both Marxist-Leninist and Maoist terms, through class struggle and cultural revolution, exercise of political power and mutation in consciousness.

Foucault did not, however, give his most detailed elaboration of "desubjectification" until the 1978 interview with Le Bitoux, in which he characterizes it in an idiom far more auspicious for cultural revolution than "class warfare." His extraordinary description both of the dynamics of the process and of its somewhat unexpected preconditions and setting urges its citation at length:

> Le Bitoux: What do you think of the sexual practices in the gay bathhouses?
> Foucault: I believe it is politically important that sexuality should be able to function as it functions in the bathhouses. There you meet men who are like you, who are like what you are for them: nothing other than bodies with which combinations, fabrications of pleasure are going to be possible. You cease to be imprisoned in your own face, in your own past, in your own identity.
>   It is regrettable that such sites of erotic experience do not still exist for heterosexuals. Wouldn't it be a marvelous state of affairs for them to be able, at any hour of the day or night, to enter into a place furnished with all the comforts and with all the possibilities they could imagine, and there to meet other bodies, present and fleeting? There the exceptional possibility of being desubjectified, of being desubjugated, still remains, perhaps not in the most radical way, but in any case, with sufficient intensity for one to take note of it.
> Le Bitoux: Why does this anonymity seem important to you?
> Foucault: Because the intensity of pleasure flows from it. It is not the affirmation of identity which is important, but the affirmation of non-identity. Not only because you leave your calling card at the door, but also because of the multiplicity of things, the heap of possibilities that you encounter there. It is an important experience in which you invent, for as long as you wish, the pleasures that you fabricate together.[136]

Foucault's figuration of bathhouse sex as a desubjectification empties the male subject of face, past, and identity. By leaving his "calling card at the door" and producing, with others like him, "combinations" and "fabrications," this nonsubject is initiated into a realm of pleasure that annihilates both the distinction between public and private space and the pseudosovereign who has taken up residence within the binarism, and leaps beyond hierarchy, borders, and limits. Like the subversive sexual practices that, according to Judith Butler, can take place "in both homosexual and heterosexual contexts," desubjectification "open[s] surfaces and orifices to erotic signification" in new ways and "effectively reinscribe[s] the boundaries of the body along new cultural lines."[137] And crucially, this process is not conceived, like the Barthesian orgasm, as a purely individualistic (or masturbatory) project. Rather, the desubjectification that Foucault describes, being founded in the sexual revolution(s) of the 1960s, is irreducibly communal and bears more than a passing resemblance to the "transpersonal libido" that Gitlin saw operating in the New Left. At its most radical, it explicitly transgresses the body's limits, divesting the individual subject of self-possession and identity and undermining the distinction between the one and the many, to produce a kind of *collective subject*. Furthermore, although dependent in Foucault's formulation on the availability of a particular quasi-bourgeois space ("a place furnished with all the comforts") and on a particular set of homosexual practices (which have, please note, radically changed complexion as a result of the AIDS epidemic), it is not categorically limited to male homosexuals inventing pleasures with each other. Rather, a process of desubjectification (striking the very "heart of humanism") might well proceed from any such practices that affirm "non-identity," that dispossess the old bourgeois ego and that take place within a new, neither public nor private "site of erotic experience," a literal utopia ("no place").

To jump from the Foucauldian gay bathhouse back to Tennessee Williams may seem perverse, and yet I know no other theorization of (male homosexual) pleasure that more lucidly glosses the raptures of Williams's texts, or that provides as clear an analogue to their most ecstatic moments and most desperate anxieties. In their atomization and dismemberment of bodies, narratives, and words, their verbal promiscuity, their unexpected combinations and fabrications of pleasure, their ability to make the reader lose his or her self-possession and identity, their opening up of a new narrative and theatrical space—neither wholly private nor public—they are paradigmatic of that desubjectification that Foucault describes (and, coincidentally, a radiant invitation to the reader or spectator to participate in the process). The passage cited above from the short story "Sand" seems to me to qualify as one of these ecstatic moments, in which the subject fantasizes its own material dissolution into grains of sand, reversing the expected relationship between self and Other, in this case, body and earth, as the latter "rises and sways" while the former "grows large," becomes "immense." Meanwhile, one of Williams's only (romantic) comedies for the stage, *The Rose Tattoo*, provides in its spirited ending a theatrical image of sexual bliss as collective subjectivity, in its call for the women of the village to toss Alvaro's *"brilliantly colored shirt"* back and forth among them so that it *"moves in a zigzag course through the pampas grass to the very top of the embankment, like a streak of flame shooting up a dry hill."*[138]

In *Moise and the World of Reason*, the process of desubjectification is much more emotionally ambivalent than in "Sand" or *The Rose Tattoo*. Here, despite the linking of sex and writing, and despite the occasional textual rapture, the dominant frame of mind is an anxious one and the dominant subjectivity, resolutely schizophrenic. Although the text uses a single narrator, it shamelessly multiplies emotional states, which change with each new narrative, discursive fragment, or dropped end stop. Furthermore, even more explicitly than *Tokyo Hotel*'s production of Miriam and Mark as doubles, *Moise* figures the narrator, that unnamed "distinguished failed writer," and the unnamed "has-been" playwright as twin portraits, in the style of "St. Oscar's boy Dorian" (Moise even admonishes the narrator that the elder playwright "is yourself grown old!"; pp. 130, 179). Sklepowich is certainly correct to see Moise, as well, as yet another "thinly veiled" version of a single subjectivity (whom, with his predisposition for a biographical reading, he identifies as the playwright himself).[139] And yet these three portraits do not add up to one full subject. Rather, they coexist in a kind of promiscuous intimacy, insistently destabilizing each other, symptomatic of a subjectivity that is always already decentered and bereft, never characterized in the ecstatic terms of the woman in "Sand" or the villagers in *The Rose Tattoo*.

Yet, ironically, this foregrounding of a schizophrenic subject, together with the preeminence of rhetorical figures of insufficiency and failure— the fractured sentence and its structural corollary, narrative disjunction— are startlingly productive of textual pleasure. Like one of the narrator's particularly ghastly rejection slips, which "depresses [him] to such a point that [he] feel[s] transfigured by it," these figures function as an alchemical agent in Williams's late works, transfiguring critical rejection—both the narrator's and his own—into gold (p. 91). As such, they become, I believe, the starkest indices of that textual "bliss," which Barthes avers is "unspeakable" and "interdicted" (and here he cites Lacan:

"Bliss is forbidden to the speaker . . . except between the lines"; p. 21).
They are the clearest signs of an almost inconceivable transaction that
passes "between the lines," and that radically reconfigures—and desub-
jectifies—the reading subject. "Lost" in the text of pleasure, this enrapt
subject "unmakes himself, like a spider dissolving in the constructive
secretions of its web" (p. 64). For what is the Barthesian text of pleasure
if not the simulacrum of Foucault's bathhouse, a place of fantasy and
nonidentity, at whose door you leave your calling card and go forth
in search of combinations and fabrications of delight? Like Foucault's
subject of pleasure, or like the stuttering—and transfigured—narrator
of *Moise*, the reader is not daunted by the sudden rupture of an imaginary
continuity. Rather, cruising each word and rhetorical figure, he or she
is always ready to turn to yet another one, always attentive to "the
multiplicity of things, the heap of possibilities," the (un)imaginable pleasures to which the incomplete sentence provides access. (I am deliberately
analogizing certain male homosexual practices with literary and theoretical texts, in the belief that the furtiveness and improvisatory quality
of these practices, their historical status as an insurrection on the cultural
margins, is deeply inscribed in certain acts of writing that have little or
nothing to do with sexuality.)

As I have tried to show, the fractured discourse of *Moise and the
World of Reason* stands at the end of a long chain of unfinished statements that reaches back (at least) to Laura's abashment *"beyond speech"*
(after Jim breaks the horn off her glass unicorn),[140] and leads to Baby
Doll's "I want to—" and Leonard's "Barman, I would like." Each of these
moments functions as the mirror image, or dialectical negation, of that
bliss it simultaneously announces and defers. In all of these cases, the
inability to finish the sentence, to name desire, has, I believe, a profoundly revolutionary potential, and the fact that these incomplete sentences are the product of a character's despair or failure does not in
any way attenuate their radical character. On the contrary, as Walter
Benjamin, Theodor Adorno, and Ernst Bloch repeatedly emphasize, the
very anguish they express yet never quite manage to encompass marks
them as infinitely precious for a politically revolutionary art.

In his last major work, *Aesthetic Theory* (published posthumously in
1970), Adorno, that most dialectical of twentieth-century Marxist theorists, makes an extraordinary observation about the apparently negative
art of "today." First he notes that during an earlier period, "in authentic
modern works" (that is, in the landmarks of high modernism), "an
appearing Utopia" is still representable—indeed, it is "as fresh as ever."
But "today," he continues, "this has become impossible; nowadays darkness is the representation of this Utopia. Art's Utopia, the counterfactual

yet-to-come, is draped in black." Adorno insists that although utopian hopes must now always confront "that catastrophe, which is world history," they are by no means extinguished. On the contrary, he emphasizes that the darkness of "today" makes all the more urgent an "imaginary restitution of that catastrophe," a restitution that, in fact, clearly informs much of the apocalyptic—that is, utopian—art that sprang out of the New Left, the counterculture and the many liberation movements of the 1960s and early 1970s.[141]

In Fredric Jameson's contemporaneous work, *Marxism and Form* (1971), he elaborates on the utopian theory of Ernst Bloch in clearly Adornian terms. In developing what he calls a Marxist hermeneutic, Jameson characterizes utopian figurations in literature and art by reference to Bloch's notion of an anticipatory illumination that prefigures and predicts a not yet even conceivable utopia. He cites Bloch's insistence that anticipation has two poles: the "darkness of the lived instant" and the principle of hope, of "material astonishment," the "very source or origin of the world itself, ever at work and ever hidden away within the darkness of the lived instant."[142] As Jameson emphasizes, because utopia is "quite impossible" to imagine, "except as the unimaginable," it will always stand revealed in allegorical figures.[143]

Among Williams's late works, *Moise and the World of Reason* is the closest to being a utopian allegory, both in its dramatization of the "darkness of the lived instant" and in its figuration of narrative closure as (un)imaginable bliss. In its final pages, all the fragments, false starts, and unfinished sentences are explicitly focused toward completion, filling the last Blue Jay—as happens in the last two luminous pages of text. In this *deus ex machina*, Moise, in "ecstasy," takes one of two cameramen as a new lover at exactly the same moment that the narrator discovers his next love in the other one, the "jacketless cameraman," standing "with delicate gleams here and there," and answering the narrator's silent proposition by nodding to him in "a soundless assent." Then, softly in the fading light, the narrator hears

> the footsteps of a giant being, as hushed as they are gigantic, footsteps
> of the Great Unknown One approaching our world of reason or
> unreason, you name it as you conceive it. And now
>   The last Blue Jay is completed. (p. 190)

Like the desires circulating promiscuously through the novel, the grammatical form that marks its fulfillment is itself rent, a statement torn and reassembled: an incomplete sentence, followed by a new paragraph that finishes it immaculately. In this cleft that closure (impossibly) opens up, the narrator's thoughts—"And now"—break off in midstream, exactly like Moise's final speech, when, enraptured, she turned "from expression to action," loosening the trousers of the other cameraman and reaching for a jar of petroleum jelly (p. 189). Like the blissful, anonymous visitors to the Foucauldian bathhouse, these four (three of whom remain nameless) prepare for "combinations, fabrications of pleasure." And as the last piece of narrative falls soundlessly into place, this (im)perfect closure, together with the desubjectification it promises, becomes the very figure of astonishment, of the (un)imaginable, fiercely charged with expectation, with preparation for action, and for the immanent approach of "the Great Unknown One."

Like the heroes of the novella "The Knightly Quest" (1965), journeying through space toward "the spot marked X on the chart of time without end," the narrative of *Moise* moves toward an impossible fulfillment, the indescribable described as ecstasy, as a gigantic hush, as a soundless assent.[144] In so doing, it demonstrates that utopia can be figured only as contradiction, nonidentity, incomplete completion, as a still unfulfilled desire that begs for the turn from expression to action. *Moise* thereby defines what is most revolutionary in Tennessee Williams's work: its ability as a text of bliss and desubjectification to lead the reader or spectator simultaneously to recognize the oppressiveness of the present historical moment and to think an unthinkable alternative. Given this idiosyncratic definition, it is little wonder that Williams found it necessary to point out to an interviewer eager to pin him down on his politics that "'revolutionary' is a misunderstood word." Carefully distinguishing his writing from propaganda, he insisted that the most revolutionary works of art do not proselytize. Rather, like *In the Bar of a Tokyo Hotel* or *Moise*, they design a revolution that is so finely "woven into the fabric of the work" that it is everywhere perceptible only as the imperceptible, as the radiant figuration of a utopia yet to come.[145]

Utopia and the Wreckage of History

Despite Williams's attempt at fashioning a "revolutionary" theater, his writing remains, in crucial ways, fatally complicit with the exigencies of the very history he was struggling to overcome. Despite the deeply utopian impulses that inform his work, despite his sympathy with the disenfranchised and the outsider, despite his deconstruction of the liberal humanist subject and his valorization of feminine desire, despite his championing of textual pleasure, his work in certain respects epitomizes the problems that weakened and finally disabled the revolutions of the late 1960s. Both *In the Bar of a Tokyo Hotel* and *Moise and the World of Reason* betray the fact that Williams was much less invested in the kind of radical structural change that the New Left was attempting to provoke than in that revolution in consciousness that was the province of the counterculture. Both play and novel seem dedicated less to political revolution than to transforming the awareness of the reader or spectator, to activating a "homosexual" mode of address, to dramatizing the utopian potential in the "darkness of the lived instant." Both works are focused on individual and personal problems, completely neglecting questions of class domination, even while calling into question the ostensible sovereignty of the individual. And although both provide this reader with intense pleasure, the stimulation of textual bliss is no guarantee of these works' progressive political function. (Not to point this out about Williams's late works would be to betray him: to forget the damning reviews that plagued him for the last twenty years of his life, to deny the power of the homophobic cultural regime of which he was unwillingly a part, to claim as unambiguously emancipatory texts that are all too obviously the product of emotional distress.)

In an important essay on the political implications of textual pleasure, Fredric Jameson makes a crucial point that helps one to critique not just the "revolutionary" works of Williams, but also the late theoretical prescriptions of Barthes and Foucault with which they have much in common. Carefully avoiding the kind of puritanical stance that has often marked leftist analyses of pleasure and the sublime, Jameson emphasizes that "the proper political use of pleasure must always be *allegorical*." Interpreted allegorically, pleasure may be understood both as a "local issue" (that is, "meaningful and desirable in and of itself") and *"at one and the same time* . . . as the *figure* for Utopia in general, and for the systematic revolutionary transformation of society as a whole."[146] In certain crucial respects, Williams's late writings never quite actualize the allegorical structure Jameson describes. Too often, his utopian figures appear exhausted by their very expression. Too often, the history of the oppression of women is neglected and women are subsumed (as Moise is) under a masculine (that is, nonvaginal) regime of sexuality. Furthermore, Williams's romanticization of androgyny, his claim that "the androgynous is the truest human being," brings to mind Foucault's dangerous sentimentalization in *Herculine Barbin* of the indetermination of the eponymous hermaphrodite, floating in a "happy limbo of a non-identity," despite overwhelming evidence to the contrary (Barbin ended as a suicide, an involuntary victim of the binary system of genders).[147] Most important, the sexual utopias that end *Moise* and "The Knightly Quest" (with its three radiant "astronauts in the full glitter of youth" drinking champagne and sailing into infinity), like the Foucauldian bathhouse, are still, I believe, organized around a phallic economy of desire.[148]

The nameless cameramen and astronauts may figuratively have left their calling cards at the door, but that act does not completely cancel their subjectivities. In these works, not the outward signs of bourgeois identity, but the masculine body itself becomes the arbiter and object of a desire that is absolutely unquenchable. And the narrator of *Moise*, like the subject of the Foucauldian bathhouse, circulating among endlessly alluring bodies, is engaged, despite the novel's ostensible closure in a happy end, in an endless search for the one who "has" the Phallus (this search, a variation on that of the hero of classic narrative, *must* be endless, because, of course, no one "has" the Phallus). More and more, I believe that Williams's configuration of sexuality, like that of Foucault, is still unequivocally within a phallic and hom(m)o-sexual economy of desire and remains, in Teresa De Lauretis's words, "manifestly" (if "not intentionally") "self-serving to the male-gendered subject."[149]

Furthermore, these late "revolutionary" texts of Williams's seem incapable of extending or even sustaining the very forces of liberation they unleash and embody. The ending of *Moise* seems aimed at providing an imaginary resolution of the very problems it raises and thereby giving the reader a vicarious satisfaction. Even the narrator's avowed sympathy for "the Gay Libs" does not spur him on to link the battle for gay liberation with other contemporaneous social and political struggles, none of which is even mentioned in the novel. As in the Foucauldian bathhouse, the emancipatory energies seems to be contained by and finally dissipated within the spaces in which they are produced. In considering the political value of Williams's erotic utopia, one must recall his own rhetorical question in his letter to Donald Windham (quoted above) that concludes his discussion of the "two times" he feels "happy and selfless and pure":

> There must be a third occasion for happiness in the world. What is it and where?

Where indeed?

In the middle of *Moise and the World of Reason* there is an unusually revealing story that comes close to suggesting an answer to this question. The narrator recalls his encounter at age fourteen with "four strange young men" who for two days cruised the streets of his hometown in their dark, new limousine, "the handsomest car" he'd ever seen. Hailed by the "blond of the four," the one with the "charming intensity of his pale eyes" (who clearly presages the blond cameraman at the end of the novel), the narrator asks them to give him a ride home. Instead, they take him out of town, where, "scared crazy" and intoxicated by the danger, his heart "beating like a wild bird," he is nearly assaulted sexually, to be rescued only by the compassion of the blond, who safeguards the narrator by holding him so tightly between his knees that he can feel the blond's erection. When the limousine finally drops him off at home, the narrator bids a loving farewell to his protector with "a soft, lingering kiss" (pp. 108–12).

Like *Cat on a Hot Tin Roof*, this passage, in its presentation of the four "strange young men" in their frightening and tantalizingly dark machine, vividly demonstrates the almost magical confluence in Williams's work of homosexuality and the commodity form. Throughout his career, his most luminous and erotic writing is always inscribed with the double-edged promise of the commodity, which pledges endless joy and boundless ecstasy, neither of which, of course, it can ever redeem. The quintessential object of unsatisfiable desire, it finally delivers neither joy nor ecstasy, but only its pure, infinitely drab objecthood. The subject in search of this Janus-faced commodity—like Big Daddy, who "buys and buys and buys" in the hope "that one of his purchases will be life everlasting"—finally acquires not the life or the eros he so desperately craves but death, the interminable flatness of things. The driver of the limousine clearly epitomizes this promise, by his attractiveness to the narrator and by the deadly mechanical quality he embodies, driving "as if he were a part of the machine, a controlling extension of it, one that owned a commanding block of units in the stock of a corporation" (p. 112). Even more unmistakably marked by the twin covenant of the commodity is the narrator's extraordinary—and, again, deeply utopian and erotic—fantasy about holding the blond "in [his] arms, over [his] lap, at the time of his passing."

> This is an erotic feeling, needless to tell you. I would like to have felt the spasmodic motions of his prone body as it surrendered its warmth of being and to have placed one hand on his forehead and the other over his groin to comfort him at the two places where he lived most intensely and would have most resisted ravishment by the non-living, by the mineral kingdom. (p. 113)

This persistent positioning of phallic sexuality in Williams's work under the sign of the commodity means that desire, like the four "strange young men," moves inexorably toward death, toward the perfection of "the machine," toward the stillness of "the mineral kingdom." This complex association in his work between homoeroticism and death is historically marked, of course, and allows one to position Williams at a particular cultural juncture. In part, the association signals the necessarily schizophrenic attitude toward his or her own desires on the part of any homosexual subject who is the product of a viciously homophobic culture. The incident with the four "strange young men" (much like the narrator's "almost pleasurable" mauling by the two brutal policemen) exemplifies the nearly sadomasochistic eroticization of violence that so often characterizes not just Williams's representations of homosexuality, but those of so many other gay men and lesbians writing when homosexual practices were—and, of course, still are in many places—punishable by imprisonment or death (p. 155).

At the same time, however, even this darkness and violence (like the wound that the incomplete sentence opens up) is subject to a twist of the dialectical knife so that it may be reconfigured yet again as Adorno's "counterfactual yet-to-come." When considered as a utopian figure, Williams's limousine driver bears witness to the modern age's reconceptualization of hope in scientific and technological terms. Bloch emphasizes the necessary link between the present and the (un)imaginable future, that "in spite of everything," utopia "cannot be removed from the world" and that "even the technological . . . will be in the great realm of the utopian" (this is particularly true as the last precapitalist sanctuaries disappear under late capitalism).[150] In light of Bloch's intuition, the association of erotic desire and the commodity form leads to a utopian figuration in Williams that is radically different from the nostalgic imaginings of most of his contemporaries, whether they be the dreams of a Willy Loman for a refuge from the terrors of industrial capitalism or the counterculture's agrarian idylls.[151] (Jameson points out that nostalgia, in fact, represents utopia "standing on its head conceptually"—a misrecognition "in which everything which in reality belongs to the future is attributed to the past.")[152] In associating bliss with the machine, Williams carefully avoids sentimentalizing the premodern past, placing his bet instead on a future that—like the thermonuclear sublime—promises both the endlessly radiant and the endlessly lethal. His use of utopian figures drawn from an urban, industrialized, and scientific culture (cameramen, astronauts) lends a distinctively modern (if not modernist) resonance to his writing, a resonance that ensures that even self-proclaimed memory plays from either end of his career, The Glass Menagerie and Vieux Carre (1978), will be more critiques than romanticizations of an unmistakably onerous and suffocating past. Both send their narrators off into futures filled with "the counterfactual yet-to-come," into a world swarming with the infinite promise and infinite disappointment of the commodity, into a world "lit by lightning," to borrow Tom's incomparable evocation.[153]

In their reconfiguration of utopia, in their conflation of homosexual desire with the commodity form, in their fear and celebration of "the mineral kingdom," in their refusal to mourn the unitary subject-that-never-was, Williams's works stand like Walter Benjamin's New Angel of progress, propelled into the future by a storm yet turned toward the past, buffeted by the wind blowing from Paradise and staring fixedly at that "single catastrophe," which is the history of the world, "which keeps piling wreckage upon wreckage and hurls it in front of his feet."[154] Like this angel, caught between the violence of the storm raging in Paradise and the growing pile of debris, Williams's works clear a tiny avenue of hope, simultaneously testifying both to the possibility of transfiguration and to the staggering difficulty of an articulation of homosexual desire and pleasure, of Paradise, among the wreckage of history. In their extraordinary ability both to arouse and contain bliss, in their subversion and reinscription of gendered categories and phallic sexuality, they attest to the continuing promise—and the failure—of the liberation movements of the late 1960s and early 1970s. In their denunciation and eroticization of sexual violence (the "head-on violence" the narrator of "Hard Candy" would avoid), they epitomize the contradictions circulating around the desires of the modern homosexual subject who has internalized homophobic cultural values. Yet, at the same time, rejecting a crippling nostalgia far more decisively than most other American works of this period, Williams's writings suggest that the path of revolution must, despite the hazards, proceed through the commodity form, through that convulsive rustle of the Blochian *novum* that the commodity simultaneously promises and defers: "the utterly and unexpectedly new, the new which astonishes by its absolute and intrinsic unpredictability."[155]

If that most misunderstood of words, *revolutionary*, is to be applied to Williams's works, they must be most prized—that is, read, directed, and acted—less as ends in themselves than as allegories, as figures for the (un)imaginable hopes they articulate so dazzlingly, and for the surrealistic theater of sexual bliss they announce. There is no question but that they cannot, despite their best attempts, cancel or transcend the hegemonic sexual ideology of Cold War America in which they are inscribed and that has vilified women, gay men, and lesbians while consistently privileging the active, heterosexualized, male subject. Perhaps Williams's most conspicuous failure as a revolutionary lies in the fact that his writing remains far more attentive to the utopian potential of masculine than feminine eroticism. Like Foucault, Williams seems to declare proudly and joyously that "homosexuality is an historic occasion to re-open affective and relational virtualities, not so much through the intrinsic qualities of the homosexual, but due to the biases against the position he occupies."[156] Like Foucault, Williams reconfigures and valorizes what has long been subjugated. Despite this recolonization, *"he,"* the homosexual subject enunciated in the writings of both men, remains the product of discourses and practices that continue to position him, however uncomfortably, within the locus of Western male privilege that, to borrow Gayatri Spivak's word, must be *unlearned* if a truly revolutionary subject is to be enunciated.[157] And the technique of unlearning must be understood in terms of *process* (the validation of which remains a precious legacy of the New Left), by making connections, for example, across the international division of labor, and among the histories of homophobia, misogyny, and racism that Williams's works so often brilliantly illuminate, yet that remain far too frequently conceptualized as autonomous narratives. More than twenty years after the exhilarating crest of the New Left and the Gay Liberation Front, the reader or spectator of Williams who dares to fulfill the utopian promise of his work— and simultaneously that of the 1960s—must look beyond even its rebellious protagonists to those figures on the margins of the texts, those resistant subjects waiting to take their pleasure: the quietly defiant Japanese Barman, the African-American waitress in *Baby Doll* intoning "I Shall Not Be Moved," or the restive lesbian women in *Something Unspoken*. In the gloom of the present historical moment, marked by an emphatic turn to the right in the First World and Eastern Europe, and by the tightening of the First World's neocolonial grip over most of the Third, the need for sites of resistance—such as a revolutionary theater— is arguably even more urgent than it was during the 1960s. The utopian pledge inscribed in Williams's work becomes all the more precious to a reader or spectator willing to see it not simply as a *substitute* for utopia, but as an incitement to commemorate what we know but too often forget, to turn from expression to action, and to redeem the promise of Mr. Gutman in *Camino Real*: "Revolution only needs good dreamers who remember their dreams."[158]

Notes

Introduction

1. James Reston, "A Debate of Politicians," *New York Times*, July 25, 1959, 3.

2. "The Two Worlds: A Day-Long Debate," *New York Times*, July 25, 1959, 1–2.

3. Byrnes and Clayton quoted in Lawrence S. Wittner, *Cold War America: From Hiroshima to Watergate* (New York: Praeger, 1974), 7. Wittner's book provides one of the very best analyses of U.S. foreign and domestic adventures during the 1940s and 1950s.

4. See William H. Chafe, *The Unfinished Journey: America Since World War II* (New York: Oxford University Press, 1986), 67–68.

5. Wittner, *Cold War America*, 15.

6. Ibid., 36–37.

7. General James Van Fleet, speaking to a Filipino delegation in 1952; quoted ibid., 79.

8. Ibid., 51, 81, 82.

9. Harrison E. Salisbury, "Nixon and Khrushchev Argue in Public as U.S. Exhibit Opens; Accuse Each Other of Threats," *New York Times*, July 25, 1959, 1.

10. "The Two Worlds," 1–2.

11. Quoted in Wittner, *Cold War America*, 95. See also Chafe, *The Unfinished Journey*, 105–8.

12. Elaine Tyler May, *Homeward Bound: American Families in the Cold War Era* (New York: Basic Books, 1988), 24.

13. Ibid., 14.

14. Morris Zelditch, Jr., "Role Differentiation in the Nuclear Family: A Comparative Study," in *Family, Socialization and Interaction Process*, ed. Talcott Parsons and Robert F. Bales (New York: Free Press, 1955), 339.

15. May, *Homeward Bound*, 193–200.

16. Joseph Burns in the *Kelly Longitudinal Study, 1935–1955*, quoted in May, *Homeward Bound*, 33.

17. See Wittner, *Cold War America*, 94.

18. Talcott Parsons, *Social Structure and Personality* (New York: Free Press, 1964), 42.

19. For a more extensive contextualization of Parsons, see R. W. Connell, *Gender and Power: Society, the Person and Sexual Politics* (Stanford, Calif.: Stanford University Press, 1987), 29–32.

20. Sue-Ellen Case, *Feminism and Theatre* (New York: Methuen, 1988), 6.

21. Suzanne J. Kessler and Wendy McKenna, *Gender: An Ethnomethodological Approach* (Chicago: University of Chicago Press, 1978), 162. An important extension of Kessler and McKenna's work that further explores the possibilities of a radical destabilization of the relationship between sex and gender can be found in Judith Butler, *Gender Trouble: Feminism and the Subversion of Identity* (New York: Routledge, 1990). See also Anne Fausto-Sterling, *Myths of Gender: Biological Theories about Women and Men* (New York: Basic Books, 1985).

22. See Gayle Rubin, "The Traffic in Women: Notes Toward a Political Economy of Sex," in *Toward an Anthropology of Women*, ed. Rayna Reiter (New York: Monthly Review Press, 1975), 157–210.

23. See Case, *Feminism and Theatre*; Jill Dolan, *The Feminist Spectator as Critic* (Ann Arbor, Mich.: UMI Research Press, 1988); Elin Diamond, "Brechtian Theory/Feminist Theory: Toward a Gestic Feminist Criticism," *TDR* 117 (Spring 1988): 82–94; Teresa De Lauretis, *Alice Doesn't: Feminism, Semiotics, Cinema* (Bloomington: Indiana University Press, 1988); idem, *Technologies of Gender: Essays on Theory, Film, and Fiction* (Bloomington: Indiana University Press, 1987). Although I have singled these four out, there are numerous other feminists who have made extremely important contributions to theater studies. For further references, see the bibliographies in Case, *Feminism and Theatre*, 139–44, and Dolan, *The Feminist Spectator*, 145–50.

24. Diamond, "Brechtian Theory/Feminist Theory," 83.

25. Dolan, *The Feminist Spectator*, 10.

26. Case, *Feminism and Theatre*, 82–83.

27. For presentations of the distinction between cultural (or radical) feminism and materialist (or Marxist) feminism, see ibid., 62–64, 82–84; Dolan, *The Feminist Spectator*, 5–17.

28. Teresa De Lauretis, "The Technology of Gender," in *Technologies of Gender*, 1–30.

29. Louis Althusser, "Ideology and Ideological State Apparatuses (Notes towards an Investigation)," in *Lenin and Philosophy*, trans. Ben Brewster (New York: Monthly Review Press, 1971), 165.

30. Diamond, "Brechtian Theory/Feminist Theory," 84.

31. Catherine Belsey, "Constructing the Subject: Deconstructing the Text," in *Feminist Criticism and Social Change: Sex, Class and Race in Literature and Culture*, ed. Judith Newton and Deborah Rosenfelt (New York: Methuen, 1985), 46. This essay provides a fine elaboration of Althusser's notion of ideology and its implications for literary analysis.

32. Butler, *Gender Trouble*, 44.

33. Catherine Belsey, *Critical Practice* (London: Routledge, 1980), 65.

34. Joan Riviere, "Womanliness as a Masquerade," in *Formations of Fantasy*, ed. Victor Burger, James Donald, and Cora Kaplan (New York: Methuen, 1986), 38, 35.

35. Butler, *Gender Trouble*, 52.

36. Riviere, "Womanliness as a Masquerade," 38.

37. Stephen Heath, "Joan Riviere and the Masquerade," in *Formations of Fantasy*, ed. Victor Burger, James Donald, and Cora Kaplan (New York: Methuen, 1986), 52.

38. See Butler, *Gender Trouble*, 43–48. The phrase "fullness of being" is Kaja Silverman's. See Silverman, *The Subject of Semiotics* (New York: Oxford University Press, 1983), 183.

39. Butler, *Gender Trouble*, 44.

40. Ibid., 47.

41. Silverman, *The Subject of Semiotics*, 139 (see also 183–86).

42. Heath, "Joan Riviere and the Masquerade," 55.

43. Butler, *Gender Trouble*, 50.

44. E. Lemoine-Luccioni, quoted in Heath, "Joan Riviere and the Masquerade," 56.

45. Butler, *Gender Trouble*, 151 n. 6.

46. Ibid., 54.

47. Connell, *Gender and Power*, 183.

48. Ibid.

49. Sue-Ellen Case, "Toward a Butch-Femme Aesthetic," in *Making a Spectacle: Feminist Essays on Contemporary Women's Theatre*, ed. Lynda Hart (Ann Arbor: University of Michigan Press, 1989), 297.

50. See also Mary Russo, "Female Grotesques: Carnival and Theory," in *Feminist Studies/Critical Studies*, ed. Teresa De Lauretis (Bloomington: Indiana University Press, 1986), 213–29; and Butler, *Gender Trouble*, 31.

51. Andrew Ross, "Cowboys, Cadillacs, Cosmonauts: Families, Film Genres, and Technocultures," in *Engendering Men: The Question of Male Feminist Criticism*, ed. Joseph A. Boone and Michael Cadden (New York: Routledge, 1990), 88.

52. Tennessee Williams, "The Mysteries of the Joy Rio," in *Collected Stories* (New York: Ballantine, 1986), 105.

One: Arthur Miller: "Why Can't I Say 'I'?"

1. U.S. Congress, House Committee on Un-American Activities, *Investigation of the Unauthorized Use of United States Passports—Part 4*, June 1956, 4686. Compare with Proctor's assertion, "I like not to spoil their names." Arthur Miller, *The Crucible* (New York: Bantam, 1959), 135.

2. U.S. Congress, *Investigation*, 4672–73.

3. Joan Holden of the San Francisco Mime Troupe, for example, remembers seeing a performance of *The Crucible* in the mid-1950s, with her mother sobbing beside her, that provided her with the first realization that "something could happen in the theatre besides lights and beautiful music and costumes." Quoted in David Savran, *In Their Own Words: Contemporary American Playwrights* (New York: Theatre Communications Group, 1988), 102.

4. C. W. E. Bigsby, *A Critical Introduction to Twentieth-Century American Drama*, vol. 2 (Cambridge: Cambridge University Press, 1984), 248.

5. Ronald Hayman, *Arthur Miller* (New York: Frederick Ungar, 1972), 111; Tom F. Driver, "Strength and Weakness in Arthur Miller," in *Arthur Miller: A Collection of Critical Essays*, ed. Robert W. Corrigan (Englewood Cliffs, N.J.: Prentice-Hall, 1969), 59; June Schlueter and James K. Flanagan, *Arthur Miller* (New York: Frederick Ungar, 1987), 143.

6. See David Caute, *The Great Fear: The Anti-Communist Purge Under Truman and Eisenhower* (New York: Simon and Schuster, 1978), 536–37; Walter Goodman, *The Committee: The Extraordinary Career of the House Committee on Un-American Activities* (New York: Farrar, Straus and Giroux, 1968), 391–94.

7. U.S. Congress, *Investigation*, 4690. According to Victor Navasky, Lillian Hellman, irked at Miller's "cozy"-ness with the committee, responded to Miller's statement, "I have had to go to hell to meet the devil" with the quip that he "must have gone as a tourist." Victor Navasky, *Naming Names* (New York: Penguin, 1981), 423.

8. U.S. Congress, *Investigation*, 4690–91.

9. This is the word Victor Navasky uses in his detailed examination of the committee's investigations. For a critical analysis of Miller's performance, see Navasky, *Naming Names*, 211–19. For a more straightforwardly journalistic account of Miller's testimony, see Benjamin Nelson, *Arthur Miller: Portrait of a Playwright* (New York: David McKay, 1970), 184–98.

10. Robert Sylvester, "Brooklyn Boy Makes Good," in *Conversations with Arthur Miller*, ed. Matthew C. Roudané (Jackson: University Press of Mississippi, 1987), 17. See also Bigsby, *A Critical Introduction*, 162.

11. Arthur Miller, *Timebends* (New York: Grove, 1987), 407.

12. Ibid., 408.

13. Bigsby, *A Critical Introduction*, 139–41, 155–63.

14. Paul Buhle, *Marxism in the United States: Remapping the History of the American Left* (London: Verso, 1991), 144–45.

15. Earl Browder, "Democracy or Fascism," in *The American Left: Radical Political Thought in the Twentieth Century*, ed. Loren Baritz (New York: Basic Books, 1971), 311.

16. For a fine summary of the fortunes of the Communist party during this period, see Buhle, *Marxism in the United States*, 195–220.

17. Anthony Arblaster, *The Rise and Decline of Western Liberalism* (Oxford: Basil Blackwell, 1984), 15, 17. Part I of Arblaster's book provides an excellent resumé and critique of the constitution of Western liberalism.

18. Ibid., 331–32.

19. Consider Wendy Brown's observation: "More than any other kind of human activity, *politics* has historically borne an explicitly masculine identity. It has been more exclusively limited to men than any other realm of endeavor and has been more intensely, self-consciously masculine than most other social practices." Wendy Brown, *Manhood and Politics: A Feminist Reading in Political Theory* (Totowa, N.J.: Rowman and Littlefield, 1988), 4.

20. See Henry Hart, "Discussion and Proceedings of the American Writers' Congress," in *The American Left: Radical Political Thought in the Twentieth Century*, 196–213.

21. Michael Gold, "Wilder: Prophet of the Genteel Christ," in *The American Left: Radical Political Thought in the Twentieth Century*, 195, 194, 192.

22. Gold is quoted at length in Buhle, *Marxism in the United States*, 173.

23. Elaine Tyler May, *Homeward Bound: American Families in the Cold War Era* (New York: Basic Books, 1988), 98.

24. U.S. Congress, *Investigation*, 4669.

25. Miller, *The Crucible*, 30–31. And consider his statement before the committee: "I believe now in facts. I look to life as to see what is happening, and I have no line. I have no preconception." U.S. Congress, *Investigation*, 4690.

26. U.S. Congress, *Investigation*, 4690.

27. While countless references to countless appellations could be cited here, I quote this phrase from Clare Booth Luce's memorial tribute to Monroe, "The 'Love Goddess' Who Never Found Any," *Life*, August 7, 1964, 70–78.

28. U.S. Congress, *Investigation*, 4684–85.

29. See Richard H. Rovere, "The Monroe Doctrine," *Spectator*, June 29, 1956, 877.

30. Allen Drury, "Arthur Miller Admits Helping Communist-Front Groups in '40's," *New York Times*, June 22, 1956, 1.

31. Rovere, "The Monroe Doctrine," 877.

32. Navasky, *Naming Names*, 216. Caute reports: "According to Miller himself, Chairman Walter of HCUA actually offered to call off the hearing in 1956 if Miller would permit a photograph of him standing with Miller and his fiancee, Marilyn Monroe." Caute, *The Great Fear*, 536.

33. Arthur Miller, "The Family in Modern Drama," in *The Theater Essays of Arthur Miller*, ed. Robert A. Martin (New York: Viking, 1978), 69–85. The distinction between private and public first assumed its modern character in the sixteenth century, coincidentally with the development of mercantile capitalism and the liberal humanist subject who was to form its principal agent. For a traditionally liberal account of the emergence of this new subject, see Lawrence Stone, *The Family, Sex and Marriage in England 1500–1800* (London: Penguin, 1979), 149–80. For more radical critiques, see Catherine Belsey, *The Subject of Tragedy: Identity and Difference in Renaissance Drama* (London: Methuen, 1985), especially pp. 5–10, 15–19; Francis Barker, *The Tremulous Private Body: Essays on Subjection* (London: Methuen, 1984).

34. Miller, "The Family in Modern Drama," 81.

35. Ibid., 76.

36. Ibid., 81–84.

37. Ibid., 82–85.

38. Sue-Ellen Case, *Feminism and Theatre* (New York: Methuen, 1988), 6–7.

39. These are the words Willy Loman and Eddie Carbone use to describe Bernard and Rodolpho, respectively. Arthur Miller, *Death of a Salesman* (New York: Penguin, 1976), 33; Arthur Miller, *A View from the Bridge* (New York: Penguin, 1977), 30.

40. Matthew C. Roudané, "An Interview with Arthur Miller," in *Conversations with Arthur Miller*, 362.

41. Arthur Miller, "Introduction to the *Collected Plays*," in *The Theater Essays of Arthur Miller*, 135. For a fine analysis of the use of memory in *Salesman*, see Peter Szondi, *Theory of the Modern Drama*, ed. and trans. Michael Hays (Minneapolis: University of Minnesota Press, 1987), 91–95.

42. Arthur Miller, *After the Fall* (New York: Penguin, 1979), 1.

43. Belsey, *The Subject of Tragedy*, 42–51.

44. See Walter H. Sokel, *Anthology of German Expressionist Drama: A Prelude to the Absurd* (Garden City, N.Y.: Anchor, 1963), ix–xxix.

45. See Renate Benson, *German Expressionist Drama: Ernst Toller and Georg Kaiser* (London: Macmillan, 1984), 7; Walter H. Sokel, *The Writer in Extremis: Expressionism in Twentieth-Century German Literature* (New York: McGraw-Hill, 1964).

46. Miller's debt to Ibsen has been widely acknowledged and studied. See, for example, Bigsby, *A Critical Introduction*, 168–72, 188–89; and Nelson, *Arthur Miller*, 79–81.

47. Phillip Gelb, "Morality and Modern Drama," in *Conversations with Arthur Miller*, 36. For an especially perspicuous account of Miller's transformation of *An Enemy of the People*, see Nelson, *Arthur Miller*, 135–45.

48. Raymond Williams, *Modern Tragedy* (Stanford, Calif.: Stanford University Press, 1966), 98. Williams's chapter on liberal tragedy, "From Hero to Victim" (pp. 87–105), is perhaps his most important contribution to dramatic criticism and urgent reading for those concerned with the development of bourgeois drama.

49. Raymond Williams describes Miller's work as representing "a late revival of liberal tragedy, on the edge (but only on the edge) of its transformation into socialism." Williams, *Modern Tragedy*, 103. In fact, liberal tragedy has been far more doggedly persistent on

the American stage than Williams's hopeful phrase "late revival" (corresponding, perhaps, to "late capitalism") would indicate. Many of the most decorated younger playwrights, from Wendy Wasserstein to August Wilson, have worked to resurrect the form, albeit in a severely debilitated condition. Both *The Heidi Chronicles* and *Fences* appropriate liberal tragedy's struggling and tortured hero for those who have traditionally been excluded from representation as heroes: women and black men. This "late" resuscitation of the sovereign subject, however, seems to me to be markedly reactionary in comparison with the work of Emily Mann, Maria Irene Fornes, Milcha Sanchez-Scott, and David Henry Hwang (among others), which seeks to produce alternative models of subjectivity. For a cogent mapping of these alternatives, see Sue-Ellen Case's important essay, "From Split Subject to Split Britches," in *Feminine Focus: The New Women Playwrights*, ed. Enoch Brater (New York: Oxford University Press, 1989), 126–46. For feminist critiques of bourgeois realism, see Case, *Feminism and Theatre*, 124; Jill Dolan, *The Feminist Spectator as Critic* (Ann Arbor, Mich.: UMI Research Press, 1988), 83–85, 106.

50. Konstantin Stanislavsky, *An Actor Prepares* (New York: Theatre Arts Books, 1936), 14–15, 43.

51. Ibid., 49.

52. Ibid., 122. For a fine analysis of the relationship between Stanislavsky and modern drama, see William Worthen, *The Idea of the Actor: Drama and the Ethics of Performance* (Princeton, N.J.: Princeton University Press, 1984), 143–72.

53. Hayman, *Arthur Miller*, 37.

54. Miller, *Death of a Salesman*, 11. All subsequent references to the play in this chapter will be to this edition. Page numbers will be noted in the text.

55. Ralph Waldo Emerson's definition of the hero, in fact, provides a startlingly accurate description not of the Miller hero, but of the Miller hero's *dreams* of his own heroism: "The hero is a mind of such balance that no disturbances can shake his will, but pleasantly, and, as it were, merrily, he advances to his own music, alike in frightful alarms, and in the tipsy mirth of universal dissoluteness." R. W. Emerson, "Heroism," in *Essays* (Boston: James Munroe, 1841), 207.

56. Talcott Parsons, "The Social Structure of the Family," in *The Family: Its Function and Destiny*, ed. Ruth Nanda Anshen (New York: Harper and Brothers, 1959), 271.

57. Robert W. Corrigan, "Introduction: The Achievement of Arthur Miller," in *Arthur Miller: A Collection of Critical Essays*, 6.

58. Luce Irigaray, *This Sex Which Is Not One*, trans. Catherine Porter with Carolyn Burke (Ithaca, N.Y.: Cornell University Press, 1985), 170–72. I am also alluding here, of course, to the work of Eve Kosofsky Sedgwick, whose theory of male homosociality has had a deservedly tremendous impact on the analysis of patriarchal relations. See Eve Kosofsky Sedgwick, *Between Men: English Literature and Male Homosocial Desire* (New York: Columbia University Press, 1985). Despite my deep admiration for Sedgwick's work, particularly her careful attention to the relationship between sexuality and social class, I prefer in this instance to deploy Irigaray's neologism, primarily because the ambiguities it encodes are, I believe, more productive and resonant for my analysis.

59. For a valuable critique of Irigaray, see Toril Moi, *Sexual/Textual Politics: Feminist Literary Theory* (London: Methuen, 1985), 147–49.

60. See Talcott Parsons, "Age and Sex in the Social Structure," in *The Family: Its Structure and Functions*, ed. Rose Laub Coser (New York: St. Martin's, 1964), 262.

61. Miller, *Timebends*, 488.

62. Sherry B. Ortner, "Is Female to Male as Nature Is to Culture?" in *Woman, Culture, and Society*, ed. Michelle Zimbalist Rosaldo and Louise Lamphere (Stanford, Calif.: Stanford University Press, 1974), 85.

63. Parsons, "The Social Structure of the Family," 270. Sue-Ellen Case also elaborates on this binarism. See Case, *Feminism and Theatre*, 6.

64. See my analysis of *The Crucible* in David Savran, *Breaking the Rules: The Wooster Group* (New York: Theatre Communications Group, 1988), 206–9.

65. Arthur Miller, *The Price* (New York: Viking, 1968), 108.

66. Victor J. Seidler, "Reason, Desire, and Male Sexuality," in *The Cultural Construction of Sexuality*, ed. Pat Caplan (London: Tavistock, 1987), 86. Seidler's essay provides a useful and brief history of the liaison between reason and masculinity.

67. See Barker, *The Tremulous Private Body*, especially pp. 45–69.

68. R. W. Connell, *Gender and Power* (Stanford, Calif.: Stanford University Press, 1987), 183.

69. Miller, *A View from the Bridge*, 19, 30, 46.

70. Ibid., 63.

71. Gerald Weales, "Arthur Miller's Shifting Image of Man," in *Arthur Miller: A Collection of Critical Essays*, 135. Mottram also describes Eddie's "nervous sexual feeling for Rodolpho." Eric Mottram, "Arthur Miller: Development of a Political Dramatist in America," in *Arthur Miller: A Collection of Critical Essays*, 39.

72. Nelson, *Arthur Miller*, 214.

73. Miller, *Timebends*, 464. At the time of the filming, Miller also referred to the work as a "present" for Monroe. James Goode, *The Making of The Misfits* (New York: Limelight, 1986), 300.

74. For a detailed account of the events that inspired the film's plot, see Goode, *The Making of The Misfits*, 17–19.

75. Carl E. Rollyson, Jr., *Marilyn Monroe: A Life of the Actress* (Ann Arbor, Mich.: UMI Research Press, 1986), 177–78.

76. John Huston, *An Open Book* (New York: Alfred A. Knopf, 1980), 288.

77. Nelson, *Arthur Miller*, 227, 237.

78. Leonard Moss, *Arthur Miller* (Boston: Twayne, 1980), 53.

79. Corrigan, "Introduction," 5.

80. Scott Hammen, *John Huston* (Boston: Twayne, 1985), 97.

81. John McCarty, *The Films of John Huston* (Secaucus, N.J.: Citadel, 1987), 131.

82. Goode, *The Making of The Misfits*, 21; Huston, *An Open Book*, 286.

83. Miller, *Timebends*, 460–61.

84. The uncut story, published in Arthur Miller, *I Don't Need You Any More* (New York: Viking, 1967), 78–113, greatly expands the characterizations of the three protagonists, filling in the details of family life omitted in the version published in *Esquire*, October 1957, 158–66. Because the unabridged version provides the men with more complex motives, it transforms them somewhat from social icons into more traditionally drawn realistic characters. In so doing, it changes the emphasis of the story, and (anticipating *After the Fall*) reconfigures, to some degree, a historical atrocity as a psychological one.

85. Miller, "The Misfits," *Esquire*, 161.

86. Ibid., 165.

87. "Perce Howland watched, his face dreamy and soft." Ibid., 158. The selection of Montgomery Clift, a homosexual, to play the role may in part have been suggested by the character's "softness."

88. Ibid., 166.

89. Miller, *The Misfits* (New York: Viking, 1961), 42, 24, 78. Unless indicated otherwise, all subsequent references will be to this edition; page numbers will be noted in the text.

90. Miller, "The Misfits," *Esquire*, 165.

91. Here I must disagree with Sue-Ellen Case, who uses *The Misfits* as an example of a text in which "women's sexuality" is "subordinate and derivative in relation to that of the leading male characters." Case, *Feminism and Theatre*, 124. Although there is certainly an attempt on the part of the men to keep her strictly dependent upon them, I believe that Roslyn has a vitality that consistently exceeds and, to some extent, undermines her subordination.

92. Stanley Kauffman, "Across the Great Divide," review of *The Misfits, New Republic*, February 20, 1961, 26. In playing these roles, she is also unmistakably an elaboration of the unnamed "girl" who rescues the sea robins from death on the beach in the story "Please Don't Kill Anything," in Miller, *I Don't Need You Any More*, 71–77.

93. See, for example, Talcott Parsons, "Family Structure and the Socialization of the Child," in *Family, Socialization and Interaction Process*, ed. Talcott Parsons and Robert F. Bales (New York: Free Press, 1955), 101.

94. This dialogue is transcribed verbatim from the film. A slightly different and more elaborate version is in Miller, *The Misfits*, 30–31.

95. Miller, *The Misfits*, 21, 34. Compare Miller's declaration: "The freedom that Nevada offers is the opposite of selling your existence for the rewards and punishments of a so-called civilized existence." Quoted in Goode, *The Making of The Misfits*, 74.

96. Goode, *The Making of The Misfits*, 74.

97. Ibid.

98. This speech is transcribed verbatim from the film. The scripted version is in Miller, *The Misfits*, 118.

99. This speech is transcribed verbatim from the film. The scripted version is in Miller, *The Misfits*, 119.

100. According to Goode, Miller and Huston "got along very well" during the making of the film. Goode, *The Making of The Misfits*, 65. Neither has left a record of any major disagreements over this particular sequence. I am not especially concerned, however, with the lack of extensive documentation because the question of individual authorship is far less important to me than the status of the film as a cultural document in which are encoded various struggles and anxieties that circulate in the society at large. It matters little to me whether the so-called author of the sequence is judged to be Miller or Huston because, I believe, neither constitutes a real origin. That hypothetical source would be located in the complex economic and ideological nexus known as society and, therefore, will always stand above and beyond the individual artist-as-producer.

101. Kauffmann, "Across the Great Divide," 26.

102. Ibid. More sensationalistic (or more naive) than Kauffmann, Goode notes admiringly how one particular shot "depended upon Marilyn jiggling properly in the saddle." Goode, *The Making of The Misfits*, 181.

103. See Laura Mulvey, "Visual Pleasure and Narrative Cinema," *Screen* 16 (Autumn 1975): 6–18; Teresa De Lauretis, *Alice Doesn't: Feminism, Semiotics, Cinema* (Bloomington: Indiana University Press, 1984), 58–69; Kaja Silverman, *The Subject of Semiotics* (New York: Oxford University Press, 1983), 222–36.

104. Miller, quoted in Goode, *The Making of The Misfits*, 76.

105. According to her personal maid, Lena Pepitone, Monroe was very unhappy with this sequence: "I convince them by throwing a fit, not by explaining anything. So I have a fit. A screaming fit. . . . And to think, *Arthur* did this to me. . . . If that's what he thinks of me, well, then I'm not for him and he's not for me." Quoted in Gloria Steinem, with photographs by George Barris, *Marilyn* (New York: Henry Holt, 1986), 79.

106. Mary P. Ryan, *Womanhood In America: From Colonial Times to the Present* (New York: New Viewpoints, 1979), 189.

107. *Life*, July 26, 1943, 10.

108. "Soldier's Wife at Work," *Life*, September 7, 1942, 39–42.

109. See Ryan, *Womanhood in America*, 188–91.

110. Joseph H. Pleck, "The Theory of Male Sex-Role Identity: Its Rise and Fall, 1936 to the Present," in *The Making of Masculinities: The New Men's Studies*, ed. Harry Brod (Boston: Allen and Unwin, 1987), 28.

111. See Nancy Woloch, *Women and the American Experience* (New York: Alfred A. Knopf, 1984), 495–506; Ryan, *Womanhood in America*, 191–209.

112. Benjamin Spock, *Baby and Child Care* (New York: Meredith, 1968), 564.

113. Cornelia Otis Skinner, "Women Are Misguided," *Life*, December 24, 1956, 73.

114. See Woloch, *Women and the American Experience*, 495–506; Ryan, *Womanhood in America*, 191–209.

115. Talcott Parsons and Robert F. Bales, eds., *Family, Socialization and Interaction Process*, 16–22.

116. May, *Homeward Bound*, 99.

117. Miller, *Timebends*, 467.

118. Ibid., 466. Frank Taylor, producer of the film, remarked about the role, "It's a spiritual autobiography. This is who she is." Quoted in Goode, *The Making of The Misfits*, 257. During the shooting one interviewer noted, "Some friends claim Roslyn is a portrait of Marilyn Monroe." W. J. Weatherby, interview with Monroe, *The Guardian*, November 3, 1960, 8.

119. Miller describes both Roslyn and Monroe as "golden girls." Miller, *The Misfits*, 7; idem, *Timebends*, 242. Also compare the following passages of dialogue between Gay and Roslyn and Miller and Monroe:

"I think you're the saddest girl I ever met."

"You're the first man ever said that." (Miller, *The Misfits*, 33)

After one of those silences I said, "You're the saddest girl I've ever met."

She first thought this a defeat; men, she had said once, only wanted happy girls. But then a smile touched her lips as she discovered the compliment I had intended. "You're the only one who ever said that to me." (Miller, *Timebends*, 369)

120. May, *Homeward Bound*, 55.

121. Miller, *Timebends*, 466. Also consider Nelson's observation: "Miller explains that the slump in his writing began before his marriage to Marilyn, but it is clear that it continued throughout the marriage and the tensions and frictions of that relationship." Nelson, *Arthur Miller*, 241.

122. Morris Zelditch, Jr., "Role Differentiation in the Nuclear Family: A Comparative Study," in *Family, Socialization and Interaction Process*, 339. According to Goode, an autograph seeker approached Miller during the filming of *The Misfits* to request the signature of "Monroe's husband." Goode, *The Making of The Misfits*, 107.

123. Quoted in Goode, *The Making of The Misfits*, 44.

124. Spock, *Baby and Child Care*, 27.

125. Howard Taubman, "Theatre: After the Fall," *New York Times*, January 24, 1964, 18.

126. Robert Brustein, "Arthur Miller's Mea Culpa," *New Republic*, February 8, 1964, 26–30.

127. Leslie Hanscom, "'After the Fall': Arther Miller's Return," *Newsweek*, February 3, 1964, 50; Taubman, "Theater: After the Fall," 18.

128. For an enumeration of the autobiographical elements in the play, see Moss, *Arthur Miller*, 66–68.

129. Mrs. Henry Reichman, letter to the *New York Times*, February 23, sec. II, p. 7; Lillian Gruber, letter to the *New York Times*, February 2, 1964, sec. II, p. 3.

130. Tom Prideaux, "A Desperate Search by a Troubled Hero," *Life*, February 7, 1964, 64D; "Marilyn's Ghost Takes the Stage," *Life*, February 7, 1964, 64A.

131. Barbara Gelb, "Question: 'Am I My Brother's Keeper?'" *New York Times*, November 29, 1964; reprinted in Roudané, *Conversations with Arthur Miller*, 79.

132. Miller, *Timebends*, 527.

133. Bigsby, *A Critical Introduction*, 216; Raymond Williams, *Drama from Ibsen to Brecht* (New York: Oxford University Press, 1969), 275.

134. As examples of these various strategies, see Hayman, *Arthur Miller*, 84–85; Moss, *Arthur Miller*, 66–70; Schlueter and Flanagan, *Arthur Miller*, 98, 157; Nelson, *Arthur Miller*, 240–70.

135. Arthur Miller, "Foreword to *After the Fall*," in *The Theater Essays of Arthur Miller*, 257.

136. Paul De Man, "Autobiography as De-facement," *MLN* 94 (December 1979): 919.

137. Ibid., 920–21.

138. Ibid., 926.

139. Ibid., 921.

140. I am here indebted to Paul Jay's discussion of the relationship between autobiography and psychoanalysis. See Jay, *Being in the Text: Self-Representation from Wordsworth to Roland Barthes* (Ithaca, N.Y.: Cornell University Press, 1984), 21–32.

141. Arthur Miller, "Arthur Miller Ad-Libs on Elia Kazan," *Conversations with Arthur Miller*, 69.

142. Miller, *After the Fall*, final stage version (Harmondsworth: Penguin, 1980), 56. Unless indicated otherwise, all subsequent references will be to this edition; page numbers will be noted in the text.

143. Miller, *After the Fall*, original version (New York: Viking, 1964), 84–85.

144. Miller, "The Family in Modern Drama," 81–84.

145. Consider, for example, the delighted tone of the short article he wrote to accompany a photo spread of Monroe, "My Wife Marilyn: Playwright Pays Affectionate Tribute to Her Feat," *Life*, December 22, 1958.

146. The original version of *After the Fall* is in many respects a much more interesting text than the revision. It is more active and less contemplative, more frankly associative in its structure, much more particularized and detailed and, as a result, somewhat less intent on "universalizing" the experience of the characters.

147. Reichman, letter to the *New York Times*.

148. Miller, *After the Fall*, original version, 77.

149. Ibid., 105.

150. Brustein, "Arthur Miller's Mea Culpa," 26.

151. "It was in 1942 that Philip Wylie coined the term 'Momism' in his best-selling book, *Generation of Vipers*. 'Momism' . . . was the result of frustrated women who smothered their children with overprotection and overaffection, making their sons in particular weak and passive." May, *Homeward Bound*, 74 (see also pp. 75, 96–97).

152. Steven R. Centola, "'The Will to Live': An Interview with Arthur Miller," in *Conversations with Arthur Miller*, 343.

153. De Lauretis, *Alice Doesn't*, 113, 121.

154. Miller, *After the Fall*, original version, 14.

155. In the original version of the play, Holga tells the story of a heroic "old soldier" who saved her from committing suicide (as Quentin did Maggie) and then "made [her] follow him" on foot through the countryside. When she "suddenly" knocked at a door,

however, and her mother opened it, the old soldier instantly and mysteriously disappeared, as though to prove the incompatibility of the maternal and the heroic. Ibid., 24.

156. De Lauretis, *Alice Doesn't*, 121.

157. Miller, "Arthur Miller Ad-Libs," 69.

158. Miller, *Timebends*, 113, 327.

159. Compare Virginia Woolf's wonderful observation: "Women have served all these centuries as looking-glasses possessing the magic and delicious power of reflecting the figure of man at twice his natural size." Quoted in De Lauretis, *Alice Doesn't*, 6.

160. Bigsby, *A Critical Introduction*, 214.

161. Arthur Miller, "With Respect for Her Agony—But with Love," *Life*, February 7, 1964, 66. This assertion of universal guilt is also connected to a founding belief of bourgeois liberalism in the innate competitiveness and corruption of the individual subject. See H. Mark Roelofs, "Hobbes, Liberalism, and America," in *Liberalism and the Modern Polity: Essays in Contemporary Political Theory*, ed. Michael J. Gargas McGrath (New York: Marcel Dekker, 1978), 119–42.

162. Miller, "Foreword to *After the Fall*," 257.

163. Bigsby, *A Critical Introduction*, 213.

164. Brustein, "Arthur Miller's Mea Culpa," 28. Somewhat more reluctantly, Bigsby also concedes that the play is "a piece of self-justification." Bigsby, *A Critical Introduction*, 216.

165. See Harry Brod, "Introduction: Themes and Theses of Men's Studies," in *The Making of Masculinities: The New Men's Studies*, 13–15.

166. Reported in Navasky, *Naming Names*, 391.

167. See Rollyson, *Marilyn Monroe*, 20.

168. Anonymous actor quoted in Navasky, *Naming Names*, 218.

169. Miller, "With Respect for Her Agony," 66.

170. Bigsby, *A Critical Introduction*, 214.

171. Arthur Miller, *The Creation of the World and Other Business* (New York: Viking, 1973), 54, 50.

172. Ibid., 56.

173. Arthur Miller, *The Archbishop's Ceiling/The American Clock* (New York: Grove, 1989), 31.

174. Miller, *The Archbishop's Ceiling/The American Clock*, 6, 25.

175. Mark Lamos, "An Afternoon with Arthur Miller," in *Conversations with Arthur Miller*, 381.

176. Arthur Miller, *Clara*, in *Danger: Memory!* (New York: Grove, 1987), 58. All subsequent references will be to this edition; page numbers will be noted in the text.

177. Arthur Miller, "The Pussycat and the Expert Plumber Who Was a Man," in *One Hundred Non-Royalty Radio Plays*, ed. William Kozlenko (New York: Greenberg, 1941), 26.

178. Roudané, "An Interview with Arthur Miller," 362.

179. Ibid., 360.

180. Miller, *Timebends*, 408.

181. Miller, *After the Fall*, original version, 62.

Two: Tennessee Williams I: "By coming suddenly into a room that I thought was empty"

1. Tennessee Williams, "The Mysteries of the Joy Rio," in *Collected Stories* (New York: Ballantine, 1986), 104, 106. All subsequent references will be to this edition; page numbers will be noted in the text.

2. Tennessee Williams, *Memoirs* (Garden City, N.Y.: Doubleday, 1975), 142. In regard to Kazan's testimony before the House Committee, Williams wrote in a 1952 letter that although he recognizes the "great hostility toward" Kazan on the part of "most theatre people," he "take[s] no attitude about it, one way or another." Tennessee Williams, with commentary by Maria St. Just, *Five O'Clock Angel: Letters of Tennessee Williams to Maria St. Just, 1948–1982* (New York: Alfred A. Knopf, 1990), 56.

3. Charles Ruas, "Tennessee Williams," in *Conversations with Tennessee Williams*, ed. Albert J. Devlin (Jackson: University Press of Mississippi, 1986), 293.

4. Tennessee Williams, *Tennessee Williams' Letters to Donald Windham, 1940–1965*, ed. Donald Windham (New York: Holt, Rinehart and Winston, 1977), 126, 106.

5. Jean Evans, "The Life and Ideas of Tennessee Williams," in *Conversations with Tennessee Williams*, 15.

6. David Frost, "Will God Talk Back to a Playwright? Tennessee Williams," in *Conversations with Tennessee Williams*, 146.

7. Williams, *Memoirs*, 238 (see also pp. 94, 115). In an interview conducted in the early 1970s, in response to the interviewer's attempt to oppose Miller's concern with "social issues" against Williams's interest in "sexual problems," Elia Kazan makes an important observation: "Williams, by the way, is political in the sense that he supports any cause that is truly liberal, in every way he can. But it's always pure, it's always immediate, it's not calculated. And it's always personal." Michel Ciment, *Kazan on Kazan* (New York: Viking, 1974), 79.

8. George Whitmore, "George Whitmore Interviews Tennessee Williams," in *Gay Sunshine Interviews*, vol. 1, ed. Winston Leyland (San Francisco: Gay Sunshine, 1984), 316.

9. Benjamin Nelson, *Tennessee Williams: The Man and His Work* (New York: Ivan Obolensky, 1961), 287–88.

10. Robert Bechtold Heilman, *The Iceman, the Arsonist, and the Troubled Agent: Tragedy and Melodrama on the Modern Stage* (Seattle: University of Washington Press, 1973), 115; Roger Boxill, *Tennessee Williams* (London: Macmillan, 1987), 1.

11. Raymond Williams, *Modern Tragedy* (Stanford, Calif.: Stanford University Press, 1966), 119.

12. C. W. E. Bigsby, *A Critical Introduction to Twentieth-Century American Drama*, vol. 2 (Cambridge: Cambridge University Press, 1984), 16, 32–33.

13. Ibid., 33.

14. John M. Clum, "'Something Cloudy, Something Clear': Homophobic Discourse in Tennessee Williams," in *Displacing Homophobia: Gay Male Perspectives in Literature and Culture*, ed. Ronald R. Butters, John M. Clum, and Michael Moon (Durham: Duke University Press, 1989), 155.

15. Williams, *Letters to Donald Windham*, 106.

16. Ibid., 105–6.

17. I want to emphasize here that I am not using *homosexual* to denote a transhistorical subject. Rather, following Jeffrey Weeks, Guy Hocquenghem, Thomas Yingling, and many others, I recognize that the "homosexual" (like all subjects) and "homosexuality" are both historical and discursive constructs, always, in Yingling's words, "multiple, culturally specific, and subject to historical change or conceptual alteration." Thomas E. Yingling, *Hart Crane and the Homosexual Text: New Thresholds, New Anatomies* (Chicago: University of Chicago Press, 1990), 227 n. 3. See also Jeffrey Weeks, "Preface," in Guy Hocquenghem, *Homosexual Desire*, trans. Daniella Dangoor (London: Allison and Busby, 1978), 10.

18. Frost, "Will God Talk Back," 146. A year later, recalling the event, Williams noted that Frost "asked me if I was a homosexual in front of millions of people. I was so mortified

I didn't know what to say, so I just blurted out, 'I cover the waterfront,' and the audience cheered me so loud he said he guessed he better break for a commercial." Rex Reed, "Tennessee Williams Turns Sixty," in *Conversations with Tennessee Williams,* 198.

19. C. Robert Jennings, "*Playboy* Interview: Tennessee Williams," in *Conversations with Tennessee Williams,* 229; Williams, *Memoirs,* 220.

20. Harold Beaver, "Homosexual Signs (*In Memory of Roland Barthes*)," *Critical Inquiry* (Autumn 1981): 99.

21. Don Lee Keith, "New Tennessee Williams Rises from 'Stoned Age,'" in *Conversations with Tennessee Williams,* 153; Williams, *Memoirs,* 50; Whitmore, "George Whitmore Interviews Tennessee Williams," 315.

22. Williams, *Memoirs,* 17; Reed, "Tennessee Williams Turns Sixty," 198; John Hicks, "Bard of Duncan Street: Scene Four," in *Conversations with Tennessee Williams,* 322.

23. Jennings, "*Playboy* Interview," 230; Williams, *Memoirs,* 142; Whitmore, "George Whitmore Interviews Tennessee Williams," 320.

24. Williams, *Memoirs,* 50; Whitmore, "George Whitmore Interviews Tennessee Williams," 315–16; Jennings, "*Playboy* Interview," 249.

25. Jennings, "*Playboy* Interview," 229. For Williams on the derivation of his name, see Mark Barron, "Newest Find on Broadway is a Mississippi Playwright Named Tennessee Williams," and Walter Wager, "Tennessee Williams," both in *Conversations with Tennessee Williams,* 4, 126.

26. See, for example, Clum's "'Something Cloudy, Something Clear'"; Edward A. Sklepowich, "In Pursuit of the Lyric Quarry: The Image of the Homosexual in Tennessee Williams' Prose Fiction," in *Tennessee Williams: A Tribute,* ed. Jac Tharpe (Jackson: University Press of Mississippi, 1977), 525–44; Kaier Curtin, "*We Can Always Call Them Bulgarians*": *The Emergence of Lesbians and Gay Men on the American Stage* (Boston: Alyson, 1987).

27. Whitmore, "George Whitmore Interviews Tennessee Williams," 313. For corroboration, see Curtin, "*We Can Always Call Them Bulgarians,*" especially pp. 250–333.

28. Williams, *Memoirs,* 3.

29. Yingling, *Hart Crane and the Homosexual Text,* 27.

30. Wager, "Tennessee Williams," 128–29.

31. Whitmore, "George Whitmore Interviews Tennessee Williams," 313; Dotson Rader, "The Art of Theatre V: Tennessee Williams," in *Conversations with Tennessee Williams,* 344.

32. James Grauerholz, "Orpheus Holds His Own: William Burroughs Talks with Tennessee Williams," in *Conversations with Tennessee Williams,* 299–300.

33. "New Play, Old Play," review of *Orpheus Descending, Time,* April 1, 1957, 61.

34. Gore Vidal, "Selected Memories of the Glorious Bird and the Golden Age," *New York Review of Books,* February 5, 1976, 15.

35. See Vito Russo, *The Celluloid Closet: Homosexuality in the Movies* (New York: Harper and Row, 1981).

36. John D'Emilio, *Sexual Politics, Sexual Communities: The Making of a Homosexual Minority in the United States, 1940–1970* (Chicago: University of Chicago Press, 1983), 19. Although the proscription of homosexuality was rather strictly enforced in the dominant culture, there did arise an active gay and lesbian subculture in connection with the Harlem Renaissance, a subculture that also produced its own distinctive arts and discourses. See Eric Garber, "A Spectacle in Color: The Lesbian and Gay Subculture of Jazz Age Harlem," in *Hidden from History: Reclaiming the Gay and Lesbian Past,* ed. Martin Bauml Duberman, Martha Vicinus, and George Chauncey, Jr. (New York: New American Library, 1989), 318–31.

37. Alan Berubé, "Marching to a Different Drummer: Lesbian and Gay GIs in World War II," in *Hidden from History: Reclaiming the Gay and Lesbian Past*, 387.

38. Weeks, "Preface," 9.

39. Berubé, "Marching to a Different Drummer," 391.

40. Guy George Garbrielson, quoted in *New York Times*, April 19, 1950, 25.

41. John D'Emilio, *Sexual Politics, Sexual Communities*, 45. D'Emilio's volume provides a valuable history of the persecution of homosexuals during the 1950s (see pp. 40–53). See also Jonathan Katz, *Gay American History: Lesbians and Gay Men in the U.S.A.* (New York: Harper and Row, 1976), 91–128.

42. See John D'Emilio and Estelle B. Freedman, *Intimate Matters: A History of Sexuality in America* (New York: Harper and Row, 1988), 294.

43. See D'Emilio, *Sexual Politics, Sexual Communities*, 48.

44. Eann MacDonald [Henry Hay], "Preliminary Concepts," quoted in Katz, *Gay American History*, 410.

45. *ONE: The Homosexual Magazine* 3 (April 1955): 4.

46. Review of *One Arm & Other Stories*, *ONE: The Homosexual Magazine* 3 (April 1955): 30.

47. Senator Kenneth Wherry, quoted by Max Lerner in the *New York Post*, July 17, 1950; reprinted in Katz, *Gay American History*, 95.

48. Ibid.

49. Weeks, "Preface," 21–22. This materialist reading of homophobia is, of course, heavily indebted to the work of Michel Foucault, in particular *The History of Sexuality*, vol. 1, *An Introduction*, trans. Robert Hurley (New York: Vintage Books, 1980). For a fine elaboration of Foucault and of the relationship between the materialist and psychoanalytical interpretations of homophobia, see Jonathan Dollimore, "Homophobia and Sexual Difference," *Oxford Literary Review* 8, nos. 1–2 (1986): 5–12.

50. *ONE: The Homosexual Magazine* 3 (April 1955): 4. See also Michael Bronski, *Culture Clash: The Making of Gay Sensibility* (Boston: South End, 1984), 81–84.

51. Interview with Henry Hay (1974) in Katz, *Gay American History*, 417.

52. See, for example, Clifford Kirkpatrick, *The Family as Process and Institution* (New York: Ronald, 1955), 328.

53. Frank Golovitz, "The Single Homosexual," *ONE: The Homosexual Magazine* 6 (April 1958): 7, 10.

54. See Curtin, "We Can Always Call Them Bulgarians," especially pp. 100–102.

55. Ruth Goetz, quoted ibid., 315.

56. Ruth Goetz and Augustus Goetz, *The Immoralist* (New York: Dramatists Play Service, 1954), 32, 79–80.

57. Ibid., 121. See also Curtin, "We Can Always Call Them Bulgarians," 291–319. The nexus of sin, disease, and racism performed by *The Immoralist* has proven distressingly hardy and vigorous in the 1990s. Given three of the horrors of the age—the AIDS crisis, the attack on the National Endowment for the Arts, and the anti-Arab racism whipped up by the recent Gulf War—*The Immoralist* would seem the perfect vehicle for any theater eager to pander to the forces of reaction and to triple its NEA funding.

58. Williams, *Memoirs*, 142.

59. Louise Davis, "That Baby Doll Man: Part I," in *Conversations with Tennessee Williams*, 43.

60. Charles P. Roland, *The Improbable Era: The South since World War II* (Lexington: University of Kentucky Press, 1975), 1–17.

61. Raymond Williams, *Drama from Ibsen to Brecht* (New York: Oxford University Press, 1969), 106.

62. Tennessee Williams, *Cat on a Hot Tin Roof* (New York: Signet, 1955), 85. All subsequent references will be to this edition; page numbers will be noted in the text.

63. "New Play in Manhattan," review of *Cat on a Hot Tin Roof*, *Time*, April 4, 1955, 98.

64. The *Time* review uses this phrase to describe the information that is revealed in the scene between Brick and Big Daddy. "New Play in Manhattan," 98.

65. Walter Benjamin, "Theses on the Philosophy of History," in *Illuminations*, trans. Harry Zohn (New York: Schocken, 1969), 262.

66. Whitmore, "George Whitmore Interviews Tennessee Williams," 319.

67. Tennessee Williams, *The Glass Menagerie* (New York: New Directions, 1970), 7. All subsequent references will be to this edition; page numbers will be noted in the text.

68. Tennessee Williams, *The Rose Tattoo* in *Three by Tennessee* (New York: Signet Classic, 1976), 140. All subsequent references will be to this edition; page numbers will be noted in the text.

69. Mary Ann Corrigan, "Beyond Verisimilitude: Echoes of Expressionism in Williams' Plays," in *Tennessee Williams: A Tribute*, 375, 383, 392, 400, 402, 409.

70. Studs Terkel, "Studs Terkel Talks with Tennessee Williams," in *Conversations with Tennessee Williams*, 80.

71. Maxime Alexandre et al., "Open Letter to M. Paul Claudel, French Ambassador to Japan," in Maurice Nadeau, *The History of Surrealism*, trans. Richard Howard (London: Jonathan Cape, 1968), 238.

72. C. W. E. Bigsby, *Dada & Surrealism* (London: Methuen, 1972), 60.

73. André Breton, "First Surrealist Manifesto," trans. Patrick Waldberg, in *Avant-Garde Drama: Major Plays and Documents Post World War I*, ed. Bernard F. Dukore and Daniel C. Gerould (New York: Bantam, 1969), 566.

74. Walter Benjamin, "Surrealism: The Last Snapshot of the European Intelligentsia," in *One-Way Street and Other Writings*, trans. Edmund Jephcott and Kingsley Shorter (London: NLB, 1979), 226.

75. Quoted in Jacqueline Chenieux-Gendron, *Surrealism*, trans. Vivian Folkenflik (New York: Columbia University Press, 1990), 146–47.

76. Benjamin, "Surrealism," 227.

77. Ibid., 236. For analyses of the politics of surrealism, see Chenieux-Gendron, *Surrealism*, 141–58; Helena Lewis, *The Politics of Surrealism* (New York: Paragon House, 1988).

78. Quoted in Chenieux-Gendron, *Surrealism*, 134.

79. Quoted in Lewis, *The Politics of Surrealism*, 73. See also Emmanuel Cooper, *The Sexual Perspective: Homosexuality and Art in the Last 100 Years in the West* (London: Routledge and Kegan Paul, 1986), 139; Julien Levy, *Memoir of an Art Gallery* (New York: G. P. Putnam's Sons, 1977), 81.

80. See Lewis, *The Politics of Surrealism*, 71–76; Mary Ann Caws, "Ladies Shot and Painted: Female Embodiment in Surrealist Art," in *The Female Body in Western Culture: Contemporary Perspectives*, ed. Susan Rubin Suleiman (Cambridge: Harvard University Press, 1986), 262–87.

81. Tennessee Williams, *Camino Real* (New York: New Directions, 1970), vii–viii. All subsequent references will be to this edition; page numbers will be noted in the text.

82. Don Ross, "Williams in Art and Morals: An Anxious Foe of Untruth," in *Conversations with Tennessee Williams*, 41.

83. See Edward B. Henning, *The Spirit of Surrealism* (Bloomington: Cleveland Museum of Art in cooperation with Indiana University Press, 1979), 138–39. In 1943, Williams

wrote that De Chirico's *Conversation among the Ruins* was his "favorite" canvas at the Art Institute of Chicago. Williams, *Letters to Donald Windham,* 63.

84. Allen Ellenzweig, "George Platt Lynes at Robert Miller," *Art in America,* March 1982, 144. See also Robert Knafo, "Illusion and Disillusion: The Photography of George Platt Lynes," *Arts Magazine,* January 1982, 78–79; Jack Woody, *George Platt Lynes Photographs 1931–1955* (Los Angeles: Twelvetrees, 1980).

85. See Kenneth Burke, *A Grammar of Motive* (Berkeley: University of California Press, 1969), 3–7.

86. Williams, *Letters to Donald Windham,* 148.

87. An entire industry of postmodernist theory has emerged during the last ten years, and the definition of postmodernism generally has become a primary site of struggle for most theorists dealing with the politics of contemporary culture. Three works that make particularly valuable contributions to the debate, in part because of their widely divergent opinions, are Andreas Huyssen, *After the Great Divide: Modernism, Mass Culture, Postmodernism* (Bloomington: Indiana University Press, 1986); Fredric Jameson, "Postmodernism, or the Cultural Logic of Late Capitalism," *New Left Review* 146 (July–August 1984): 53–92; Andrew Ross, ed., *Universal Abandon? The Politics of Postmodernism* (Minneapolis: University of Minnesota Press, 1988).

88. Terkel, "Studs Terkel Talks with Tennessee Williams," 86.

89. Arthur Miller, "The Shadows of the Gods," in *The Theater Essays of Arthur Miller,* ed. Robert A. Martin (New York: Viking, 1978), 189–93. This passage is also quoted at length in Bigsby, *A Critical Introduction,* 88–92.

90. Miller, "The Shadows of the Gods," 190.

91. Eric Bentley, "Theatre," review of *Cat on a Hot Tin Roof, New Republic,* 11 April 1955, 28.

92. Although Howard Davies's 1989 Broadway production (starring Kathleen Turner) restored Williams's original ending, its style was rather stolidly realistic, and it played down the various sonic intrusions.

93. Roland Barthes, *On Racine,* trans. Richard Howard (New York: Hill and Wang, 1964), 4. Although there is considerable violence between Maggie and Brick in act 1, the room is still a kind of haven for them.

94. Tennessee Williams, *A Streetcar Named Desire* (New York: Signet, 1947), 95.

95. Eve Kosofsky Sedgwick, *Epistemology of the Closet* (Berkeley: University of California Press, 1990), 56.

96. Ibid., 85.

97. In *The Night of the Iguana,* Williams constructs a more overt scene of fetishism (that again dramatizes the commodity status of sexuality) in Hannah's story of her sexual "encounter" with an Australian salesman in Singapore who begs her for a "piece of [her] clothes" just to "hold" for "a few seconds" while he takes "his satisfaction." Tennessee Williams, *The Night of the Iguana* (New York: Signet, 1961), 114–16.

98. Jacques Lacan, *Ecrits,* trans. Alan Sheridan (New York: W. W. Norton, 1977), 11.

99. Williams, *Letters to Donald Windham,* 91–93.

Three: Tennessee Williams II: "'Revolutionary' is a misunderstood word"

1. The editors of Williams's *Collected Stories* refer to "Hard Candy," with some justification, as being "really a variation of the earlier 'The Mysteries of the Joy Rio.'" Tennessee Williams, *Collected Stories* (New York: Ballantine, 1986), 608.

2. Edward A. Sklepowich, "In Pursuit of the Lyric Quarry: The Image of the Homosexual in Tennessee Williams' Prose Fiction," in *Tennessee Williams: A Tribute,* ed. Jac Tharpe (Jackson: University Press of Mississippi, 1977), 531.

3. Even Williams's short stories came under intense fire during the 1950s. When *One Arm* was published in a commercial edition in 1954, the excoriating review in *Time* magazine began, "This collection of short stories wears the scent of human garbage as if it were the latest Parisian perfume." *Time*, January 3, 1955, 76. Mercifully for Williams, *Hard Candy* was not submitted for review during the 1950s.

4. Tennessee Williams, "Hard Candy," in *Collected Stories*, 362. All subsequent references will be to this edition; page numbers will be noted in the text.

5. Although they recognize Williams's narrative equivocations, both Sklepowich and Clum believe that the story foregrounds Williams's own internalization of guilt. See Sklepowich, "In Pursuit of the Lyric Quarry," 533–34; John M. Clum, "'Something Cloudy, Something Clear': Homophobic Discourse in Tennessee Williams," in *Displacing Homophobia: Gay Male Perspectives in Literature and Culture*, ed. Ronald R. Butters, John M. Clum, and Michael Moon (Durham, N.C.: Duke University Press, 1989) 153–56.

6. Clum, "'Something Cloudy, Something Clear,'" 156.

7. Stanley Edgar Hyman, "Some Trends in the Novel," *College English* (October 1958): 1–3.

8. Stephen S. Stanton, "Introduction," in *Tennessee Williams: A Collection of Critical Essays*, ed. Stephen S. Stanton (Englewood Cliffs, N.J.: Prentice-Hall, 1977), 3–4.

9. Nancy M. Tischler, *Tennessee Williams: Rebellious Puritan* (New York: Citadel, 1961), 213.

10. See Sklepowich, "In Pursuit of the Lyric Quarry," 542, 544 n. 18.

11. Sedgwick writes: "If Albertine and the narrator are of the same gender, should the supposed outside loves of Albertine, which the narrator obsessively images as imaginatively inaccessible to himself, then, maintaining the female *gender* of their love object, be transposed in *orientation* into heterosexual desires? Or, maintaining the transgressive same-sex *orientation*, would they have to change the *gender* of their love object and be transposed into male homosexual desires? Or, in a homosexual framework, would the heterosexual orientation after all be more transgressive?" Eve Kosofsky Sedgwick, *Epistemology of the Closet* (Berkeley: University of California Press, 1990), 233. See also J. E. Rivers, *Proust & the Art of Love: The Aesthetics of Sexuality in the Life, Times, & Art of Marcel Proust* (New York: Columbia University Press, 1980), 1–9.

12. Stanton, "Introduction," 4.

13. For a fine elaboration of this paradigm shift, see George Chauncey, Jr., "From Sexual Inversion to Homosexuality: Medicine and the Changing Conceptualization of Female Deviance," *Salmagundi*, 58–59 (Fall 1982–Winter 1983): 114–46.

14. George Whitmore, "George Whitmore Interviews Tennessee Williams," in *Gay Sunshine Interviews*, vol. 1, ed. Winston Leyland (San Francisco: Gay Sunshine, 1984), 312. See also Rex Reed, "Tennessee Williams Turns Sixty," and Dotson Rader, "The Art of Theatre V: Tennessee Williams," both in *Conversations with Tennessee Williams*, ed. Albert J. Devlin (Jackson: University Press of Mississippi, 1986), 189, 344.

15. Tennessee Williams, *The Roman Spring of Mrs. Stone* (New York: New Directions, 1950), 10. All subsequent references will be to this edition; page numbers will be noted in the text.

16. For a history of the "Ganymede," see Alan Bray, *Homosexuality in Renaissance England* (London: Gay Men's Press, 1982), 58–67.

17. Susan Sontag, "Notes on 'Camp,'" in *Against Interpretation and Other Essays* (New York: Dell, 1966), 277, 286.

18. Morris Zelditch, Jr., "Role Differentiation in the Nuclear Family: A Comparative Study," in *Family, Socialization and Interaction Process*, ed. Talcott Parsons and Robert F. Bales (New York: Free Press, 1955), 339.

19. In his *Memoirs* Williams announces, "Of course, 'swish' and 'camp' are products of self-mockery, imposed upon homosexuals by our society." Curiously, Williams appears not to recognize any emancipatory or resistant force in these strategies. Tennessee Williams, *Memoirs* (Garden City, N.Y.: Doubleday, 1975), 50.

20. See Sue-Ellen Case, "Gender as Play," *Women & Performance* (Winter 1984): 21-24.

21. "Cardinal Scores 'Baby Doll' Film," *New York Times*, December 17, 1956, 28.

22. Quoted in "The Bitter Dispute over 'Baby Doll,'" *Life*, January 7, 1957, 60.

23. "The Trouble with *Baby Doll*," *Time*, January 14, 1957, 100.

24. "New Picture," review of *Baby Doll*, *Time* December 24, 1956, 61.

25. Michel Ciment, *Kazan on Kazan* (New York: Viking, 1974), 81.

26. Sy Kahn, "*Baby Doll*: A Comic Fable," in *Tennessee Williams: A Tribute*, 307.

27. "New Picture," 61.

28. "The Bitter Dispute over 'Baby Doll,'" 64-65.

29. Tennessee Williams, *Baby Doll* (London: Secker and Warburg, 1957), 30. All subsequent references will be to this edition; page numbers will be noted in the text. For an account of the weaving together of the two plays and the differences between the film and its sources, see Gene D. Phillips, *The Films of Tennessee Williams* (Philadelphia: Art Alliance, 1980), 87-92.

30. Kahn, "*Baby Doll*," 294.

31. Tennessee Williams, *Kingdom of Earth*, in *The Theatre of Tennessee Williams*, vol. 5 (New York: New Directions, 1976), 126; idem, *Battle of Angels*, in *Orpheus Descending with Battle of Angels* (New York: New Directions, 1958), 132; idem, *In the Bar of a Tokyo Hotel*, in *Dragon Country* (New York: New Directions, 1970), 3. All subsequent references will be to these editions; page numbers will be noted in the text.

32. Ciment, *Kazan on Kazan*, 76.

33. Teresa De Lauretis, *Alice Doesn't: Feminism, Semiotics, Cinema* (Bloomington: Indiana University Press, 1988), 119. For my analysis of Miller's use of this mythical narrative, see chapter 1.

34. Zelditch, "Role Differentiation in the Nuclear Family," 339.

35. Mark Crispin Miller, "Deride and Conquer," in *Watching Television: A Pantheon Guide to Popular Culture*, ed. Todd Gitlin (New York: Pantheon, 1986), 197. Crispin's article provides a fine analysis of the changing image of "Dad" on American television.

36. John Gruen, "Tennessee Williams," in *Conversations with Tennessee Williams*, 116.

37. De Lauretis, *Alice Doesn't*, 121.

38. Tennessee Williams, *The Night of the Iguana* (New York: Signet, 1961), 58.

39. Tennessee Williams, "Big Black: A Mississippi Idyll," in *Collected Stories*, 29-30.

40. Tennessee Williams, "Rubio y Morena," in *Collected Stories*, 273.

41. Williams, *Battle of Angels*, 185.

42. Tennessee Williams, *Sweet Bird of Youth* (New York: New Directions, 1972), 71, 107.

43. Cecil Brown, "Interview with Tennessee Williams," in *Conversations with Tennessee Williams*, 267. See also Studs Terkel, "Studs Terkel Talks with Tennessee Williams," and Walter Wager, "Tennessee Williams," both also in *Conversations with Tennessee Williams*, 92, 128.

44. Brown, "Interview with Tennessee Williams," 266.

45. Calvin C. Hernton, *Sex and Racism in America* (New York: Grove, 1965), 39. For further references, see Earle V. Bryant, "The Sexualization of Racism in Richard Wright's 'The Man Who Killed a Shadow,'" *Black American Literature Forum*, 16 (Fall 1982): 119-21.

46. Tennessee Williams, "Miss Coynte of Greene," in *Collected Stories*, 521-23.

47. "Blunt and Banned," *Newsweek*, December 17, 1956, 106; "The Bitter Dispute over 'Baby Doll,'" 61.

48. "Should It Be Suppressed?," *Newsweek*, December 31, 1956, 59.

49. "The Bitter Dispute over 'Baby Doll,'" 60-61. According to Benjamin Muse, "Negroes might be 'Southern Negroes,' but a 'Southerner' in common parlance was emphatically a white person." Muse, *Ten Years of Prelude: The Story of Integration since the Supreme Court's 1954 Decision* (New York: Viking, 1964), 38.

50. Charles P. Roland, *The Improbable Era: The South since World War II* (Lexington: University of Kentucky Press, 1975), 30-35.

51. Ibid., 35. For accounts of the ruling and its impact on the South, see Muse, *Ten Years of Prelude*; Hubert H. Humphrey, *Integration vs Segregation* (New York: Thomas Y. Crowell, 1964); Numan V. Bartley, *The Rise of Massive Resistance: Race and Politics in the South During the 1950's* (Baton Rouge: Louisiana State University Press, 1969).

52. Muse, *Ten Years of Prelude*, 40-50.

53. Roland, *The Improbable Era*, 35-39.

54. Thomas P. Brady, *Black Monday* (1955), quoted in Muse, *Ten Years of Prelude*, 42.

55. "New Picture," 61.

56. Kazan explains: "Because I meant to keep a certain mystery in the film, it was never made clear what happened. When Silva (Eli Wallach) lies in the crib and she's tucking him in, there's a fade-out. Then he's fast asleep and she's sitting at the foot of the crib.... Because so much was made of her thumb in her mouth, there was the assumption by some people that she went down on him during the fade-out; or that some sort of overt physical sexual act had been performed. But it really doesn't matter at all, because that's not what the picture is about, and *I* never thought anything did happen. I just thought of him at first teasing her then falling asleep in the crib and taking a nap." Ciment, *Kazan on Kazan*, 79-80.

57. "New Picture," 61.

58. "Cardinal Scores 'Baby Doll' Film," 28.

59. In the script, Williams calls for Vacarro to strip off his shirt shortly after his arrival at the Meighan plantation (p. 55), thereby allowing him to play the seduction scene in a state of partial undress. Kazan, however, less attuned to the erotic possibilities of the male body, disregards Williams's direction.

60. "The Bitter Dispute over 'Baby Doll,'" 65.

61. C. W. E. Bigsby, *A Critical Introduction to Twentieth-Century American Drama*, vol. 2 (Cambridge: Cambridge University Press, 1984), 133.

62. See ibid., 111-34; Ruby Cohn, "Late Tennessee Williams," *Modern Drama*, September 1984, 336-44.

63. Signi Falk, *Tennessee Williams*, 2d ed. (Boston: Twayne, 1978), 153, 157-58.

64. Ibid., 128.

65. See, for example, Bigsby, *A Critical Introduction*, 111-14, 121-23; Roger Boxill, *Tennessee Williams* (London: Macmillan, 1987), 145-65.

66. Frank Rich, "A Playwright Whose Greatest Act Was His First," *New York Times*, February 26, 1983, 10.

67. Clive Barnes, "Theater: 'In the Bar of a Tokyo Hotel,'" *New York Times*, May 12, 1969, 54.

68. "Torpid Tennessee," *Time*, May 23, 1969, 75; Jack Kroll, "Life Is a Bitch," *Newsweek*, May 26, 1969, 133; Harold Clurman, "Theatre," *The Nation*, June 2, 1969, 709-10.

69. Stefan Kanfer, "White Dwarf's Tragic Fade-out," *Life*, June 13, 1969, 10. According to one biographer, Williams was so "devastated" by this review that he refused to leave

his hotel room for three days. Donald Spoto, *The Kindness of Strangers: The Life of Tennessee Williams* (New York: Ballantine, 1986), 311.

70. Clurman, "Theatre," 710.

71. "Torpid Tennessee," 75; Henry Hewes, "Tennessee's Quest," *Saturday Review*, May 31, 1969.

72. George Niesen, "The Artist against the Reality in the Plays of Tennessee Williams," in *Tennessee Williams: A Tribute*, 486–87.

73. Boxill, *Tennessee Williams*, 154.

74. Bigsby, *A Critical Introduction*, 114.

75. Tennessee Williams, *The Demolition Downtown*, in *The Theatre of Tennessee Williams*, vol. 6 (New York: New Directions, 1981), 343.

76. Roland Barthes, *The Pleasure of the Text*, trans. Richard Miller (New York: Hill and Wang, 1975), 50.

77. Williams, *Memoirs*, 220. For his own spirited description (remarkably free of self-pity) of his "Stoned Age" and subsequent hospitalization, see pp. 195–229.

78. Stanley Kauffmann, "Homosexual Drama and Its Disguises," *New York Times*, January 23, 1966, sec. II, p. 1; see also Kauffmann, "On the Acceptability of the Homosexual," and "Drama Mailbag," *New York Times*, February 6, 1966, sec. II, pp. 1, 5–15. For a resumé of the debate sparked by Kauffmann's article, see Kaier Curtin, *"We Can Always Call Them Bulgarians": The Emergence of Lesbians and Gay Men on the American Stage* (Boston: Alyson, 1987), 320–33.

79. See Lawrence S. Wittner, *Cold War America: From Hiroshima to Watergate* (New York: Praeger, 1974), 278–81.

80. Quoted ibid., 280.

81. Ibid., 279.

82. Quoted in Judith Clavir Albert and Stewart Edward Albert, eds., *The Sixties Papers: Documents of a Rebellious Decade* (New York: Praeger, 1984), 17.

83. In its single-minded fury, Mark's paranoid and aggressive rhetoric is oddly reminiscent of the remarks of Assistant Secretary of Defense John McNaughton in 1967: "We seem to be proceeding on the assumption that the way to eradicate the Vietcong is to destroy all the village structures, defoliate all the jungles, and then cover the entire surface of South Vietnam with asphalt." Quoted in Wittner, *Cold War America*, 279.

84. Clurman, "Theatre," 709.

85. Bigsby, *A Critical Introduction*, 32–33.

86. Fredric Jameson, "Periodizing the 60s," in *The Ideologies of Theory, Essays 1971–1986*, vol. 2, *The Syntax of History* (Minneapolis: University of Minnesota Press, 1988), 206–8. Neil Lazarus has pointed out to me that although Jameson sees the neocolonialist order as a more effective means of subjugation than the older imperialist system, it could be argued that, in fact, the new order (of hegemony rather than domination) allows for and, indeed, produces more numerous and potent sites of resistance than the old. And while Jameson is certainly correct to note that rebellion in the 1980s or 1990s is not likely to be figured as a "universal liberation," *nationalism* remains a profoundly revolutionary (that is, antineocolonialist) force in many parts of the Third World.

87. Wager, "Tennessee Williams," 132.

88. Stanley Aronowitz, "When the New Left Was New," in *The 60s without Apology*, ed. Sohnya Sayres, Anders Stephanson, Stanley Aronowitz, and Fredric Jameson (Minneapolis: University of Minnesota Press, 1984), 20.

89. "The Port Huron Statement," in Albert and Albert, *The Sixties Papers*, 176, 181.

90. Paul Buhle, *Marxism in the United States: Remapping the History of the American Left* (London: Verso, 1991), 231.

91. Ibid., 237.

92. Quoted in Wittner, *Cold War America*, 285.

93. Stokely Carmichael, "What We Want," in Albert and Albert, *The Sixties Papers*, 139–40.

94. Jameson, "Periodizing the 60s," 180.

95. Todd Gitlin, *The Sixties: Years of Hope, Days of Rage* (New York: Bantam, 1989), 350.

96. James Weinstein, "The Fortunes of the Old Left Compared to the Fortunes of the New," in *Failure of a Dream? Essays in the History of American Socialism*, ed. John H. M. Laslett and Seymour Martin Lipset (Garden City, N.Y.: Anchor/Doubleday, 1974), 707. A particularly good account of the various splinters of SDS can be found in Aronowitz, "When the New Left Was New," 35–39.

97. Buhle, *Marxism in the United States*, 249.

98. Jameson, "Periodizing the 60s," 181.

99. Buhle, *Marxism in the United States*, 235–37.

100. Gitlin, *The Sixties*, 28. His chapter 8, "'Everybody Get Together,'" provides a particularly good resumé of the counterculture. See also Martin A. Lee and Bruce Shlain, *Acid Dreams: The CIA, LSD, and the Sixties Rebellion* (New York: Grove, 1985); Abe Peck, *Uncovering the Sixties: The Life and Times of the Underground Press* (New York: Pantheon, 1985).

101. Quoted in Lee and Shlain, *Acid Dreams*, 166.

102. Gitlin, *The Sixties*, 213.

103. Abbie Hoffman, "Revolution for the Hell of It," in Albert and Albert, *The Sixties Papers*, 421.

104. Jameson, "Periodizing the 60s," 188–89. For a useful summary of the founding principles and history of American Maoism, see Noel Ignatiev, "'Antirevisionism' (Maoism)," in *Encyclopedia of the American Left*, ed. Mari Jo Buhle, Paul Buhle, and Don Georgakas (New York: Garland, 1990), 48–51.

105. Jerry Rubin, quoted in Lee and Shlain, *Acid Dreams*, 207.

106. Jameson, "Periodizing the 60s," 189.

107. Gitlin, *The Sixties*, 108–9.

108. Ibid., 108–9, 372.

109. Ibid., 108–9, 371–73. See also Weinstein, "The Fortunes of the Old Left," 708–10.

110. Weinstein, "The Fortunes of the Old Left," 709.

111. Konstanin Berlandt, "Been Down So Long It Looks Up to Me," in Albert and Albert, *The Sixties Papers*, 450–55. An SDS statement of 1969, although singling out "male supremacy" as an oppressive system, ignores homophobia. "Bring the War Home," in Albert and Albert, *The Sixties Papers*, 247–53.

112. See Gitlin, *The Sixties*, 372.

113. Kate Millett, "Sexual Politics: A Manifesto for Revolution," in Albert and Albert, *The Sixties Papers*, 476–77.

114. John D'Emilio, *Sexual Politics, Sexual Communities: The Making of a Homosexual Minority in the United States, 1940–1970* (Chicago: University of Chicago Press, 1983), 233.

115. The Gay Liberation Front's statement of purpose (1969), quoted in D'Emilio, *Sexual Politics, Sexual Communities*, 234.

116. Len Richmond and Gary Noguera, "Random Notes from the Editors," in *The Gay Liberation Book*, ed. Len Richmond and Gary Noguera (San Francisco: Ramparts, 1973), 11–13.

117. Dennis Altman, "Introduction," in *The Gay Liberation Book*, 15–17.

118. Huey Newton, "A Letter from Huey," in *The Gay Liberation Book*, 142–45.

119. Arthur Evans, "How to Zap Straights," in *The Gay Liberation Book*, 115.

120. Sklepowich, "In Pursuit of the Lyric Quarry," 538.

121. Tennessee Williams, *Moise and the World of Reason* (New York: Simon and Schuster, 1975), 16, 18. All further references will be to this edition; page numbers will be noted in the text.

122. Tennessee Williams, "One Arm," in *Collected Stories*, 191–92, 197–98.

123. Tennessee Williams, *Tennessee Williams' Letters to Donald Windham, 1940–1965*, ed. Donald Windham (New York: Holt, Rinehart and Winston, 1977), 105.

124. Barthes, *The Pleasure of the Text*, 38. All further citations will be to this edition; page numbers will be noted in the text. For an incisive critique of the elitism and conservatism of Barthes's volume, see Andreas Huyssen, *After the Great Divide: Modernism, Mass Culture, Postmodernism* (Bloomington: Indiana University Press, 1986), 209–13.

125. Tennessee Williams, "Sand," in *Collected Stories*, 54–55.

126. Tennessee Williams, "Desire and the Black Masseur," in *Collected Stories*, 216.

127. Ibid.

128. Although the "heterosexual" address is very much like what Laura Mulvey identifies as the mode of classic narrative cinema, my notion of "homosexual" address and "homosexual" pleasure is very different from the alternative that Mulvey offers: the "destruction of pleasure as a radical weapon." Laura Mulvey, "Visual Pleasure and Narrative Cinema," *Screen* (Autumn 1975): 7. Rather than abjuring visual pleasure, I am trying to demonstrate how it can be reconfigured and mobilized for a progressive (and even revolutionary) art.

129. See Belden Fields, "French Maoism," in *The 60s without Apology*, 154–55; Fredric Jameson, "Pleasure: A Political Issue," in *The Ideologies of Theory, Essays 1971–1986*, vol. 2, *The Syntax of History*, 65–66.

130. Huyssen, *After the Great Divide*, 212.

131. Michel Foucault, "Two Lectures," in *Power/Knowledge: Selected Interviews and Other Writings, 1972–1977*, ed. Colin Gordon, trans. Colin Gordon, Leo Marshall, John Mepham, and Kate Soper (New York: Pantheon, 1980), 89.

132. Michel Foucault, *The History of Sexuality*, vol. 1, *An Introduction*, trans. Robert Hurley (New York: Vintage Books, 1980), 92–95.

133. For critiques of Foucault, see Peter Dews, *Logics of Disintegration: Post-Structuralist Thought and the Claims of Critical Theory* (London: Verso, 1987), 144–99; Gayatri Chakravorty Spivak, "Can the Subaltern Speak?" in *Marxism and the Interpretation of Culture*, ed. Cary Nelson and Lawrence Grossberg (Urbana: University of Illinois Press, 1988), 271–313.

134. Michel Foucault, "Le Gai Savoir," interview with Jean Le Bitoux (part II), *Mec*, July 1988, 32 (my translation). My thanks to Michael West for drawing this interview to my attention and providing me with a copy of it.

135. Michel Foucault, "Revolutionary Action: 'Until Now,'" in *Language, Counter-Memory, Practice: Selected Essays and Interviews*, ed. Donald F. Bouchard (Ithaca, N.Y.: Cornell University Press, 1977), 221–22.

136. Michel Foucault, "Le Gai Savoir" (part I), *Mec*, June 1988, 36 (my translation).

137. Judith Butler, *Gender Trouble: Feminism and the Subversion of Identity* (New York: Routledge, 1990), 132.

138. Tennessee Williams, *The Rose Tattoo*, in *Three by Tennessee* (New York; Signet Classic, 1976), 252.

139. Sklepowich, "In Pursuit of the Lyric Quarry," 538.

140. Tennessee Williams, *The Glass Menagerie* (New York: New Directions, 1970), 105.

141. Theodor Adorno, *Aesthetic Theory*, trans. C. Lenhardt, ed. Gretel Adorno and Rolf Tiedmann (London: Routledge and Kegan Paul, 1984), 196.

142. Fredric Jameson, *Marxism and Form: Twentieth-Century Dialectical Theories of Literature* (Princeton, N.J.: Princeton University Press, 1971), 122–24.

143. Ibid., 142.

144. Tennessee Williams, "The Knightly Quest," in *Collected Stories*, 483.

145. Whitmore, "George Whitmore Interviews Tennessee Williams," 316.

146. Jameson, "Pleasure: A Political Issue," 73.

147. Jeanne Fayard, "Meeting with Tennessee Williams," in *Conversations with Tennessee Williams*, 212; Michel Foucault, *Herculine Barbin*, trans. Richard McDongall (New York: Colophon, 1980), xiii. For important feminist critiques of Foucault, see Butler, *Gender Trouble*, 93–106; Naomi Schor, "Dreaming Dissymmetry: Barthes, Foucault, and Sexual Difference," in *Men in Feminism*, ed. Alice Jardine and Paul Smith (New York: Methuen, 1987), 98–110.

148. Williams, "The Knightly Quest," 482.

149. Teresa De Lauretis, "The Technology of Gender," in *Technologies of Gender: Essays on Theory, Film, and Fiction* (Bloomington: Indiana University Press, 1987), 15.

150. "Something's Missing: A Discussion between Ernst Bloch and Theodor W. Adorno on the Contradictions of Utopian Longing," in Ernst Bloch, *The Utopian Function of Art and Literature*, trans. Jack Zipes and Frank Mecklenburg (Cambridge: MIT Press, 1988), 15.

151. In the late 1980s and early 1990s, the so-called men's movement (populated almost exclusively by white, heterosexual men) has been perhaps the most pernicious exemplum of this reactionary nostalgia, with its attempt to recuperate a traditional masculinity by appeal to ritual practices: drumming ceremonies and the use of Native American sweat lodges. (These appropriations blithely ignore the histories of these practices and the fact that they are the product of the very cultures that white American men have tried over the centuries to exterminate.) Moreover, the movement's championing of male bonding coupled with its militant (if guilty) homophobia clearly indicate that, in relation to the noxious heritage of American masculinity, the movement simply represents business as usual. The most currently fashionable literary product of the movement is Robert Bly's *Iron John* (New York: Addison-Wesley, 1990).

152. Jameson, *Marxism and Form*, 128.

153. Williams, *The Glass Menagerie*, 115.

154. Walter Benjamin, "Theses on the Philosophy of History," in *Illuminations*, trans. Harry Zohn (New York: Schocken, 1969), 257.

155. Jameson, *Marxism and Form*, 126.

156. Michel Foucault, "Friendship as a Way of Life," in *Foucault Live: Interviews, 1966–84*, trans. John Johnston, ed. Sylvere Lotringer (New York: Semiotext[e] Foreign Agents Series, 1989), 207.

157. For Spivak's figuration of unlearning, see "Criticism, Feminism and the Institution," interview with Elizabeth Grosz, and "Questions on Multi-culturalism," interview with Sneja Gunew, both in Gayatri Chakravorty Spivak, *The Post-Colonial Critic* (New York: Routledge, 1990), 1–16, 59–66.

158. Tennessee Williams, *Camino Real* (New York: New Directions, 1953), 20.

Index

David Savran is the author of the only book-length study of New York's most radical theater company, *Breaking the Rules: The Wooster Group* (1986), and of a collection of interviews, *In Their Own Words: Contemporary American Playwrights* (1988), both published by Theatre Communications Group. He has contributed articles to many journals and essay collections. Additionally, he has directed more than thirty productions of plays and operas at universities in the United States and Canada, at BACA Downtown in New York, at the Kennedy Center, and at the Edinburgh Festival Fringe. He is Associate Professor of English at Brown University.